The Coaching Connection

The Coaching Connection

A Manager's Guide to Developing Individual Potential in the Context of the Organization

Paul Gorrell and John Hoover

AMACOM
American Management Association
New York • Atlanta • Brussels • Chicago • Mexico City • San Francisco
Shanghai • Tokyo • Toronto • Washington, D. C.

Special discounts on bulk quantities of AMACOM books are available to corporations, professional associations, and other organizations. For details, contact Special Sales Department,
AMACOM, a division of American Management Association, 1601 Broadway, New York, NY 10019.
Tel.: 800-250-5308. Fax: 518-891-2372.
E-Mail: specialsls@amanet.org
Website: www.amacombooks.org/go/specialsales
To view all AMACOM titles, go to: www.amacombooks.org

Library of Congress Cataloging-in-Publication Data

Gorrell, Paul.
The coaching connection : a manager's guide to developing individual potential in the context of the organization / Paul Gorrell and John Hoover.
p. cm.
Includes bibliographical references and index.
ISBN-13: 978-0-8144-1414-9
ISBN-10: 0-8144-1414-1
1. Employees—Coaching of. 2. Organizational learning. 3. Career development. 4. Management—Study and teaching. I. Hoover, John, 1952- II. Title.

HF5549.5.C53G67 2009
658.3'124—dc22

2009003030

Printing Number
10 9 8 7 6 5 4 3 2 1

This book is dedicated to Amy Friedman, founder and Chief Executive Officer of Partners in Human Resources International, headquartered in New York City (www.WemakeTalentWork.com). Amy's was one of the first woman-owned Human Capital Consulting firms to take on the male-dominated Wall Street and media/entertainment human resources consulting industry in the mid-1990s. From her firm's inception, Amy has championed the balance of premier career transition services with executive coaching. Amy's responsive leadership and responsiveness to industry needs and her close relationships with her clients helped inspire us to define Contextual Coaching and many of the other guiding principles in this book.

Contents

INTRODUCTION

The Tale of Two Clients, or The Coaching Conundrum

"Engaging in an executive coach for your high performing talent tells them that they are valued and that you are investing in their future. A coach builds awareness around successes and failures and provides a supportive partner who reflects the commitment to your executive's personal and professional long-term success."

—Judy Jackson
Senior Vice President
Head of Human Resources
Digitas

Executive coaching has often in the past been used to remediate damaging behaviors demonstrated by those with enough institutional authority to do significant damage to people and to the organization that employs them. When powerful executives behave badly by making ill-advised financial or organizational gambles, their organizations suffer. When an organization suffers, the suffering trickles down to a variety of constituency groups.

Profits can be lost, benefits can be lost, jobs can be lost, and whatever good things customers and the community at large derive from the organization's goods and services are diminished or disappear altogether. Anything, such as coaching, that helps managers and executives make good decisions is worth the investment, whether that means turning around a manager's or executive's thinking and/or involving them in more productive habits, skills, and activities.

The emerging trend that is eclipsing the mostly remedial approach to coaching is to identify high-potential leaders inside organizations and engage them with skilled coaches early on. The emergent practice is to use the guidance of a business coach to make high-potential individuals more effective businesspeople the same way a sports coach improves the performance of a gifted athlete: transforming natural talent and ability into highly refined skills and capabilities. While coaches in business and sports spend time reprogramming bad habits, addressing skills gaps, and establishing the most productive and efficient activities to enhance the businessperson's or athlete's ultimate goals and objectives, coaches prefer to (and should) enter the equation sooner rather than later.

The Coaching Connection is, in part, about connecting the dots between the need for highly skilled, knowledgeable, and wise coaches and the exponentially increased benefits of preemptive managerial and executive skill and competency building as opposed to reactive, after-the-fact interventions. If we have learned anything from the history of coaching, it is that effective leadership does not come naturally to the vast majority of people who are promoted into leadership positions and *are paid to lead.* We have also learned that leading is not easy for *anyone* facing high-pressure demands from employee, customer, and the board, internal and external economic challenges, and complex marketplace competition.

The Conundrum

Who, then, is the coaching client? Is it the individual or small team receiving the coaching or the organization that is paying for it?

Reread the opening paragraphs of this introduction and note how many times the individual manager's or executive's fortunes are tied directly to the fortunes of the organization and vice versa. Throughout this book you will hear us discuss this symbiotic relationship, this interdependence, if you will, between the organization and the members of its organizational population.

That makes our final answer: The individual *and* the organization that employs the individual are *co-clients*. We are not talking about someone who has been referred to professional therapy by the human resources department to be treated for depression or to receive marriage and family therapy, although even those referrals have a potential benefit to the organization by helping to develop a happier and healthier employee. We are talking about the growth and development of individuals specifically in how they do their jobs and interact professionally with others now and in the future, both of which are directly and inexorably linked to the health and well-being of the organization that employs them.

Conundrum solved. The tale of two clients unfolds. In marriage counseling, neither partner is the client. The *relationship* between them is the client. So it is with business coaching. The highest value a coach or a manager who coaches can bring to the individual or to a small team is to find the place where the best interests of both converge.

The diagram of the contextual coaching process illustrates how the individual and the organization are considered separate at first but begin to merge as the coaching process progresses. Ultimately, if the coaching is successful, the individual's and the organization's interests become one—or as blended as humanly possible. A well-coached employee who has experienced such convergence will be able to articulate how his or her function adds value to the organization.

Look no farther than a commonly held definition of organizational culture to discover why the organization functions the way it does. Organizational culture is the driving, guiding—often unspoken—force that defines how an organization conducts business, treats its internal and external customers, and positions itself in the marketplace. Organizational culture is also defined as the shared beliefs, values, and behaviors that inform the real organizational environment and the real organizational conduct behind the rhetoric.

If espoused organizational goals and objectives are consistently aligned with organizational culture, an organization has a reasonable chance of achieving those goals and objectives. If organizational goals and objectives are at cross purposes with the shared beliefs, values, and behaviors that constitute organizational culture, the best efforts to act in spite of the culture or in ways contrary to the true culture are likely to produce entropy as the organization grinds to a halt (productivity-wise) in its own inertia. The *AMA/Institute for Corporate Productivity Corporate Culture Survey 2008*, commissioned and published by the American Management Association, concluded, among other things, that organizations with cultures that considered the individual needs of their employees tended to prosper more than those that did not.

The bottom line is this: You cannot coach a culture. But you can coach the individuals who create and sustain a culture. As a result, both individual and organization can, and should, win. Such is the basis of the Contextual Coaching process model.

***Contextual Coaching*™ Process**

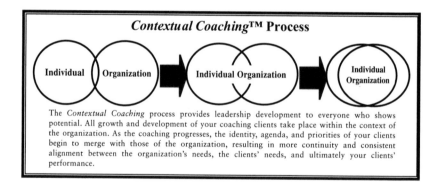

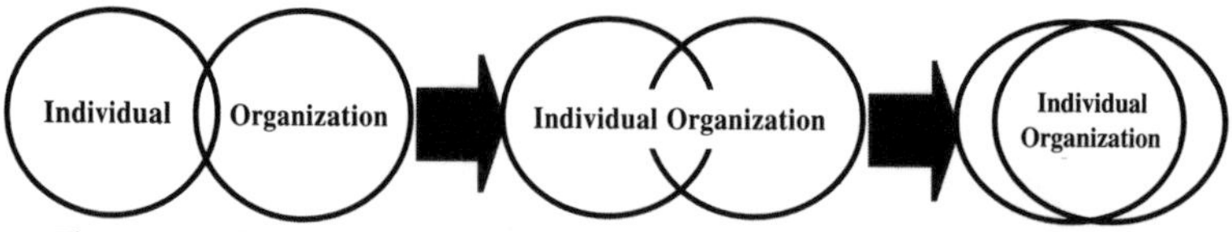

The *Contextual Coaching* process provides leadership development to everyone who shows potential. All growth and development of your coaching clients take place within the context of the organization. As the coaching progresses, the identity, agenda, and priorities of your clients begin to merge with those of the organization, resulting in more continuity and consistent alignment between the organization's needs, the clients' needs, and ultimately your clients' performance.

The Benefits of Using the Contextual Coaching Model

Although you work or will be working individually with your coaching clients or coaching a small team, the Contextual Coaching model is a true organizational process. We developed Contextual Coaching to be a comprehensive way to expand traditional executive coaching into an organization development process based on alignment. Using a systems approach, Contextual Coaching produces simultaneous growth and development opportunities for the organization and the executive. Your individual clients' contexts remain fundamental aspects of the coaching engagement and drive the developmental process for the individuals while, at the same time, enhancing your clients' roles in the broader growth and development of the organization.

This dual focus means that you, as a coach or a manager who coaches, will address multiple contexts that affect your client's unique situation as well as aligning the coaching process with the strategies, cultural imperatives, talent management systems, and competency requirements of the entire organization. As a contextual coach, you will map the coaching process to a changing organizational landscape, complete with enterprise-wide strategic agendas and individual issues, revealing how each one complements the other.

One of the greatest challenges that coaches face is the complexity of having two customers who need to be satisfied through one process. The coaching process remains an individual development process that focuses primarily on the growth of one particular employee. Yet, the organization's expectations need to be satisfied, as they have either funded the program or otherwise supported it through their resources.

Great coaches try to manage this process through good stakeholder management. This means establishing and sustaining relationships with their coaching clients' key constituents, such as their human resources partners and their manager(s), if the latter is not indeed the coach. By clearly expressing expectations of these constituents and checking in with them regularly to ensure that the process is tracking with those expectations, the coach is able to manage expectations and provide important communication relative to the coaching success.

The return on investment from these engagements is maximized when both the coaching client and the organization are seen as customers in the process. Because of this, the Contextual Coaching model is well positioned to satisfy both customers and to achieve overall success within the engagement. You, like all contextual coaches, will learn to balance the needs of the individual with the requirements of key constituents, including your client's manager (if that is not you), learning and development groups, and human resources departments, in each assignment.

The diagram of the Contextual Coaching model will be with you for the rest of this book. As we will explain in greater detail in Chapter 1 and beyond, the ten components of the Contextual Coaching model represent a structured approach to developmental coaching that, once studied, will result in a well-balanced coaching client who is aware of, and skilled at addressing, the major areas of complete and comprehensive organizational focus.

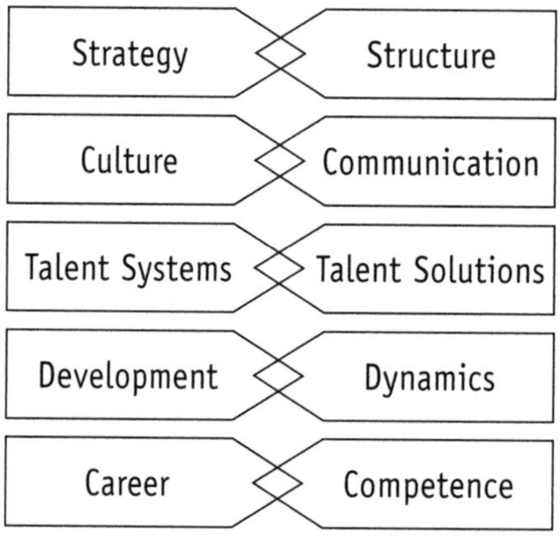

The ten components of the Contextual Coaching model shouldn't be thought of as the Ten Commandments of Coaching. They represent architectural knowledge for a well-balanced organizational leader. However, you should be knowledgeable about all ten if you want to serve the organization well and help it become an employer of choice filled with well-balanced employees-of-choice.

Another Part of the Trend

So far, we have mentioned trends toward blending the benefits of business coaching and the advantages of using it primarily for leadership and performance development and using it sooner rather than later. This book will teach you the essentials of what we call Contextual Coaching, which is the underpinning philosophical approach to developmental coaching that we present throughout this book for producing well-balanced managers and executives.

We will talk about acting as a coach as well as acting, at times, as a manager who coaches. You might be coaching someone else's direct reports, or you might be coaching your own. Sometimes you might be doing both, depending on your caseload. The underlying approach to creating well-balanced coaching clients is the same in any case, although the exact execution may vary slightly from one scenario to the next.

Executive coaching is increasingly popular for all the reasons we have mentioned thus far. That's the good news. The bad news is that the use of external coaches remains among the most expensive of all external organizational interventions. Thus, the trend to bring the coaching function inside the organization. There are advantages to that, as well as disadvantages, upon which we will also elaborate in Chapter 1.

For now, suffice it to say that business coaching, at least for midlevel managers and possibly for people working for them, will be increasingly delivered by people inside the organization. We are especially close to this practice because our firm is called upon to prepare internal candidates to provide coaching services—mostly in Fortune 100 and Fortune 50 companies as well as major not-for-profits. These coaches are sometimes specially-trained HR professionals. At other times they can be managers or executives who have expressed interest in developing coaching skills and who often have naturally empathic and advanced emotional intelligence coefficients that help them to help others.

This book is officially a manager's guide because it targets internal coaches and managers who coach. As we mentioned, we will refer to the reader as both. Regardless of the precise distinction, anyone who coaches is engaged in a noble cause—developing and aligning what individuals do best with what their organizations need most. Nothing could be more important to the health and well-being of an organization and all the constituencies that rely upon the organization's success.

Join the Excitement

Our prediction for you, albeit admittedly biased, is that you will enjoy a rewarding coaching experience if you are new to it or, if you are an experienced coach, you will enjoy it even more as you become a contextual coach. As a coach, particularly as a contextual coach, you will deal with things that people who do conventional training and development do not deal with. You will engage more individual and personal aspects of your clients than a classroom or online instructor can. When people less intimately affiliated with your clients broach a subject that is as potentially sensitive as competence (for example), your clients might shut them out. Improperly or insensitively approached, your clients might disconnect from or push back against even you until you sharpen your coaching skills.

Rewarded behavior is repeated behavior; therefore, you want to reward the right behavior through your coaching. That is logical. What makes just as much sense (although we seldom stop to think about it) is that inappropriate or nonproductive habits and behaviors are also rewarded. Why else would your clients engage in them? People do things for only two reasons: (1) to gain something as a result of the behavior or (2) to avoid something as a result of the behavior.

If your clients become extremely competent at what they do, they might get recognition, a raise, or a promotion. If your clients are hanging onto their jobs by a thread, becoming more competent through your help might mean little more than not getting yelled at, reprimanded, or terminated. The first is intentional behavior, which is behavior intended to produce something good. The second example is avoidant behavior, behavior aimed at avoiding a negative consequence.

If your clients' behaviors have been suspect for a long time, you might need to help them engage in avoidant remediation in the near term. Once you have been able to stabilize their position in the organization, the two of you can refocus on moving toward intentional growth and development in the far term. To build the tallest skyscraper in the world, you must begin by excavating a deep hole in the ground. In other words, begin building in the opposite direction. A building needs to be anchored deep in bedrock to have the strength to stand tall. Similarly, as a coach or a manager who coaches, you must secure a strong foundation before your clients can grow their careers.

Contextual Coaching helps your clients to reach their full potential within the context of the organization, as illustrated in the diagram. Contextual Coaching forges a stronger partnership between the individual's immediate needs and long-term career strategy and the organization's immediate needs and long-term success strategy. Contextual Coaching transforms a potential individual or organizational disconnect into a thriving partnership. It transforms dissonance into resonance, contradiction into cultural compatibility, and mutual exclusivity into mutual interest.

When all is said and done, you will have played a critical role in helping the individual and the organization develop. It is to be hoped that you did it soon enough to avoid the kind of damage people with institutional authority can do when not grounded in good leadership skills and management science. Certainly, the good you do for your clients and for the organization will have a ripple effect—even so much as a trickle-*up* effect—on more people than you probably realize. That is the power of *The Coaching Connection*.

CHAPTER 1
A Coaching Culture

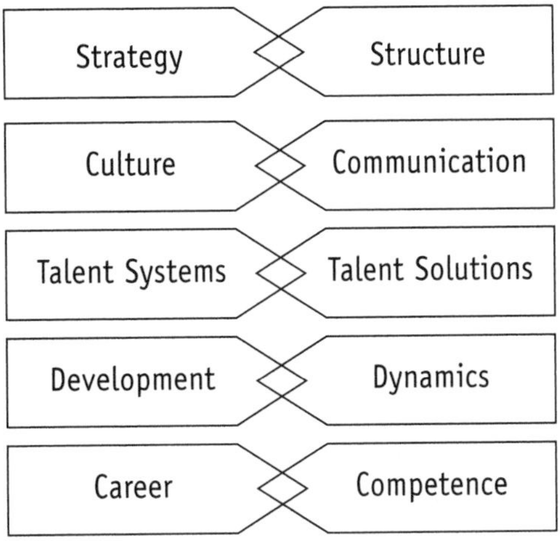

"Executive coaching is the most powerful tool we have to transform a good leader into a great one, and is one of the best investments we can make. A leader who doesn't embrace coaching is a leader who's likely reached his or her peak."

—Mark Effron
VP, Talent Management
Avon Products

If you are a manager or executive who is responsible for the performance of others, one of the most critical functions you can perform on behalf of your organization is to provide the guidance, encouragement, and support to bring out the best that your people have to offer your organization and the customers you serve. Whether you are an experienced coach in the workplace or a manager who is in the process of developing or improving this invaluable individual-

and organization-enhancing practice, coaching places you and the individual recipient (or small group of recipients) at the flashpoint where individuals and teams come face to face with their real potential.

Although coaching for executives and midlevel people has become increasingly popular, especially over the past twenty years, we still find it remarkable that many businesspeople have yet to be directly involved with business coaching, on either side of the equation. That means there is a huge growth opportunity for those who can produce the type of tremendous individual and organizational improvement that coaching is capable of yielding.

The Contextual Coaching model that you will become familiar with throughout this book is a balanced approach to developing a well-rounded leadership skill set to establish and maintain reasonable expectations among individuals, teams, and the leaders who represent the thinking and strategy of the organization. When expectations are reasonable, attainable, and worthwhile, people find it far easier to maintain their own equilibriums and to engage more consistently in positive and productive behavior.

Not only will this book be extremely helpful to you as a coach, but it can also help your coaching clients to understand and derive greater benefit from the process. Coaching is a dance of sorts between you and those you coach. However, that does not necessarily mean that the coach always leads.

Ginger Rogers, apparently tired of hearing endless accolades about her perennial dance partner, Fred Astaire, is said to have pointed out, "Anything he does, I do backwards and in high heels." The coaching engagement is a relationship, primarily between two people or between a coach and a small group or team. Whereas the coach often leads, the one being coached is doing anything *but* moving backward. What is true for one is true for the other. The benefits of Contextual Coaching accrue to everyone, regardless of whether they are dancing forward, backward, to the right, or to the left. So read on, absorb, and learn, regardless of your role in the coaching engagement.

Coaching, as an enterprise-wide, organizational initiative, might have tapped you as a coach-at-large, a mentor, an onboarding specialist, or a career coach or put you in some other advisory or guidance role. Although you already coach your direct reports in various ways, if you are to craft an organization-wide culture of coaching, you'll need to become part of a deliberate, methodical, systematic, and strategic application of coaching to do these and other functions:

- Onboard a new team member.[1]
- Address specific performance and productivity issues.
  - Improve a person's habits.
  - Expand a person's knowledge and skill set.
  - Help someone choose more productive activities in which to engage.
- Develop leadership potential.
- Prepare a high-potential person for promotion.
- Prepare a high-potential person for succession.
- Help people make domestic and international geographical transitions.
- Help a colleague or direct report deal with stress and anxiety on the job.
- Help a colleague or direct report find assistance with personal problems.
- Help a person understand and put to good use personality assessment data.
- Help people understand their 360-degree feedback and put it to good use.
- Help people understand and better fulfill their roles in the big-picture strategy.
- Help people get to the core of their dysfunctional attitudes and revise perceptions and expectations until those attitudes improve.

1. "Onboarding" is a relatively new term for many people. However, as early as the 1940s and 1950s, Walt Disney had become a huge believer in acclimating his new hires to the Disney organizational culture. According to Mike Vance, author of *Think Out of the Box* and first Dean of Disney University, Walt assigned each new management and executive hire a mentor for one year. Each mentor was a longtime and trusted employee. Disney felt it was that important to immerse new hires in the Disney culture to ensure that they not only fully bought into the Disney Way but also became skilled practitioners and tireless advocates for the organization and its unique way of doing business internally and externally. Now many companies use formal onboarding programs to do the same things.

Other leading demands for coaching arise from a number of the other issues mentioned in the preceding list. Acceleration or developmental coaching is usually a matter of taking people from the productive place where they are and expanding their skill sets, developing more of their potential, strengthening their competencies, and increasing their capabilities. Acceleration or developmental business coaching makes something that is good even better.

A 2008 study conducted by the American Management Association (AMA) found that most coaching engagements are for acceleration purposes rather than remedial work. The study, "Coaching: A Global Study of Successful Practices," surveyed more than 1,000 business leaders around the world and found increasing use of coaching as a means of improving individual productivity. Nearly 60 percent of North American companies use coaching for high potentials frequently or a great deal, and about 42 percent use coaching of executives to the same extent. These percentages were higher in the international sample. Only 37 percent of North American respondents and fewer than 30 percent of international respondents said they used coaching to help problem employees.

No matter what precipitates or drives the coaching engagement, the thing that makes the coaching *contextual* is the alignment between the design and execution of the coaching and the overarching strategy of the organization. Coaching in business environments is not about making a client feel good. We stipulate that a quality coaching engagement will more than likely leave everyone involved feeling better about themselves and what they do in the organization. However, the individual and the organization that pays for the coaching must both benefit for the engagement to be considered a true success.

An individual's success in business begins with adding value to the organization. To coach your people without regard for the organization's needs does a disservice to the individual by limiting the value he or she can add. Limiting the value an individual or team of individuals can add also diminishes their career potential. In any of these cases, the organization loses right along with the individual. When coaching clients get seriously better at what they do, both they and the organization win.

Keeping the Coach in Context

You will soon learn and understand how coaching people within the context of their working environments and their organizational cultures positions them and their organizations for the most positive outcomes. If performance or behavioral issues are in question, the modifications must also be in the context of organizational strategy to do the most good for the organization and your client's career. If career acceleration is the goal, the coaching must always be done in the context of the organization's needs, since career enhancement is inexorably tied to organizational success. Sometimes, business coaching is simply a matter of making periodic course corrections. As with performance improvement and career acceleration, course corrections must be calibrated to the flight plan and navigational markers of the organization.

For coaching to be most effective and to provide the best return on the coaching investment, regardless of the immediate rationale, every aspect of the coaching engagement must resonate with the grand organizational scheme. Organizations have mission statements that describe what they do and vision statements that describe where they want to grow. What organizations need to stay true to their mission and vision statements varies from organization to organization, depending upon their individual charters. Contextual Coaching can be described as *aligning what people do best with what organizations need most.* As a coach or a manager who coaches, you must always be sensitive to both sides of that equation.

When an organization embarks on creating and sustaining a coaching culture, such alignment is never left to chance. It is deliberate, intentional, and strategically planned. If your organization is adopting a coaching culture, the alignment between what your people do best with what your organization needs most is the big-picture agenda in which you are being asked to participate.

It is the perfect symbiotic relationship. Each one needs the other. In Contextual Coaching, the individual's coaching is always in the context of the organization and the organization's goals, needs, and/or strategic agenda. If the organization is not considered, you are talking about therapy, not coaching. The coaching culture you are engendering in your organization must first account for the context of the prevailing culture. It is only when an individual's attitudes or behaviors are assessed against the context of the prevailing culture that you can measure gaps in performance or the potential for leadership development.

Helping the Organization Through Habits, Skills, and Activities

Besides generally educating and raising awareness, there are three primary categories within which people contribute to or detract from the success of the organization—three ways they enhance or inhibit the alignment between what individuals do best and what their organizations need most: habits, skills, and activities.

Habits

Habits are those things that people do repeatedly (good or bad, positive or negative, helpful or a hindrance) until they become second nature. As the saying goes: Good habits are hard to adopt and easy to abandon; bad habits are easy to adopt and hard to abandon. Unfortunately, we have not come across a magical solution to reverse this truth.

Habits play out unconsciously most of the time. Every one of us does any number of things unconsciously each day. How often have you stopped yourself or had a colleague stop you and ask, "What are you doing?" or "Why are you doing that?" without having a good answer? If this happens to you, it is probably because you are doing something out of unconscious routine that does not make sense in the moment or under the circumstances. You are so oblivious to your own actions at that moment that you never notice that there is no connection between what you are unconsciously doing and anything appropriate or productive.

Other habits, such as what time you arrive at the office or the first fifteen activities you engage in day in and day out, are sometimes things you are aware of but stopped thinking about a long time ago. Neither do you have much incentive to change them. They have become comfortable. Coaches can help all of us take a closer, more objective look at ourselves and make an inventory of what we do. As coaches, we can help our clients discover where, when, and how their habits are enhancing their careers.

We can also help our coaching clients successfully alter habits and/or adopt new ones in order to overcome old behaviors that impede their growth and development. As coaching clients, we must press our coaches for feedback. We should repeatedly ask what we are habitually doing that blocks us from the results and outcomes we want.

Skills

Like habits, skills can be taught and learned. Raw, natural talent is often a consideration in hiring, placement, and career path choices. The same is true for natural inclinations and predispositions. These types of character attributes are most often identified through psychological and aptitude testing such as temperament sorters, type indicators, and personality assessments. Instruments such as these can be helpful to you as you coach, just as they are helpful as you are being coached.

Unlike skills, personality preferences cannot be taught. They can be identified, exposed, and even drawn out—but not taught. If a person loves to work with wood, is gifted with patience and attention to detail, and therefore becomes a carpenter, he or she is capitalizing on a natural aptitude that did not result from education. Skills enhancement, however, turns an ordinary carpenter into a skilled carpenter. As a coach, you play a critical role in assessing the kinds of skills that will help your coaching clients move forward and add value to the organization that employs them by enhancing their natural abilities.

One way you will help your coaching clients is to help them to make better choices in developing and applying their skills and natural talents. This is where your internal and external training and development resources become your trusted allies (not that they aren't already). Some organizations now call these learning and development functions "organizational learning" and have established "learning organizations" to champion them. Whatever you call it in your organization, effective coaches help their clients draft and execute a learning plan that will enhance the skills that are most beneficial to them and to the organization. They will also continuously identify new skills to be acquired that will have the same positive effect on individual growth and organizational excellence.

Activities

Whereas habits are largely unconscious actions or routines that do not seem to require immediate change, activities are totally deliberate. Activities are actions that are chosen because of their functional purpose and their tactical and strategic benefits. Whether you are coaching a direct report or someone else in the organization, the choice of activities is crucial to individual and organizational success. It is possible to have the right people on the bus, as Jim Collins would say, but still have them doing the wrong things.

Many managers will tolerate a lot of unproductive behavior as long as it is not causing major train wrecks. However, disaster avoidance is not a formula for individual or organizational achievement. As a coach who is dedicated to exponentially increasing the effectiveness of your coaching clients and the organization that pays them, it is incumbent upon you to play an active role in identifying more productive activities—even if that means invoking the "C" word (change) and instigating the transformational power that change brings about.

Three Portals into the Big Ten

Change starts with "C," and so does coaching. There is virtually nothing you will do as a coach that is not about creating or sustaining positive change in your organization. There is nothing individuals do in the coaching process that is not about changing habits, skills, and/or activities. When you think of peering into your coaching clients' behaviors through the lenses of habits, skills, and activities, you are inevitably preparing to initiate and support change in those behaviors. You will bring an out-of-focus picture of productivity into clear focus as you establish the platforms and processes upon which your clients can continuously improve their level of contribution to the organization.

FIGURE 1

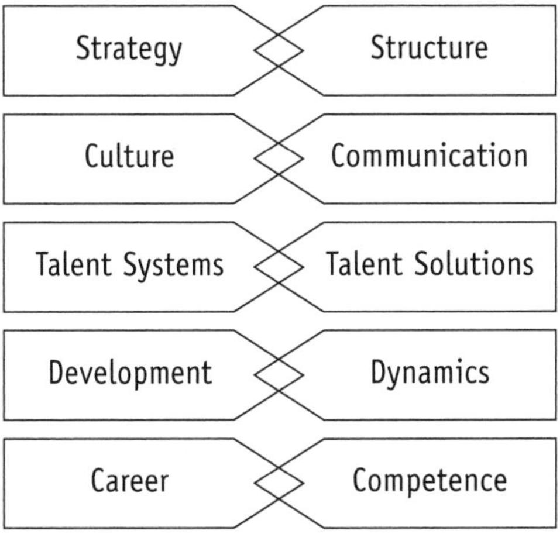

In the chapters to come, you will become expert in each of the ten Contextual Coaching categories (see Figure 1) that constitute a well-balanced, enterprise-wide corporate consciousness and make up a well-balanced team member. The ten categories, which represent competencies in well-balanced leadership, are paired into five dyads as follows:

STRATEGY ↔ STRUCTURE

How the organization's strategy creates an impact on leaders and how they manage relationships across different levels of authority within the structure

CULTURE ↔ COMMUNICATIONS

How cultural markers of the organization create challenges and opportunities and how communication style impacts success

TALENT SYSTEMS ↔ TALENT SOLUTIONS

The use of processes related to the acquisition, management, and successioning of talent and the learning and development opportunities created by the organization

DEVELOPMENT ↔ DYNAMICS

Specific areas of individual development for the coaching process and the impact of any change in behavior on the dynamics of the leaders' team

CAREER ↔ COMPETENCE

The career plan of the leader and the gaps the leader has vis-à-vis the organizational definitions of leadership

You will also be prepared to examine each of these ten essential elements through the separate lenses of habits, skills, and activities. In most cases, in each of the ten categories there will be a fragment of habit, skill, or activity, defined as:

- The dominant behavioral issue to be addressed
- The primary focus of growth and development
- The platform for career acceleration

As you deal with each of the ten Contextual Coaching categories, you will consider habits, skills, and activities and how they affect your coaching client's success in each category. Here is a practical example: When considering competency in communication, you must investigate whether the person you are coaching has well-developed communication habits, skills, and activities.

As a case in point, our firm, Partners in Human Resources International, often receives requests to provide business coaching to remedy major dysfunctions in someone's habits, skills, and activities as reflected in that person's personal communication style. When someone complains that a manager or executive needs to learn to communicate because he or she constantly yells at subordinates, telling them how upset he or she is with their low productivity, we remind them that this high-decibel manager is, in fact, a competent communicator. He or she seems to be in the habit of consistently communicating clearly and expressing precisely what he or she feels in the moment with little ambiguity. He or she can be heard and understood. What's the problem?

Seriously, the new client is in the habit of communicating—something many human resources and training partners wish they could get more people to do, especially in technology organizations. Yet, while the habit of communicating is healthy enough, the *skills* around communicating are lacking. As a quick aside, when we find executives (even very senior executives) throwing tantrums like two-year-olds, the reason is likely that they have exhausted their skills sets and, in their frustration over not being listened to or heard (as they interpret it), they are reduced to their most base natures.

To take someone who wants to be heard and understood and does not hesitate to say so and to develop his or her communication *skills* is doing the individual and the organization a tremendous service, almost beyond description. We have built enormous skill sets with people who are expressive to begin with. What they most desperately want is an affirming response. We help them to discover and employ many techniques that bring lots of affirmation. Top that off with a proactive and appropriate regimen of communications *activities* and these screamers (sometimes passive-aggressive silent types) become much-improved communicators, getting the response they want. The Contextual Coaching model provides the winning formula:

- It addresses the *habits* that will put people in the right place at the right time to do the things that will make both them and their organizations successful.
- It develops the *skills* that will refine and enhance an existing desire to communicate (as well as be successful in the other nine categories defining the organization's context).
- It promotes the *activities* of the most affirming and appropriate variety to ensure the success of both the individual and organization—all in the context of the organization's goals, strategies, and desired outcomes.

Correcting Unforced Errors

Imbalance among the ten Contextual Coaching categories, as well as an imbalance in the habits, skills, and activities associated with each one, can cause managers, executives, and employees in general to cripple or defeat themselves and the organizations that pay them. In tennis, it is called an unforced error. Returning a shot that you can easily handle and hitting it out of bounds or, worse yet, committing a double fault on your serve is a way of beating yourself without any help from your opponent.

Bowlers bowl gutter balls, golfers slice drives out of bounds, and basketball players miss free throws. When it is up to you and you alone to make the shot, it is nobody's fault (pun intended) but your own when you land outside the line, add penalty strokes, bounce off the rim, or put the ball in the gutter. Athletes, especially professionals, employ coaches to reduce the incidence of unforced errors. Why should any of your coaching clients behave any differently?

The Case for Coaching

As business coaches, we are always on the new frontier looking to help our coaching clients add value to the organizations that employ them. Working to develop a culture of coaching across the organization makes habit, skill, and activity correction and enhancement preemptive, rather than reactive. Instead of waiting until the damage has been done, relationships broken, and dissention spread far and wide, a deliberate and healthy culture of coaching helps to keep people at all levels of the organization engaged and working on habits, skills, and activities to deal with problematic issues, individually and across the corporation, as a way of doing business—not exceptional behavior.

Unless your organization is consciously, systematically, and strategically building and sustaining a culture of coaching, summoning an internal or external coach to contend with a dysfunctional behavior is likely to resemble an emergency call rather than a call for strength training. A proactive culture of coaching focuses energy and resources on accelerating performance and on making good work better, instead of waiting for things and people to need correction.

We have already listed the most frequently cited reasons for coaching:

- To help deal with stress
- To develop leadership potential
- To prepare someone for promotion
- To prepare someone for succession
- To address habits, skills, and activities
- To help find assistance with personal problems
- To help people understand and better fulfill their roles
- To interpret 360-degree feedback and put it to good use
- To interpret and put to good use personality assessment data
- To help with perceptions and expectations that will improve attitudes and relationships

But why should an organization adopt one-on-one coaching? Are not training and development or organizational learning activities enough? You will never get anyone in our business to diss the practice of organizational learning. We occupy as much space in the organizational education universe as we do in executive coaching. There has never been an executive, artist, or athlete who could not improve on his or her natural talents and abilities with expanded knowledge and practice. There has never been an organization that performed better over time in a state of ignorance than in a state of enlightenment.

Training and development activities are good. Coaching is better. It is the difference between classroom learning for children and having a private mentor who is an expert on the subject at hand. It is the difference between attending a golf or tennis class and taking private lessons. The best possible outcome results from a combination of both training and development opportunities *and* one-on-one coaching. As we indicate in our Action Coaching model, it is the combining of real-time learning activities with individual coaching that gives the entire learning experience maximum traction. If organizational learning is an effective topical gel, coaching is a fast-acting, quick-dissolving gel tablet with a concentrated dosage.

No single form of training and development gets a businessperson's attention as completely as coaching. No single form of organizational learning addresses an individual businessperson's complete range of developmental issues as completely or comprehensively as coaching. No other form of workplace intervention offers more hope of radical performance improvement.

FIGURE 2

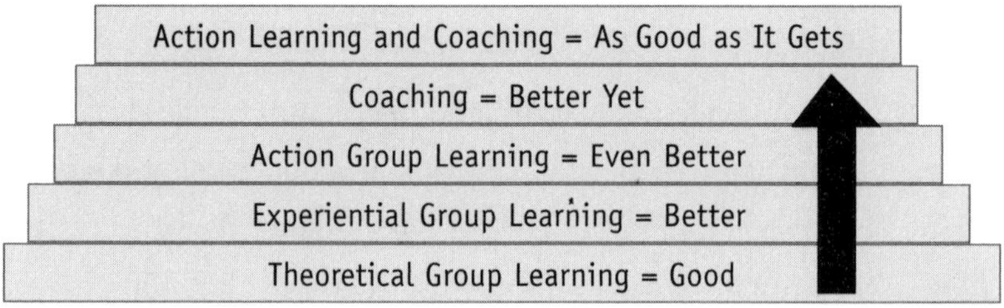

As the hierarchy in Figure 2 indicates, theoretical learning (what old-schoolers call "book learning") is good. Action learning continues to increase in popularity with our client organizations because it uses real-time, real-world organizational challenges to be worked on as living case studies.

Coaching is action learning at its very best. Completely real-time and real-world, individual coaching is a continuous living tutorial on habits, skills, and activities—all in the context of the organization—especially in the social and professional interactions of organizational life

Consider what executive coaching is most commonly called upon to do: to fully groom and prepare people for the new roles and responsibilities the organization needs them to assume or to help out when disruptive executive behavior has reached critical proportions and organizational policymakers are faced with the daunting prospect of severing ties with an expensive sample of senior talent. When there are only seconds left on the clock to preserve this monumental investment in human capital, they pull out all the stops. Pulling out all the stops does not mean using an instructor-led classroom or online course to bring about change. It means calling in an executive coach. When the whole team needs a powerful intervention or acceleration, the answer to the problem is dialing up action learning with coaching for each team member.

Your Place in the Process

As a manager or executive responsible for the performance of others or as a designated coach-at-large, you have a major responsibility: to accomplish for your clients what no classroom course, online course, or business bestseller can achieve. You have to facilitate performance improvement, enhancement of habits, skills, and activities, and/or attitude transformation that mainstream learning activities cannot. Is it any wonder that more and more progressive organizations are training internal coaches? That is, they are training internal managers and executives to provide coaching services to their direct reports and developing these and other managers and executives to act as coaches-at-large within the organization. As a coach or a manager who coaches, you should be encouraged that your organization has realized the extreme value of coaching and is making it available across the overall organizational population.

We endorse this move and support it through both training and supervision of internal coaches on a regular basis and through leadership in the field. This book and other materials we publish and distribute are examples of this commitment. Even so, our enthusiasm for internal coaching is slightly guarded. We offer the caveat that being penny-wise and pound-foolish with coaching can lead to some unpleasant experiences. The table in Figure 3 outlines some of the comparative advantages and disadvantages of using internal coaches and external coaches.

FIGURE 3

Issue	External Coach Preferred	Internal Coach Preferred
Price		√
Loyalty to the Company		√
Knowledge of the Company		√
Confidentiality	√	
Coaching Expertise	√	
Coaching Experience	√	
Objectivity	√	

Price

The AMA study we mentioned earlier supports the cost-efficiency of internal coaches. The study found that, while external coaches can be more individually effective, internal coaches tend to be more cost-efficient in the long term. "Internal coaches often provide lower cost of services, exhibit more consistency in methods, and understand the organizational culture," the AMA study noted. Despite the cost savings with internal coaches, the study's authors cited a 2007 report titled "Executive Coaching for Results," in which 59 percent of leaders indicated a preference for external coaches, while only 12 percent preferred internal coaches.

Loyalty to the Company

As a rule, external coaches are extremely loyal to their customers. After all, they are highly paid professionals. However, the dynamic is different when you are internal to the company or agency. There is a bond when the paycheck comes from the same bank account. It grows in part from being on the payroll and in part from seeing the same people year in and year out at the office, at company events, and on company softball and bowling teams. The bond also comes from being continuously immersed in the organization's culture. People seem to have a natural desire to be part of something bigger than they are. They like wearing their favorite team's jerseys. They want to cheer for something. They want to feel included and have a sense of belonging. Loyalty is a natural state. It takes consistent broken promises, lack of recognition or support, or C-suite greediness (among other things) to deplete employees' loyalty to the company that pays them. However, it can be done. Suffice it to say that managers and coaches at large inside an organization have more and deeper reasons to be loyal than an independent, outside coach.

Knowledge of the Company

Good coaches from outside the organization study up on organizational history and learn as much about the ins and outs of the company or agency as they can reasonably be expected to do. They certainly learn a great deal about the organization while engaged with their coaching clients and gathering 360-degree feedback. With the benefit of a more objective perspective, coaches can often make a more comprehensive and objective assessment of an organization than can its internal people.

However, when people are actually on the organizational food chain, a "Survivor (your organization name here)" mentality sets in. Employees have inside-out knowledge of the company. Their view of the marketplace and of the outside world in general is framed in their immense inside knowledge. So much of an organization's true culture is unwritten and even subverbal that an outsider simply cannot fully appreciate it. Think about a time when you have been on an alien campus or among the population of another organization and there was a sudden mood shift. The whole atmosphere became electrified, and people started exchanging knowing glances. It probably had nothing to do with you. Nevertheless, you could instantly sense that you were outside the loop in that place.

You were not copied on whatever virtual memo was circulating like lightning. No amount of study and research would have tapped you into what everybody employed there simply "knew." Without discussing it, at least in your presence, they understood where the skeletons were buried, who could be trusted, who could not be, who was in cahoots with whom, and how long it usually took for a flavor-of-the-month training initiative to evaporate into midair. Outsiders only think they know. People who work there know who and what is sacred.

Confidentiality

As a carryover from the world of clinical psychology and pastoral counseling, confidentiality is essential if people are going to open up about thoughts, feelings, and experiences that are too sensitive for prime time but are critical to understanding and assessing the full challenge facing the coach and coaching client. The coach and coaching client must establish a deep level of trust in a short period of time.

The more the client trusts the coach, the more he or she will reveal. The more he or she reveals, the more accurately the coach can diagnose the cause of problems, identify opportunities for growth, and help the coaching client craft an action agenda for achieving the results and outcomes that will best serve the coaching client and the organization he or she belongs to. An outside coach has a strong yet balanced loyalty to both the coaching client and the parent organization.

Whereas an independent coach has no direct career stake in the outcome of the engagement, if the person doing the coaching is on the same payroll as is the coaching client, all of that unwritten and unspoken cultural anthropology comes into play. The internal coach's loyalty is decidedly tilted toward the organization. Where is the coach on the organizational food chain vis-à-vis the coaching client? If the coach is the client's manager, there is no question. Complete confidentiality is out the window. Coaching will be limited to "safe" conversations that can excavate the contaminated soil only down to "safe" levels.

At "Survivor (your organization name here)," the object is to be the last person standing. Clients will never give up their ace in the hole, as the country singer George Strait calls it. When the client and the coach are part of the same team, they may be collegial, but the client also knows that the information the client least wants revealed could be coerced out of the coach. Understand, if you are a manager coaching a direct report or you are a coach-at-large in the organization, there will always be some suspicion as to your allegiances and your ability to keep a secret amid the political intrigue on "(your organization name here) Island." Even the AMA study on coaching found that leaders surveyed consider internal coaches to be "less confidential."

Coaching Expertise

Many people internal to organizations have natural instincts and abilities to coach others. They may even receive excellent instruction on the basic skills of coaching. However, true expertise comes from a combination of an individual's passion for a subject, formal training, networking with others in the field, and staying on top of the latest research and related literature.

Coaches whose primary jobs are in a field other than coaching can do excellent work. However, they will probably not be as expert in the field as a full-time professional coach. Would you be comfortable with a physician who did something else for his or her primary income—with medicine being a secondary or ancillary function—as you would be with a physician who is not only formally trained but engaged primarily in the practice of medicine?

Accordingly, it is incumbent on you, the provider of coaching services, to be aware of these potential limitations. Learn from the experts. Apply their knowledge whenever you can. When you are wearing the coaching hat, be the coach, and think and act like a coach. For example, exercise empathy at all times and in all things. But never let your empathy turn into sympathy.

Coaching Experience

Formal education, particularly in psychology, along with basic skills training and awareness of all the most recent and relevant research, will not replace experience. Working repeatedly with a wide variety of coaching clients, their managers, and their human resources sponsors builds knowledge and experience. The experience that best enables coaches to be effective lies in the relationships that their coaching clients have with their constituents.

The more exposure coaches have to the ways in which expectations are established, either overtly or covertly, the more skilled they become at alerting their clients to the opportunities and pitfalls that expectations represent in their professional lives. Good coaches put their coaching clients on a steep learning curve. There is a sense of urgency about getting better in a hurry. The coaches themselves are also quick studies and transform their coaching experiences into enhanced and advanced coaching skills. Full-time coaches simply have more miles on their odometers and more proven techniques to employ than do their less-experienced counterparts. The authors of the 2008 AMA coaching research report wrote that "Internal coaches may be perceived as less credible."

Objectivity

"External coaches can bring greater objectivity, fresher perspectives, higher levels of confidentiality and experience in many different organizations, industries and business environments," the authors of the AMA study continued. This has long been a popular line of reasoning. Writing in the August 1994 *Los Angeles Business Journal,* Angelo M. Troisi maintained that "All too often it is perceived that the internal coach is being overly influenced by those who are indicating a need for coaching. Objectivity is seen as lacking. On the other side of the equation, there are those who believe that a nearness to the nuances of the organization is paramount in the coaching process. There are certainly grains of truth in both arguments." External coaches also bring the flip side of inside-out organizational knowledge. Their external or "outside-in" knowledge of marketplace conditions and the world-at-large is not limited by the constraints of the internal organizational perspective and can be extremely helpful.

Just because different people working for the same employer have a stake in the outcome of the coaching engagement does not mean that the successful coaching engagement will serve them all in the same way. A coaching client might be angling for a promotion that the coach might want (unlikely) or that someone the coach knows might want (much more likely).

When coach and coaching client belong to the same organizational population, it can be difficult to keep all potential conflicts of interest out of the picture. It can also be hard to completely separate the coach's success metrics from the coaching client's success in the engagement. For an outside coach, it pays to stay objective, and it helps that there are no complementary or conflicting internal agendas. External coaches want to show results so that they will live to coach again. That gives the outside coach an extra incentive to ensure that the coaching client and the organization both win. The authors of the AMA coaching study concluded: "Regardless of what kind of coaches an organization chooses (internal or external), organizations likely will find more value than ever in leveraging coaching."

The Great Debate

In case there remains any doubt, it should be obvious by now that we are not talking about sports coaching or life coaching as they might manifest themselves in yoga, Pilates, or personal finance. These disciplines can help people excel in their business lives or their personal lives in general, and we do not want to discourage anyone from having a yoga, Pilates, or financial coach. The truth is that any type of coaching or therapeutic intervention is bound to affect other forms of coaching. Just the fact that a clinical therapy client needs a driver's license and the therapist is instrumental in helping her acquire one, however, does not make the clinician a driving instructor.

It is very important to realize and accept that the practice of business coaching is distinctly different from life coaching. We will catch a lot of flak for that statement because so many independent coaching practitioners move seamlessly back and forth between the two, depending on the coach's theoretical orientation or, to put it bluntly, who is paying the fee and why. If an individual seeks out a coach to help straighten out some part of his or her personal life, we would argue that this is a request for life coaching. If human resources leaders or other management or executive talent in an organization request coaching for themselves or others for whose performance they are responsible, within the context of the organization, we consider that business coaching.

The difference is in the *context*. Personal or life coaching can and often does deal with self-actualization, personal growth, life balance, and so on in the context of or *independent* of the environment in which the coaching client functions. Business coaching is always done in the context of the organization that is sponsoring the coaching engagement. Contextual Coaching, as we use the term and apply it to our professional practice at Partners in Human Resources International, is used in for-profit and not-for-profit organizations.

The ultimate criteria for life coaching are the coaching client's happiness and sense of fulfillment, regardless of context. While happiness and a sense of fulfillment might factor into the benefits of a business coaching engagement, the degree of success is measured by how well the best interests of the individual *and* the organization are realized—with deference to the organization. Having a model for coaching, such as Contextual Coaching, invokes a systemic process that accommodates the complex system of people and processes that make up an organization.

The Responsibility of the Coach

There can be factors at play other than those we mentioned in Figure 2 as you strive to create and sustain a coaching culture based on the balanced needs of your coaching clients and the organization. However, you can see from the figure how the most significant considerations organizations face when it comes to coaching—price, loyalty to and knowledge of the company, coaching expertise and experience, and objectivity—are split—pro and con—almost evenly between internal and external coaches. It is up to you and your internal coaching colleagues to work as hard and as skillfully as you can to minimize the gaps between concerns and benefits as they arise in relation to price, loyalty, company knowledge, confidentiality, coaching expertise and experience, and objectivity.

It is precisely because these particular gaps exist that external coaches will probably be called in to work with the most senior employees in your organization regardless of how well-developed your internal coaching pool happens to be. Nevertheless, your contribution to the excellence of your organization, given the enormous impact you have through your coaching relationships now and in the future, cannot be stressed enough. Perhaps more than any other individual in your organization, you will exert influence by the positive outcomes you facilitate for your coaching clients. Less dramatic, perhaps, but just as true, as a coach you will, at the very least, make the difference between a coaching client's growth and development and the client's stagnation. Your responsibility as a coach is enormous.

Managers and Direct Reports: The Critical Connection

Managers and their direct reports have the potential to develop the most trusting bonds outside of peer relationships at work. Peers, facing the same fate and occupying a similar place on the power spectrum, do not have much to fear from each other, at least in terms of power disparity. Peers trust one another the most. However, the linkage is not necessarily critical to organizational performance.

Between rank-and-file and upper management, where the gulf is wide and sometimes deep, there exists the least trust. The lives led by most workers, both personally and professionally, bear little resemblance to the personal and professional lives of upper management. They do not really speak the same language, their incentives are far different, and in most organizations they do not even dress the same. Like the gap between peers, the disparity between upper management and other workers is not generally considered to be mission critical.

Enter middle (or front-line) managers. This is the flashpoint where C-suite strategy meets boots-on-the-ground execution. If change and progress have any chance of gaining traction, it is at this critical juncture. Despite the fact that so many manager/direct report relationships are awkward, tenuous, and even contentious, the manager/direct report relationship is the most vital in the entire organization.

In the June 2008 issue of *Talent Management Magazine,* managing editor Kellye Whitney wrote up Procter & Gamble's research finding that manager-employee relationships are a pivotal component in performance management. This point of contact between the manager and direct report is where the essential strategy from the most senior organizational policymakers is translated into the employees' language and is framed in the context of their roles in the organization. If a critical communication is bungled at this handoff, C-suite strategy is, at best, diminished. At worst, it is doomed.

Keith Lawrence, Procter & Gamble's director of human resources for beauty, health, and well-being, told Whitney that strained relationships between managers and their direct reports are the number one reason people leave their jobs. Confirming and echoing what previous studies have chronicled, our experience in providing career transition services, as well as a preponderance of the accumulated evidence, suggests that the opposite is also true. People will stick with a job even if they can get more money elsewhere because of how highly they value their relationship with their bosses.

Either way, the relationship between managers and their direct reports is the pivot point, the sweet spot, or the lightning rod of the working population's ability and willingness to reach farther, work harder, and tolerate more discomfort as they strive to achieve the organization's goals and objectives. There is no other point at which a powerful intervention such as coaching can do more good. Ideally, coaching should not be regarded as a quick fix. However, organizations that need change and performance improvement usually need it quickly or, at least, sooner rather than later. If coaching is indeed a concentrated dosage of everything good about learning and development, then knowing where and when to apply it is essential to maximizing its positive impact.

When those responsible for the performance of others understand this message—truly get it— they will beg to be trained and developed to be the most effective coaches they can be. When managers or executives are directly responsible for the performance of direct reports, they understand and appreciate, perhaps more than anyone else, that a successful coaching engagement must account for the expressed goals, outcomes, and strategies of the organization every bit as much as the individual growth and development of the coaching client.

The Two-Sided Coin

There are no one-sided coins. Everything has a balancing consideration, if not an equal and opposite energy. We have found that, if you are providing coaching for the right reasons and with the right collegial and collaborative spirit, you will not fall victim to insular (one-sided coin) thinking. When people believe there are credible ideas and concepts on every side of an issue, there is a greater willingness to acknowledge and accept the opinions and perceptions of others. Sometimes your initial challenge as a coach or a manager who coaches is to convince your coaching clients that there are multiple considerations in almost any scenario.

In our work, we meet many people who think that they have been nominated to receive performance or remedial coaching because people simply do not understand them or how hard they work. These clients sign on to the engagement and eagerly begin with the premise that the coaching is meant to exonerate them from false accusations. On the opposite side of that unfortunate coin is the organization that hires an executive coach as window dressing in an effort to protect themselves by appearing to be supporting a person they have already decided to terminate. In this case, the only motivation is to build a litigation-proof termination story.

Of those who believe that their coaching—and especially the 360-degree assessment that is so often a part of the coaching process—will exonerate them from mass discrimination (read: everybody in the organization is against them), very few come right out and share that expectation with us. There is no room for such insular thinking in a true coaching engagement. Coaching and the act of being coached are two sides of a coin; said another way, coaches and their coaching clients constitute the currency of coaching engagements.

When you, as a coach or a manager who coaches, begin to suspect that your clients are seeking such exoneration, you need to refocus their attention on the strengths that have brought them as far as they have come and make a compelling case that the investment the organization is making by having them coached is testament to their value. Moreover, the coaching is meant to expand on their individual strengths in an effort to build a stronger organization. The more focused coaches and their coaching clients are on resolving issues and building leadership potential in the service of the organization that pays them, the more valuable that coin becomes.

The Magic Coin

Coaches and coaching clients come in all shapes, sizes, colors, and ages. One thing that all coaches have in common is that they are all different. The same applies to those who are receiving coaching. Tall ones, short ones, wide ones, and narrow ones all bring unique individuality and qualifications to the fine art of coaching. There are also those in this widely varied population of coaching clients who are looking for a single magical answer that solves everything. Nevertheless, it does not take long for even the most naïve coaching clients to accept that there is no universal magic solution to every tall, short, wide, or narrow challenge that might be facing them.

Whatever challenges your clients face, they must be considered in the context of the organization. You, your clients, and your coaching engagements are on one side of the coin; organizational context is on the other. One side can have no real value without the other side.

Summary

Whether it comes fast or slow, in a clap of thunder or as a barel detectable organizational hiccup—whether the coaching outcor rides in on the crest of a tsunami or limps across the finish line the freezing drizzle of a marathon in miserable weather—if you clients' new habits, skills, and activities are demonstrably improved, everybody wins. The bottom line to coaching businesspeople in a business environment is aligning what people do best with what the organization needs most. When that happens, it feels like magic, because the invisible hand of synergy takes over and the Contextual Coaching outcomes are greater than the sum of the parts.

Once you experience the magical feeling that accompanies helping someone else overcome a career obstacle, make a breakthrough in his or her growth and development, or move to a new level of proficiency, you will be a coaching advocate for life. Creating a coaching culture in your organization might mean pushing back the boundaries of everything you ever thought about coaching and venturing into a space where it is never about either only the organization or about only individuals in isolation. It is about all of it, all of the time.

In Chapter 2 and thereafter, everything we discuss will be squarely positioned on the Contextual Coaching platform. We will begin with an overview and review of some basics in the practice of coaching. Although this book assumes that you have studied and been trained in coaching elsewhere, it is important to reframe some of those learned principles in the context of the Contextual Coaching model.

CHAPTER 2

The Basics of Contextual Coaching

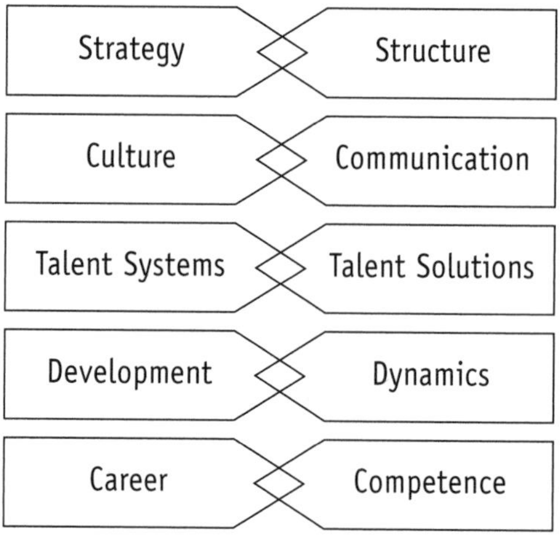

"Coaching is a key differential that can be used to help unlock the full potential of the people at every level of an organization."

—**Cynthia Augustine**
Senior Vice President, Human Resources and Employee Services Scholastic

This book is not a primer on basic coaching techniques; there is abundant existing literature to cover that ground, much of it in the extensive bibliography available at our Web site, www.WeMakeTalentWork.com. We want to remind you nonetheless of what you have learned or will soon learn about the craft of coaching through training and practice. To a coach or a manager who coaches, continuing education is every bit as important as initial training. In fact, organizations such as the International Coaching Federation (ICF) require members to accrue substantial continuing education credits to maintain their coaching credentials.

Coaching, like its parallel universe psychological therapy, is an art form, unable to meet the infinite replication requirements to hold up under scientific scrutiny. As such, we do our best to apply the most time-honored and consistently effective techniques and methodologies, practicing ceaselessly to stay current and grow our skills. While every coaching engagement is defined by the uniqueness of the coach, the client, the particular circumstances, and the truly unique composite of all three, we can still approach the engagement with the best toolkit we can assemble.

In addition to the list of reasons to request coaching we provided in Chapter 1, here are some more reasons to initiate a coaching engagement:

- Building tomorrow's leaders
- Building champions for change
- Building high-performing individuals
- Building high-performing work teams
- Recruiting and retaining the best talent
- Demanding that more be done with less
- Resolving problems blocking performance
- Helping managers engage more individuals
- Increasing job satisfaction and output capacity
- Resolving conflicts between individuals and groups
- Providing career guidance, including succession planning
- Closing the gaps between current and desired performance
- Breaking down performance-wrecking barriers between individuals and groups
- Identifying and bringing clarity to blind spots in leadership or personal performance

Begin with Trust

To accomplish any of these things, a coach must begin engaging the client, as well as the client's manager and human resources sponsor, on the level of trust. If the key constituents do not trust the coach, very little will be accomplished. In their most professional manner, coaches must demonstrate that they are trustworthy. This requires being as authentic, consistent, and as transparent as possible. Everything a coach does must be tempered with discretion and reason. By modeling openness, acceptance, and dignity, you will start your clients on the pathway to success.

Everything you have ever learned about effective and active listening comes into play when coaching. Do not expect your clients to trust you without a concerted and consistent effort on your part to repeatedly prove that you have your clients' best interests at heart and can be counted on to keep confidential information confidential. The same things that cause you to trust someone in a business situation will probably work well in the coaching relationship, with a few subtle (or not so subtle) nuances added to create a unique flavor for your engagement.

Hear Your Clients' Stories

One of the most important elements in earning the trust of others is to hear how they think and feel. Do not just listen; *hear* what they are saying, even if the message is between the lines. Repeat back to them what you think you have heard and let them confirm if you are right or wrong. If you are well practiced and pay close attention, your feedback will be increasingly accurate over time. Your clients will become more comfortable with your coaching, and the relationship will be on its way to becoming truly functional. After you have opened your ears to hearing your clients' stories, it is incumbent upon you to help your clients find their rightful place in the *organization's story*.

Most coaching organizations, like the ICF, are deeply committed to nondirective approaches wherein coaches provide safe and reflective environments in which clients discover their own answers and solutions. In reality, among coaches and managers who coach, there is a continuum of styles that runs the spectrum from highly directive to the officially sanctioned client directed. At the highly directive end of that spectrum, coaches give advice and preach a hard line about what clients should and should not do to accelerate their careers or to correct troubling behaviors. At the client-directed end of the continuum, coaches refrain from giving advice, preferring instead to gently guide clients to self-discovery of their own answers. You can imagine that the latter requires enormous patience and commitment to the process.

Whichever style you adopt as a coach—highly directive, nondirective, or somewhere in between—you must consider the type of environment and relationship you are creating. Are the environment and the relationship best for the individual and best for the organization, given the current and ongoing needs of both? Like so many things in management and human development, the exact style and content of the coaching engagement is situational.

When time is of the essence, it might be best to err toward directiveness. Organizations often face urgent situations and need performance acceleration or behavior modification in a hurry. As we intimated in Chapter 1, coaching should never be thought of as a quick fix, but organizations and individuals often need things fixed quickly. Often, there is too little time for clients to venture through the issues and causes for their stuckness, stagnation, or developmental ramp-up to arrive at their own conclusions without some gentle nudging from the coach. One danger in being a highly directive or even a gently nudging coach is that your clients will not feel personally connected to the solutions—at least the part of the solution that came from you. It might seem to them like they are following orders, which they can do without a coach. Of course, if they excelled at following orders, you might not have been called in to begin with.

When possible, you want clients to truly internalize the solutions, take ownership, and even become energized by exploring new frontiers in their habits, skills, and activities. This happens best when clients are led (often through skilled, Socratic questioning) to discover the answers that they probably knew all along but for which they were never adequately reinforced. An expert coach will skillfully lay the questions out there and patiently listen as the client connects the dots. Often, clients come up with better, more efficient, and more effective solutions than a highly directive coach would have advised. If your clients settle for less effective solutions because you strongly suggested them, you have not helped your clients or your organization as much as you could have. When you demonstrate the patience to allow your clients to come up with their best solutions, you have most likely allowed the individual and the organization to win big time.

Dispensing advice, sometimes necessary when issues are urgent, presupposes that the coach somehow knows better how to do something than does the client. That is a dangerous assumption and might severely limit your clients' creative capacity for problem solving. Dispensing advice does not teach problem solving, which is one of the richest and most rewarding outcomes of a coaching engagement. Senior executives are rarely more satisfied than when their people learn to be better problem solvers.

Never say, "If I were you. . . ." You are not them. They know you are not them. And they will resent the implication that you know how to be them better than they do (even if you believe that is true). Coaching is about skillfully leading people to their own discoveries. Their own personal epiphanies will be much more powerful and long lasting than any pontification you can offer. You must have the patience and the prescience to resist the urge to spew advice in hopes of a mythical quick fix.

Create the Context and Set Expectations

Once you have achieved initial traction with the trust issue, thoroughly explain that this coaching is being conducted in the context of the organization and the culture within which your client is functioning. This is all about establishing realistic and achievable expectations. There are two reasons people support change and will take the risk of modifying their behavior:

1. They believe in their hearts that they will be happier and more successful with the new way of doing things than they are with the old way. If you do not instill this belief in

people, they will never take the leap of faith that is inevitable in making meaningful and lasting changes.

2. They believe that what you are urging them to do, what you are urging them to sign on for, or what you are urging them to support is, in fact, *possible*. Even if people believe they will feel better and truly enjoy the new outcome you are describing, if they do not believe in their hearts that it is attainable, they will hold back and not extend themselves. Your cause will be lost.

Be very up front and honest about how this engagement is about them and about the organization. Your goal is to help clients succeed in the best possible way within the context of the organization's best strategy and agenda. This early education will expose whether or not a client even cares about the organization's best strategies and agenda. If not, you have a more complex challenge ahead of you and a longer row to hoe.

Explain How the Process Works

Make sure that you complete the expectation setting by explaining to your clients and their managers (if that is not you) how things work in a coaching engagement. Explain what will be involved, how often you will meet, how many reports you will write, and to whom they will be distributed. Assure them that the entire process is confidential. Answer any questions they might have about your qualifications. The more your clients are familiar with the process and familiar with you, the less chance they will be derailed by surprises and choose to disengage.

Empower your clients. Give them maximum opportunity to control the process. If they are uncomfortable about any aspect of the engagement, alter it until they are comfortable. To achieve maximum buy-in, offer maximum control without compromising the engagement. You want your clients to be as energized and enthusiastic as possible. Giving them knowledge and eliminating surprises will help get the job done.

Collect Objective Feedback from Selected Constituents

One of the things you will do to empower your clients is to involve them in the design of their own 360-degree assessment. Allow them to craft questions for the structured interviews you will conduct with the feedback providers they choose. Allow them to nominate the first list of feedback providers, and then negotiate the list with your client's manager and human resources leader.

Many organizations and business coaching providers use standardized, purely qualitative instruments. We make the 360-degree assessment as individualized as possible whenever we can. This takes extra time, but it puts your client at the epicenter of the process.

You can also use personality assessments and other psychometric instruments that you are qualified to administer and interpret. The Myers-Briggs Type Indicator is perhaps the most widely used type indicator. Others are the Caliper Profile, the DiSC, the Birkman Method, the Kersey Temperament Sorter, and the Herman Brain Dominance instrument. You want as much data on your client as you can reasonably gather. If you are not certified to use these instruments, get your client's permission to enlist the assistance of a human resources or learning organization partner. HR can help guide you toward certification in one or more of the instruments if you want to increase your skill level in that area.

Create an Action Plan

Once the issue(s) you and your clients need to address are clearly defined, once you have heard and understood your clients' stories, once you have gathered self-reporting and objective third-party feedback, and once you have the context of the organization clearly articulated by your clients' managers and human resources leaders, you are ready to craft an action plan for change. This will be the blueprint for your clients' behavioral changes. It is the roadmap that shows how to get to where your clients need to go, starting with where they are at present.

Your clients should ideally write up the action plan, but that can be an enormous battle because of limits on time and perhaps a low level of comfort about writing. Our business coaches usually help facilitate the writing of action plans with their clients by providing input, revision suggestions, and guidance along the way. Your clients must be intimately involved with their plan creation or they will not accept the necessary accountability.

Your plan should include timelines for accomplishing intermediate and long-term goals. It must make clear how accomplishment will be recognized along the way. Most of all, the plan must make clear the habits, skills, and activities that will come into play in order to produce the desired changes. It is important to agree in advance how improvements in those habits, skills, and activities will be measured and documented. The use of the Contextual Coaching model to accomplish a balanced approach is detailed throughout this book and provides a structure for habit, skill, and activity development in order to build and expand well-balanced leadership abilities.

Monitoring Progress, Asking Questions, and Providing Ongoing Feedback

As a contextual coach, one of your most important tasks is making sure that the coaching engagement does not lose momentum. Tracking improvement across the five dyads of the Contextual Coaching model (Figure 1) requires focus. You must keep the engagement fresh and anticipate those sticky spots when your clients will get tired, frustrated, and even resentful of the workload.

Along with providing ongoing feedback, you want to offer as much encouragement and reward as possible and is appropriate. Rewarded behavior is repeated behavior, so pour it on. Do not miss an opportunity to recognize and applaud the type of behavior toward which you hope your client is moving. If you have not met with your client's manager already—probably in the action-planning stage—this is the time to do it.

Check in and find out how the manager is taking to the engagement. You might find out that your client's manager did not expect this amount of work and focus. You may need to manage these expectations. Moreover, you might need to do some coaching with your client's manager to get the type of reward and recognition your client deserves and to keep the process moving forward.

Circle Back on the 360-Degree Feedback

When the designated period of months has elapsed, usually six, re-administer the 360-degree feedback assessment. If you cannot redo the entire assessment, do a significant portion of it so that your client can see clearly how successful he or she has been at altering perceptions among various constituencies, including colleagues, direct reports, and managers. This sort of feedback is essential, and knowing that it is coming keeps a fire lit under your client's boiler.

Prepare your clients for the possible bad news that not much has changed in terms of perceptions. When you were describing the process early on, it is helpful to have described how large and visible your clients' behavioral changes must be to change answers to 360-degree feedback questions. Changing the answers can be achieved, and one of the biggest goals you and your clients will want to work toward is changing those answers. If your coaching is successful, your preparation for bad news will turn out to have been merely precautionary.

Wrap Up the Engagement

Revisit the entire engagement with your client. Start with the reasons the engagement was requested in the first place, and retrace every step and how your client was involved the entire way. Note what worked best and what did not. Make sure your client is well aware of *how* things have improved and *why* so that the new behaviors will not be lost.

Even as you bring closure to the process, make sure you schedule time in the future to check in and monitor progress. If additional coaching is required, you can schedule it at that time. It is vital for your client to know that he or she is not being abandoned but will receive continuing support and reinforcement in the months and even years ahead. Establish with your client's manager how the manager and your client can work together in a robust way to reinforce and sustain the behavioral improvements as they move forward.

If all is well done, there will be measurable improvements in habits, skills, and activities, based on the metrics you originally established. There will also be difficult-to-quantify-but-extremely-noticeable improvements in attitudes, as well as improvements in confidence where leadership skill and capacity building are the main coaching agenda.

The Fastest Overview in Coaching

All of the elements of a coaching engagement, as we have explained them so far, have been fairly high level. What follows is a more close-up, hands-on version. This is as close to the nuts and bolts of basic coaching practices as you will get from us in this book before we introduce you to the Contextual Coaching model of totally balanced employee and managerial development.

In Chapter 3, we begin taking you individually through each one of the ten Contextual Coaching categories. You will come out the other end well versed in the principles and practices of Contextual Coaching. You will be a big-picture coach. The Contextual Coaching model will help to ensure success as you coach others to grow and achieve their full potentials as leaders or soon-to-be leaders. Remember that the following characteristics are essential to successful coaching:

- A client-driven approach at all times
- Sensitivity to the context of each project
- Respectfulness of each person's individuality
- A deep knowledge of and respect for organizational culture
- Strategic guidance that creates a "values-based" partnership
- Attention to the full life cycle of contemporary organizational needs
- A flexible approach in light of organizational needs and changing strategies

Introduction to the Coaching Process

The idea of working with a client may seem threatening at first. If you are an experienced coach or manager who coaches, you know the feeling. You also know that your clients just as often feel threatened. Some people initially believe that they have been singled out as having a problem or are being sent for coaching because of something they did wrong. The truth is that high-potential leaders like most of your clients have been singled out as worthy of a substantial investment by the organization in their leadership potential. Decision makers obviously believe that your clients bring great value to the organization and want to help enhance their leadership capabilities by having them participate in this intense and intimate personal process. By investing in developing your clients' potential, they are also helping to align your clients' capabilities with the organization's culture, concept of leadership, and strategic agenda.

Two key points to remember and share with your clients:

- Executive coaching represents a major investment in your clients.
- Truly effective coaching must be conducted within the context of your organization.

Explain to your clients right up front that Contextual Coaching is a balanced and holistic approach to executive development that will engender a unique and cutting-edge partnership among you, your clients, and organizational stakeholders of all kinds. This is what makes it contextual, unlike more traditional forms of executive coaching that usually focus only on an individual's developmental needs without regard for the organization's overarching goals and objectives.

Constituents in This Process

Constituents are important individuals committed to your clients' leadership development who will invest time and energy in helping to manage the coaching process. These constituents provide insight into your clients' goals as well as information throughout the coaching engagement that can deepen the experience for your clients and help to monitor personal and professional development. Constituents can vary from coaching scenario to coaching scenario. Generally speaking, your clients' primary constituents include but are not limited to:

Client

Client's Peers

Client's Superiors

Client's Direct Reports

Client's Human Resource or Learning and Development Partners

You will create a plan for regular communication to keep your clients' managers, other key constituents, and your HR partners abreast of the progress of the engagement.

The Manager's Role

Coaching engagements that achieve the best results require the commitment of the client's manager throughout the process. In this process, the manager will help to identify coaching goals that influence the action plan created for the engagement. You need the manager engaged early on to help define expectations and how success will be measured. Throughout the process, you want your clients' managers to provide support and feedback. As a coach, you will encourage your client to seek out that feedback and to ask for any information that can guide your clients' leadership development. Meanwhile, the manager (and/or HR partner) represents institutional authority for the engagement, providing sign-offs on contracts and steps in the process. The manager also informs you, as the coach, of the manager's perspective on the organizational context so that the engagement can be rich, focused, and holistic.

Confidentiality

Confidentiality is the cornerstone of any effective coaching engagement. Your clients must be assured that what is discussed between the two of you stays between the two of you unless your client decides to share information with others and/or expressly grants you permission to discuss selected information. Otherwise, as a contextual coach, you will report only general observations about how the engagement is progressing. Even though the client and organization are co-clients, the client is in charge of the coach-client relationship at all times. A guarantee of complete confidentiality for clients is essential to provide them with a sense of complete control.

As a coach, you must understand how necessary confidentiality is to the success of your coaching engagements. Without confidentiality, your clients have no assurance that what is shared with you will not come back to haunt them. The coaching you are providing is your clients' process and no one else's. The information and data gathered about your clients in various assessments and 360-degree instruments and interviews belong to your clients, despite the fact that the organization pays the bills.

Steps in the Contextual Coaching Process

We cannot emphasize enough that a well-managed Contextual Coaching process will accelerate the development of your clients' leadership potential and provide a connection between what your clients do best and what the organization needs most. The program comprises five key stages, each with a specific focus:

Engagement Launch

⇩

Assessment and Exploration

⇩

Strategy and Goal Setting

⇩

Ongoing Development and Reinforcement

⇩

Engagement Conclusion

First Step in the Process: Engagement Launch

This introductory phase begins with a dialogue involving you as the coach, your client's human resource partner, and/or the client's direct supervisor regarding a general set of objectives for the engagement. If your clients have pertinent data such as job descriptions, previously taken personality assessments such as the Caliper, MBTI, or DiSC, and/or biographical sketches, this information can help to identify you as the right coach to work with each particular client on the basis of the client's skills, background, and competencies. When selected as the coach (that final decision often is made by the client after reviewing credentials of several coaches suggested by HR and interviewing them), you will meet with your new clients and their main constituents to discuss the engagement and to communicate the preliminary goals for the program.

Once selected as the coach, in the initial coaching meeting between you and your new client, discuss the coaching process, identify initial goal(s), make plans for the assessment process, and begin to build rapport and trust. In the ensuing sessions, you and your client will focus on initiating the assessment process, often including 360-degree feedback and/or personality assessment(s). Here are the steps:

- The organization initiates the executive coaching assignment.
- The executive coach is selected and prepared for the assignment.
- The coach conducts introductory meetings with client and key constituents.
- The coach and client begin building a relationship based on trust and transparency.
- All parties deepen their understanding of the coaching process purpose and agree on initial goals.
- All parties agree on key development areas to be addressed, and the coach and client craft a development plan.
- Your clients' managers sign off on the plan, and you're off and running.

This all leads to the deeper exploration that is required to ignite and fuel your clients' leadership acceleration processes. Following the engagement launch, you will have sessions with your client. Coaching sessions occur during regularly scheduled one-on-one meetings, supplemented, if necessary, by contacts either by telephone or by e-mail.[1] The frequency and length of each session will depend upon the situation and the business schedule but will generally take place every other week and last sixty to ninety minutes per session.

Second Step in the Process: Assessment and Exploration

Assessment and exploration are used to gather the data necessary for a successful coaching process. In a sense, the success of the coaching process is contingent on (1) a deeper analysis of your client's strengths; (2) areas where strengths may be overused, causing confusion or dissatisfaction with others; and (3) areas of weakness that can create gaps in overall performance and effectiveness. This process is, in effect, a gap analysis that includes multiple ways of gathering helpful information about your client and the work environment. This assessment and analysis will eventually lead to an expanded coaching plan.

The initial steps in the assessment process include data gathering that (1) deploys personality-based assessment instruments; (2) interviews the client about personal style, goals, and challenges; (3) discusses organizational culture and communication styles related to success with your clients and key constituents; and (4) structures and conducts interviews with your clients' key constituents (360-degree feedback) on leadership and/or performance behaviors across the ten Contextual Coaching leadership competencies.

The Use of Assessments

As we have mentioned, the use of assessments is extremely helpful for increasing self-awareness, gaining deeper appreciation for your clients' styles and ways of behaving and solving problems, and for defining your clients' unique emotional intelligence, which is something we have not mentioned before. Emotional intelligence (or EI) is a person's innate emotional sensitivity, emotional memory, emotional processing,

1. Many coaching engagements are conducted by telephone, e-mail, or some combination of the two, with no face-to-face contact. If this is absolutely necessary, we urge you to do the best you can. However, our preference is always to spend as much time as possible in your clients' presence to build trust, be fully present for your clients, and truly be a partner in your clients' journeys.

and emotional learning ability. Some think of EI as a way to measure maturity. In a work setting, EI references potential for learning healthy emotional management skills. Four inborn components—emotional sensitivity, emotional memory, emotional processing, and emotional learning ability—form the core of emotional intelligence.

By understanding your clients' tendencies and preferences, you as the coach can delve into the ways that others respond to your clients' thoughts, words, and actions and learn how to adjust your clients' presentational and leadership styles to be more effective and widely recognized. As a contextual coach, it will help if you are trained in the interpretation of assessment tools, even if you are not credentialed to administer the assessments. That kind of training is available through your internal learning organization or through training resources such as the American Management Association.

Assessment tools fall into two broad categories: (1) those that guide your clients toward self-knowledge through directed self-insight (personality, aptitude, behavioral, and similar self-reporting instruments), and (2) those that provide your clients with the objective observations of others (360-degree assessments). These assessments are incorporated into the coaching process early on so that the engagement can be used to address issues that the assessments identify.

The combination of these tools can offer concrete data about your clients' personalities—aspects that may already be known, but that your clients may not have been able to acknowledge or work on in any productive way. Here are some examples:

- Strengths that your clients have not effectively brought forward in the workplace
- Negative behaviors that must be modified
- Talents, aptitudes, and preferences that have not been pursued in a meaningful way
- Things your clients might not know about themselves
- Perceptions that others may have of your clients' personalities

When skillfully analyzed and communicated, the data from the assessment process helps your clients to examine:

- Life experiences
- Things that have been done well and been found especially satisfying (to increase the chances of repeating good experiences and not repeating bad ones)
- Experiences that may not have gone well (to help identify areas for improvement)
- Relationships with managers, peers, and direct reports
- A wide variety of job-related values
- Special interests and subject-matter knowledge
- Job-related satisfaction and dissatisfaction

The Third Step in the Process: Strategy and Goal Setting

Using information gathered during the assessment and exploration stage, you can now identify and analyze issues critical to your clients' progress. From that analysis, you and your clients can identify goals and objectives that will be reported to the organization for this engagement—the manager and the HR partners responsible for this coaching and development process. Meanwhile, these strategies for growth become the content of the action plan, including the material that will be emphasized during your one-on-one coaching sessions.

As the coaching process progresses, your clients will be challenged to grow in personal performance as well as leadership capability and capacity through a personalized experiential learning process. Coaching is always all about learning. This step involves clarification of goals for the engagement and involves these steps:

- You and your clients finalize the coaching plans that will guide the overall engagements.
- You and your clients present the coaching plans to the key constituents for agreement.

The next step includes the "guts" of the coaching process. As the coach, you will help your client to:

- Establish long-term behavioral change goals.
- Practice exercises to build awareness of behavior patterns.
- Seek out feedback on new behaviors demonstrated on the job.
- Determine development strategies and set weekly performance targets.
- Identify options for different communication styles and behavior patterns.

The Coaching Action Plan

The coaching action plan is a pivotal component of the entire coaching process. The action plan takes into account several factors:

- The coaching context
- The sponsoring manager's expectations
- The clients' personal and professional goals
- The company's cultural standards and values for success

While the assessment phase of the coaching process is critical for identifying and documenting your clients' behavioral tendencies as identified through personality instruments and 360-degree feedback, the action plan creates a road map for how change, adjustments, and adaptations will take place in order to accelerate an increase in leadership capabilities, competencies, and capacity. The plan outlines which of the behaviors identified in the assessments and stakeholder interviews need to improve the most during the coaching process. It also communicates the approach that will be used to make adjustments that can deepen your client's success within the context of the organization. Having a detailed and measurable action plan—with a time line—will guide the process and move it toward the desired outcomes.

The plan will enable all of the constituents, your clients, and you to monitor progress toward the specific goals that have been highlighted. Both you and your clients have a responsibility to each other and to the organization to show measurable progress throughout the coaching engagement. An action plan outlines this responsibility.

Coaching action plans also identify valuable resources that can be used in the coaching process, beginning with the manager. It is helpful to identify, where applicable, which actions or behaviors the manager can demonstrate and model to support needed behavior modifications. This includes providing honest and direct reinforcement and feedback when positive new behaviors appear and when older, unproductive patterns disappear. Other resources might include internal and external development opportunities (workshops, conferences, task forces, and committees) to reinforce positive behaviors and to develop new ones.

Elements of the Action Plan

The coaching action plan can provide all of the constituents with valuable information that can be referred to not only as guideposts but also as a source of valuable behavior-tracking progress markers for you and your client. Not only all contact information but also the start date and the projected end date of the engagement should be recorded. The fixed and limited time period helps ensure focus on the goals and serves to keep everyone on track.

As mentioned, your action plan identifies key competencies and behaviors that have been targeted for development. The plan is further broken down into specific actions and incremental accomplishments that will make the individual's progress seem realistic and doable. The progress also needs to be measurable. As the old axiom says, "If it can't be measured, it can't be managed." Every step of this process is taken in collaboration with your client.

Sharing Your Plan with Constituents

One of the most important functions of a contextual coach is to craft critical communications about the coaching engagement for distribution to concerned constituents. Comprehensive contextual coaching reports at the launch, midpoint, and end of the coaching engagement document the progress your client has made and the ways your client has enhanced a leadership skill set across the five dyads in the Contextual Coaching model. Your client should always be aware of who is receiving this information and what kind of information is being released.

In order for your clients to receive proper recognition for efforts and changes made during the coaching process, the manager and other key constituents must be involved in the formalization of the coaching action plan. This ensures that your clients are developing and growing in areas that they value. Once created, the action plan should be brought to managers and other key constituents (i.e., your clients' HR partners and/or learning and development sponsors).

We recommend that you submit the coaching action plan to your individual client's manager in preparation for a joint meeting that will include your client. This gives the manager time to review and think about the goals and desired outcomes you and your client have documented. All of this sharing is subject to your clients' approval.

When you and your individual client meet with that client's manager, the HR partner can also participate in the meeting, either in person or by providing written feedback on the action plan. Input from all key constituents is critical to ensure that everyone agrees about how your client's success will be evaluated. This is an opportunity for an open and honest dialogue between the manager and your client, which you as the coach will facilitate, with perhaps the help of the HR partner. The bottom line is this: Your clients should never feel they are alone in this.

As a coach or a manager who coaches, you must constantly remind your clients that their growth and development will be in the context of the organization. You must also remind them that the progress and improvements they are making should not be hidden under a basket. To receive proper recognition and acknowledgment for their efforts to grow and develop, your clients' accomplishments should be shared with as many key stakeholders as is practical and appropriate.

Fourth Step in the Process: Ongoing Development and Reinforcement

As your client progresses deeper into the process, you can both create more opportunity for self-awareness and engage in discussions on the new leadership behaviors being demonstrated and any refinements to those behaviors that are being practiced. This stage involves several steps:

- Tracking of behavioral changes
- Ongoing development and reinforcement
- Modification of goals and strategies to adapt to changing conditions
- Filing of a midterm report on your client's progress with the key stakeholders identified at the coaching plan stage in step three

Manager Meeting: Midterm Review

You and your clients should meet with their managers and any other appropriate key constituents midway through the coaching engagement to get feedback about how your client is doing. This meeting is sometimes called a management roundtable, especially if you involve the HR partners. This is an opportunity for your clients to share with their managers, you, and their HR partners how the development process is proceeding. Some information to be shared may have already been observed and commented on by others. However, hearing this feedback from your clients' perspectives enables their managers and other key constituents to provide additional support, continued positive reinforcement, and even more feedback.

As previously mentioned, one of the important functions of a contextual coach is to prepare communications (reports) about the coaching engagement for the appropriate constituents. As a coach or manager who coaches, you will write a comprehensive midterm report to document the progress your clients have made to that point. This is also a way to document how your clients' progress has addressed each of the leadership skill sets across the five dyads of the Contextual Coaching model.

A sentence or two about how your clients' behaviors demonstrate a growing knowledge and applicability of these dyads:

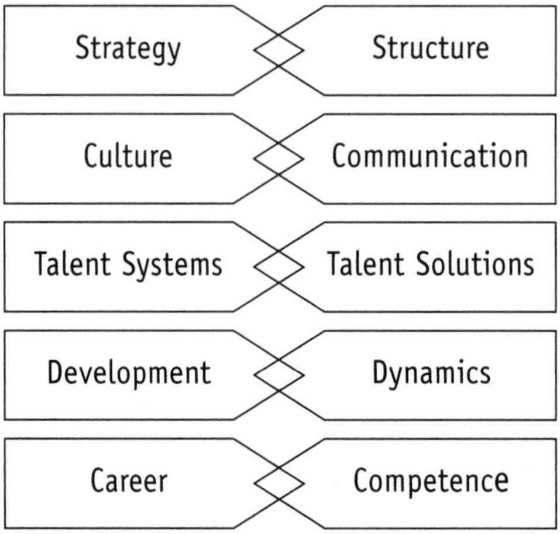

Fifth Step in the Process: Engagement Conclusion

You and your clients will prepare for completion of the coaching engagement by exploring ways to reinforce the new behaviors and reduce the use of older, less productive patterns. Together, you will build reminders and reinforcements into your clients' environments. You will eventually transfer the supportive role you have played to the individual's constituents, including the manager, peers, and others.

It is important to gain closure on the process and identify strategies for continuing your clients' growth after the formal coaching program has ended. This stage involves several steps:

- Evaluation of coaching program with HR
- Assessment of your performance as the coach
- Identification of strategies for your client to use in the post-coaching process
- Additional structured interviews to determine the impact/value of coaching
- Roundtable discussions with your clients, the HR partners, and your clients' manager

Summary

The Contextual Coaching process is based on the principle that all people operate and interact with the world on the basis of their perceptions and thinking patterns. These patterns, or mental models, are subjective and may be loaded with biases and blind spots. These blind spots often prevent people from seeing the impact of their behavior on others and on their own careers—and may inhibit their ability to find more productive alternatives.

As a coach or a manager who coaches, you will help create deeper self-awareness in others, allowing them to see themselves from a variety of perspectives. As a coach, you will become a bridge between organizational concerns and the individual needs of the people you coach. To ensure that everyone, individual and organization, derives the full benefit of the craft of coaching, you must focus on the two primary dimensions of Contextual Coaching. The first is the coaching basics, beginning with the engagement launch and all of its critical components, such as trust building, through assessing, action planning, practicing, progress reporting, and closing the engagement. The second is making sure that your clients develop awareness, understanding, and the ability to apply principles of each Contextual Coaching component in their current work or the work they are preparing themselves for in the future.

In Chapter 3 you will be introduced, in depth, to the first Contextual Coaching category: Strategy. You will learn what it is and how you can relate strategic issues to your clients' habits, skills, and activities. You will be exposed to the most appropriate behaviors your clients can adopt related to strategy. You will also be given questions for your clients and for their 360-degree feedback providers to answer that will result in an object assessment of your clients' competencies around strategy and the ability to think, converse, and act strategically. This is the first building block in the platform for a well-balanced future executive, and it adds value to what your clients can offer their organization.

CHAPTER 3

Area of Behavioral Focus: Strategy

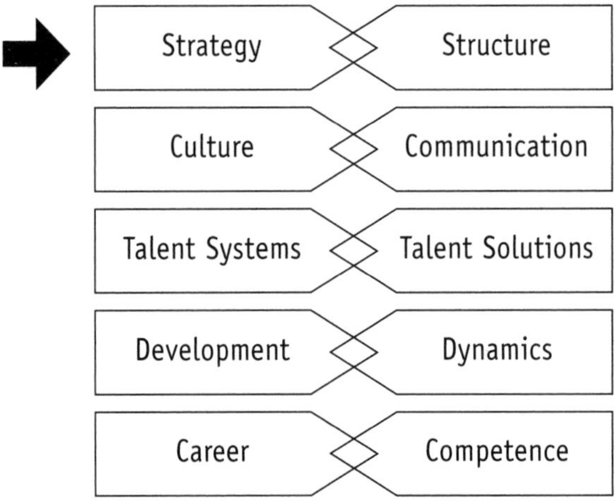

"As business models continuously change, as the workforce and workplace take on a very different look, and as economies and borders meld, coaching is a key component to help establish the appropriate personal and business framework for success."

—Steve Schloss
VP, Global People Development
Time Inc.

A strategy is a systematic, methodical, and intentional plan of action or nonaction, depending on your goal. While sometimes the best strategy is to do nothing, in most cases and in most organizations, doing nothing will accomplish just that—nothing. Whether the strategy is elaborate or simple, it must involve a plan (yes, even doing nothing requires a plan), method, technique, and series of actions (or nonactions) to achieve a specific goal or desired outcome.

The key here, as with all aspects of coaching, is the goal or desired outcome. Individuals and organizations will experience outcomes from their actions or nonactions. That is ensured. The question is, "Will the outcome be desirable?" That depends on how thoughtfully and skillfully the strategy is conceived, developed, and executed. Investing thought, analysis, research, and discussion in determining the most desirable outcome constitutes strategic thinking. Thought, analysis, research, and discussion that produce a plan to achieve the most desirable outcome is strategic planning. Both strategic thinking and strategic planning are leadership behaviors—and very coachable. Strategic thinking and planning are future-focused activities intended to produce predetermined results. As a coach, you need to focus on strategic issues, because this will make you and the people who receive your coaching all the more effective at thinking, planning, and acting in a strategic manner.

Why Strategy Is Important to the Individual

Individuals, especially those responsible for the performance of others, have strategic responsibilities that take them beyond mere operations and tactical concerns. Strategic awareness among managers and executives is essential to individual and organizational success. Without an understanding of and an appreciation for the larger organizational, future-focused picture, it is difficult to measure whether the ways individual goals and strengths are being coached are in the best interests of the organization. We like to assume they are, but how can we be sure? We assume that any personal growth and development of individuals within organizations is good for the organization. But that's not always the case, *unless* the growth and development of individuals takes place in the context of the overarching organizational strategy.

Strategy is a concern for individuals at all levels of the organization. For those who operate on the CEO level, setting the overall corporate direction is a key responsibility and an obvious marker of long-term success or failure. The company's chief executives—the CEO, COO, CFO, and so on (collectively known as the C-level)—need to be visionary and custodial at the same time. They need to look into the future and understand where the organization needs to go in light of trends and market forces while, at the same time, preserving their company's operational integrity and day-to-day position in a volatile market.

Other individuals at other levels in the organization also need to fully understand what the overall corporate strategy is and to become deft at explaining it to others. They need to develop the ability to represent the vision to other employees and to persuasively articulate its value proposition to win over their fellow team members and gain buy-in. There are undoubtedly localized strategic agendas connected to particular business units or divisions, which must also be reconciled while executing aspects of the larger strategy. These substrategies help to define the goals for the particular business units and to drive individuals toward performance and business results.

As a contextual coach, you help your coaching clients understand these corporate and local strategies, especially when it comes time for them to sell these strategies into the organization and to assign priorities. If you develop your clients without a complete understanding of these strategies, you risk leading them down the wrong path toward severe limitation or ultimate failure. Therefore, the coaching action plan for an individual must always be balanced with the strategic interests of the organization. Contextual coaches always position individual development plans within the context of the business strategy.

If your client is newly hired to your organization, the coaching process can be uniquely helpful. Newly hired individuals often face unique challenges when moving into strategic responsibilities and often require assimilation coaching. They most likely have limited experience in determining corporate direction for themselves or their teams—especially in your organization's culture. By assisting new individuals with strategic planning and with the process of tying their coaching plan to the larger corporate and business unit strategies, you further prepare individuals for future roles and help them to effectively integrate the corporate vision at whatever level they are currently functioning.

Moving from strategic thinking to action, however, can be a

challenge for many individuals who are more visionary than custodial in orientation. As a contextual coach, you may therefore assist your client to map specific tactics as a means to manage the effective execution of strategic initiatives.

Why Strategy Is Important to the Organization

An organization is, by definition, people and necessary resources brought together for a purpose. It naturally follows that these people have a collective interest in the success of the organization. Strategy is the bridge that connects the original purpose and the successful realization of that purpose. A group of people without purpose can't really be called an organization in the true sense of the word. A purpose without a strategy for its execution is almost as meaningless. An unorganized group of people can complete something sans intentionality or by chance. But can that really be called an accomplishment?

Investments of time, money, and other resources in executive coaching are too precious to leave the organizational benefits of coaching to chance. Considering that the time, money, and other resources come from the organization, it makes no sense for the organization's interests to be left out of the equation. Coaching that emphasizes the strategic context of the individual's *and* organization's work life pays exponentially greater dividends than coaching that focuses too narrowly on the individual. The strategic component of Contextual Coaching increases awareness and sharpens skills around those issues that affect the internal organizational population, as well as all outside stakeholders.

The Objectives and Goals for Strategy

Setting strategy for an organization, as well as breaking out all of the individual components and contributors to the execution of that strategy, is an organizing process in and of itself. As a contextual coach, you will help your clients become much more valuable and highly contributing members of the organizational population as you expose them to the purposes and best practices in strategic thinking and planning.

That means helping your clients look up and forward. Strategic vision is by nature out of the weeds, above the sightline clutter of details and minutia. Until people are introduced to a loftier perspective, it is rare that they will find it on their own. That's where your coaching comes in. Your objective is to challenge your clients to think more broadly, at a higher level, with consideration of future implications. Your goal is to get their thinking out where the organization is heading, not where it is or has been.

Teach your clients the difference between a mission statement and a vision statement. A mission statement is about what is—how things are done at present. It is operational and tactical in nature. Your goal is to elevate your clients' perspective to a visionary level. The vision statement is not about what is; it is about *what if*. Another strategic objective is to stimulate "possibility thinking" in your clients. This capacity for transcendent reflection will enhance their individual career possibilities while committing another pair of eyes to watching out for the organization's future.

Behaviors Related to Strategy

As you track the Contextual Coaching process, you will identify behaviors associated with the individual, as well as with the organizational results you want to produce. Strategy is the first of ten areas of behavioral focus. To prepare yourself, as a contextual coach, to provide practical and effective guidance to the individuals who receive your coaching, you must pay attention to the ways your organization establishes and executes strategy.

Coaching your clients around theoretical strategic planning and execution will produce limited results, benefiting neither the individual nor the organization. The best opportunity and incentive for your clients' growth and development related to strategic thinking, planning, and execution takes place in real time and, of course, within the context of the organization.

In examining, tracking, and modifying your clients' habits, skills, and activities, you are looking to identify ways in which they can benefit immediately from the forward-looking piece of strategy as a powerful personal awareness and goal-setting exercise. You might also inquire as to how your clients are using strategy in team building, depending on the number of their direct reports. There are specific behaviors that are part of the Contextual Coaching 360-degree assessment that measures your clients' proficiency in using strategy as a tool for developing their own careers and/or the careers of their direct reports. These include:

- Successfully managing resistance to new ideas
- Formulating a strategy related to business goals
- Articulating the strategic vision of the organization
- Applying organizational strategy to area of responsibility
- Managing strategic planning process within area of responsibility

If you were to place these behaviors before a group of feedback providers and ask them to rank your client, what would they say? Would they say that the behaviors listed are overused, underused, or used optimally by your client? If you use the Contextual Coaching 360-degree assessment, you and your client will get those answers. Even though using the Contextual Coaching 360-degree assessment is a formal way to assess the overuse, underuse, or optimal use of each behavior in a survey format, you can also use these questions to conduct your own structured interviews with feedback providers, sitting down with them face to face and discussing each behavior. How do your clients rate themselves on these behaviors?

Optimal Behavior for Strategy

As with the other nine components of the Contextual Coaching model, strategy comes to life through behaviors like those you just read. Like any behavior associated with living and working, strategic behavior can be underused to the point that few, if any, benefits are derived. It can also be overused to the point that few, if any, benefits are derived. Ideally, you can coach your client's behavior to its optimal level, for maximum benefit.

To fully understand the concept of optimal use, think of it as the Goldilocks syndrome. A chair that is too small, a bed that is too soft, and porridge that is too cold won't get the job done. Neither will furniture that is too big and hard or porridge that is too hot. As a contextual coach, you help engender and sustain strategic behavior in your clients that is "just right" to produce the most productive personal performance possible, as well as the greatest organizational gain.

Underuse of Strategy

People can underuse strategic behaviors for several legitimate reasons: (1) They might simply be unaware of what strategy is and the role it plays in their professional lives and the health and well-being of the organization; (2) they might understand on a conceptual level what strategy is and the purpose it serves but fail to see themselves as strategists or to understand how forward-looking and generally visionary thinking involves them; (3) they might "get" all of the above but not be sufficiently invested in making the behavior meaningful.

In the first case, education is the answer. Your job as coach is to create awareness of how important strategy is to the individual and the organization by leading your clients to the fountain of knowledge and encouraging them to splash around and consume the information in whatever way works best. If your clients are aware of how important strategy is to them as individuals and to the organization, help them to accept their responsibility to think and act strategically. This is where habits, skills, and activities are particularly important in establishing and maintaining the strategic behaviors you are looking for out of your clients.

If attitude and motivation are the issues, education, habits, skills, and activities are all likely to be part of the solution. The "I don't get paid to think strategically" attitude is usually a ruse or a red herring for "I don't understand" and/or "I don't know how to engage in" strategic thinking and behavior. Your clients will become comfortable with strategy through some combination of education, habits, skills, and activities. Don't wait until your clients "feel" like becoming strategic; get them actively involved in the behaviors, and the sense of familiarity, the comfort, and the mastery will come with time and reinforcement.

Overuse of Strategy

The future can be a place to hide from the responsibilities of today. It can also be a fun place about which to speculate, if your clients are given to such things. In either case, being too far out there or so far out there that the practical, tactical, or operational needs of today are being neglected will not benefit the individual or the organization. As a coach, it is your challenge to help people create the optimal balance of past, present, and future vision, with a decided prejudice in favor of future vision.

It might be that you need to paint a picture for your clients that illustrates a future vision for your organization but where the present is being neglected. What are the consequences of that? How will the future suffer? You certainly don't want to frighten your clients away from future-focused strategic behaviors. So err on the side of letting them remain eyes up and out. But teach them to keep their finger on the pulse of the organization's ongoing needs. As with everything else, optimal behavior is about balance. And balance is not about complete exclusion as much as it is about moderation in all things, from underuse to overuse of the prescribed behavior. (For examples of the underuse, overuse, and optimal use of strategy behaviors, as well as for suggested reading on strategy, visit www.WeMakeTalentWork.com and click on "The Coaching Connection.")

How Your Coaching Client Fits into Strategy

Coaching itself is strategic. It is up to you to make that clear to your clients. The organization is making an investment in them—sometimes a hefty investment—in order to derive a future benefit.

You and your client both need to understand that you are both building for the future.

The action plan for the coaching process is, by its nature, strategic. Whether the reason for your coaching is developmental or remedial, the target behaviors are ahead of you and your clients. You are moving toward improvement and, even though action begets benefits immediately, the larger and more significant benefits will follow the establishment of new habits, the adoption of new skills, and a consistent engagement in strategically rich activities.

How to Introduce Strategy to Your Coaching Client

Your clients' receptiveness to learning about and developing new behaviors around strategy will have a great deal to do with how attractive you make the discussion and how compelling you make your argument. In the end, you want your clients to be apologists for strategy, so it needs to be a client-friendly concept from the start. To that end, use your future-focused coaching to consistently point out the connection between strategic planning and execution and your clients' career success.

Remember that people buy into new ideas and behaviors (read: Change) only after they (1) believe that they will be happier with the new behaviors than with the present situation, and (2) believe that the better future you speak of is attainable. This all begins with the realistic and promising way you describe your clients' shift from an operational focus toward a visionary, strategic focus. To be a successful contextual coach, you must begin as a strategy salesperson. Once you've successfully mastered that, there are nine more categories to sell—each one important to creating a well-balanced executive in a well-balanced organization.

Connecting Strategy to the Coaching Process

We've mentioned specific ways that you can connect the topic of strategy to the coaching process: (1) Use it as an illustration of how your present relationship with your clients is a future-focused—and therefore strategic—activity; (2) raise your clients' collective consciousnesses about how strategy is the fascia tissue that connects their career ambitions to the ongoing health and well-being of the organization; and (3) make sure that strategy is understood, acted upon, and discussed in the language of optimal, well-balanced use. To keep strategy in perfect perspective, consider how it has been a past and present influence.

360-Degree Feedback Questions for Strategy

Our favorite coaching assessment is the well-executed 360-degree structured interview. Sitting and talking through these questions and noting the answers (verbal and nonverbal) of your clients and their feedback providers is a terrific way to assess the state of your clients' relationship and mastery of the ten Contextual Coaching components.

Questions for the Coaching Client

Here are questions specific to strategy that we recommend you ask your clients:

- How would you describe your management of strategic responsibilities?
- Can you provide some examples to illustrate this description?
- Who looks to you for strategic guidance and sees you as a resource for information related to the company's strategy?

- Can you explain why people look to you or do not look to you as a resource for information related to the company's strategy?

If your client is an individual contributor, the first question relates to your client's own understanding of strategic issues. Employees have a major stake in understanding their own roles in the strategy of the organization and must work to ensure that their individual efforts are aligned with the organization's strategic plan. If your coaching client has direct reports, you want to know how your client's management style supports the strategic imperatives of the organization.

The second question also works for both individual contributors and those with teams to manage. Individual contributors will choose examples to illustrate the depth of their own understanding of strategic issues, as well as examples of how the client aligns personal as well as team efforts with strategic objectives. For individual contributors, the third question relates perhaps to peers and might expose where a person is lacking influence. You might want to set up ways that clients that fall into this group might be able to demonstrate their understanding and savvy around strategic issues. This is also a training opportunity for future management responsibilities. For those clients with direct reports, this is a good time to discuss what an important opportunity this can be to achieve strategic alignment among those reporting to your client.

Even if your clients do not manage teams, this is a good exercise to illustrate that being a strategic leader has a positive influence on peers. Part of being a good coach is teaching others to coach. It can be good practice in exercising influence without authority. The earlier people in the organization start talking strategy, the better. Knowing who is tuned into organizational strategy and who is not will ensure that your clients' coaching engagements are aligned with your strategy and the organization's strategy.

Questions for the Feedback Provider

If you are using the Contextual Coaching 360-degree assessment, these will be the questions that your feedback providers will need to answer with regard to your coaching client:

- How would you describe the client's management of strategic responsibilities?
- What are some examples to illustrate this description?
- Do other individuals look to the client for strategic guidance and see the client as a resource for information related to the company's strategy?
- Can you explain why they look to the client or don't look to the client as a resource for information related to the company's strategy?

You are looking for rich answers that will give you and your coaching clients material to work with as together you design their coaching action plans. The answers you receive to these questions will spell out whether your clients have gaps in the area of strategy and, if so, the type of remedy that is called for. It should be obvious that just exploring these topics with your clients and gathering data about them will heighten clients' awareness of the many hats a manager must wear—whether your client is a manager at present or aspires to become one. If your coaching client is on track to become a manager, this is a good opportunity for your client to learn about strategy in the context of the organization.

How to Use the Responses to the 360-Degree Assessment Questions for Strategy

Don't judge the responses your clients give you. Don't judge the responses your clients' feedback providers offer. Solid input, honestly acquired, is all helpful as you design a positive course of action for leadership development, performance improvement, or remedial course correction. Information is information. Put it to good use. Help your clients understand and accept that people provide feedback through their personal filters and framed in the context of their personal comfort zones and biases. Assessments can reveal as much about the feedback providers as they do about your coaching clients, or more.

Identify the Gaps

Let the concept of optimal guide you. There is a best practice/optimal outcome scenario that you, your clients, and your clients' bosses can negotiate. What do you ideally want your client to do? To accomplish? To achieve? Once that is done, you can use the 360-feedback data, as well as other performance measures that might be available to you, as a sort of global positioning satellite to plot where your clients are now, where you want them to go, and any detours that might be encountered along the way. Comparing what you have at present and what you want in the future will provide you with some gaps to be filled.

Habits

How can the gaps be filled by removing bad habits that your clients have acquired over the years? Are your clients even aware that they might have counterproductive habits? Note any such habits in the action plan. What can you do to replace bad habits with positive habits? Note that in the action plan, too. It's not enough to remove a habit. It must be replaced with a positive habit, or the bad habit will reclaim its space, stronger than it was before.

Skills

How can the enhancement of existing skills and/or the development of new skills fill in or bridge the gaps? You have access to quite a large and impressible brain trust when you consider all of the combined experience and wisdom in your pool of feedback providers. Identify what skills are required, research how to access the necessary learning and practice opportunities, and put the program for skills acquisition in the action plan.

Activities

What can your clients begin doing in real time, right now, to begin filling or bridging the gaps exposed by the 360-degree assessment? Try to get your clients involved quickly in working on activities that get them going in the right direction. One important reason for getting your clients engaged in new and positively focused activities is to hasten the day when they are comfortable with the new behaviors. The fastest way to feel comfortable is to feel competent. Competency is often achieved through practice, practice, and more practice.

How to Discuss the Strategy Gaps with Your Coaching Client

Rather than portray the performance gaps you've identified as deficiencies, you're probably better off referring to them as "growth opportunities." If your clients think that terms such as "growth opportunities" sound maudlin or contrived, simply point out that the crevasse between where your clients are at this moment in the organization and where they want to be can be crossed only on a bridge built upon pillars that don't yet exist. A growth opportunity is a chance to build a bridge to span the place between where your clients currently reside and where they want to be. The notion of growth and development will make a lot more sense in that context.

"The organization needs you to step up and take on bigger responsibilities," you tell your clients. "You want to assume a larger and more vital role in the success of this organization. The action plan we are drafting based on your 360-degree feedback is the roadmap for getting there. Let's get started." Rather than focus on the gaps, focus instead on what will fill them.

Strategy Summary

From the beginning, we have maintained that strategy is a systematic, methodical, and intentional plan of action or nonaction, depending on what you want the outcome of your plan to be. Thinking something through and deciding upon the best course of action is a strategy. Doing something bold and outrageous or sitting tight and not doing anything at all are both strategies. What makes them brilliant or disastrous is how well the premeditated strategy meets or misses the goals the strategy was intended to achieve. A strategy is about where you are going and how you're going to get there. To that end, strategists commonly ask the journalist's questions: Who? What? When? Where? Why? How? Plus the bean counters' favorite: How much?

We have identified specific strategic behaviors for you and your clients to use as a guideline for your coaching engagement. By following those behaviors and rating what they look like when underused, overused, and optimally used, you will create a clear and powerful roadmap to follow in helping your clients to improve their performance significantly, which in turn contributes to a significantly improved organization. Part of what strengthens the organization is the way that strategy informs every other component in the model, especially structural decisions.

In Chapter 4, our focus shifts from strategy to the structure of the organization. As with every component of the Contextual Coaching model, organizational structure must be aligned with all the other components so that the components do not cancel one another out. The interrelationships among elements points to the dominance of systems theory over the whole organization. If, for example, organizational strategy is inconsistent or antithetical to organizational structure, the structure will become an impediment to the strategy, if it doesn't undermine it completely.

CHAPTER 4

Area of Behavioral Focus: Structure

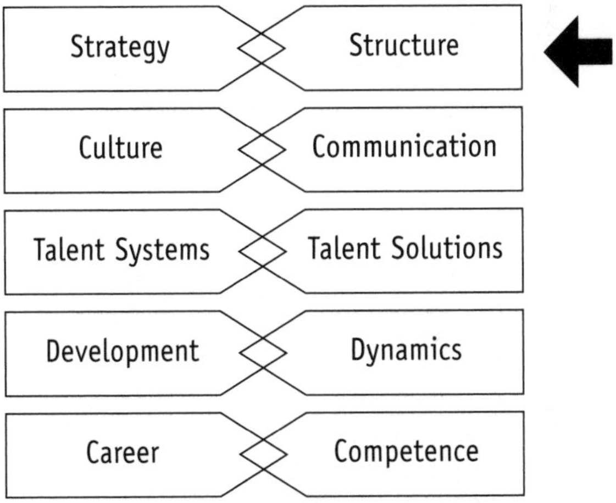

"In these challenging times, nonprofit CEOs need a safety net. A coach becomes the one person with whom they can test ideas, honestly share their moments of uncertainty, and then together construct how the CEO will lead forward with vision and confidence."

—Cathy Tisdale
Vice President, Council Partnerships
Mission to Market
Girl Scouts of the USA

Structure is the second of the ten components in the Contextual Coaching model and can be defined as a mode of organizing (in our case, people, places, and resources), an arrangement of parts, elements, or constituents—or, perhaps most importantly, a complex system considered from the point of view of the whole, rather than of any single part. Does that sound like the organization you work for? While the organization is considered from the point of view of the whole rather than from the point of any single individual, the Contextual Coaching model claims that both the individual and the organization are important; neither can be fully known without fully knowing the other.

Depending on your coaching client's level within the organization, the strategy of your client's area of responsibility must roll up and integrate with larger business units and/or the overarching corporate strategy. This requires enhanced awareness of the intentional design and structure of the organization. It is critical that the individual coaching process relate to the structure of the organization to both illustrate and understand how your coaching client's efforts will be blended with (and enhance) the work of others. Just as the coaching process must be carried out in the context of the organization, it must also roll down to the strategic concerns of those who report into the coaching client's area of the business. In pursuit of flawless execution, the organizational structure must be built to support the goals and expectations set forth in its strategic plan. As the contextual coach, you keep the coaching process focused on the organization by identifying the position of your coaching client within the corporate structure and help your client understand all the intentional and incidental strategies at play. If you know the reporting relationships, the expectations for your coaching client and other team members, and how structural strategies can best be integrated and communicated, you will be able to provide a powerful service to your coaching client and to the larger corporate constituencies being served.

When considering the structure of the organization, you should place emphasis on your coaching clients' relationship with the appropriate managing executive. Key to your coaching clients' success is the relationship they have with their manager(s)—especially if that's you. As a coach or a manager who coaches, there will be times when you will be your clients' manager and times when you will deal with clients who report to other managers.

Regardless of whether you are the manager, your clients' managers are critical constituents in this process and should be included in the communication process that surrounds the coaching engagement, including action plans, midterm and final reports, and periodic meetings. Having numerous pairs of eyes scrutinizing the engagement from time to time will help ensure the effective management of this important relationship in your coaching client's work life.

Focusing on the organizational structure will also help you to identify the lines of authority that exist inside your coaching client's organization. The use of appropriate power is crucial for your clients in managing their leadership roles. As the coach, you need to help your coaching clients focus on their leadership roles within the context of the organization. What works for leaders in some places might not work in your environment. It will also be important to identify ways your coaching clients can gain positive exposure to different levels in the organization. Knowing and understanding the organization's structure is vital for identifying where the power brokers are located.

Reorganizations

Many of us have received that eerie email that announces some sort of reorganization. You know— the one that causes a big lump in your throat, tightness in your chest, and concern about "what will happen to me?" Although you hope the reorganization won't affect your area at all, you know it will. You know that roles and responsibilities are about to change.

The Law of Gravity asserts that what goes up must come down. The same seems to be true of organizational life. What can be organized can become disorganized. Does that sound at all like your organization? What can be organized once, can be reorganized as often as the wind blows. Reorganizations have become comic fodder for Dilbert because some organizations overuse the reorganization process, hoping that changes in structure will provide all the answers to the problems that can emerge from the other nine Contextual Coaching topics.

Reorganizations are often about downsizing staff numbers, better aligning the business in light of new strategic goals, or thrusting new energies into the organization by shaking things up. Those of you in big companies have probably watched the blue-suited consultants hovering as they make plans for the company to march in a new direction. The consultants are specialists in creating appropriate structures for living the strategy in the day-to-day operations and operating in a way that creates new efficiencies and opportunities.

But, what about the times when the blue-suited consultants are not around? It is important to focus on structural needs of organizations all of the time, not just when a reorganization is in order. The way that you create an architecture for your organization or your team is critical to your process of executing your business strategy and coming through with the commitments and relationships you have to others within the organization.

All managers are challenged to look at the goals and objectives of their departments and to align people and processes to meet those goals as effectively as possible. Perhaps neither you nor your coaching cli[illegible]e organizational design specialists; you may not even ow[illegible] suit. It is nevertheless the fundamental responsibility of [illegible]o structure their staffs to fill the appropriate roles and ful-[illegible] responsibilities needed to achieve the desired outcomes.

[illegible]tructure is the way an organization sets up its employees, [illegible]operty, and other resources to manage process, determine lines of authority, identify workflow within and between departments, and create a management architecture that maximizes opportunity while minimizing risk. When you hear people refer to "drawing it up on paper," they are talking about designing structure. Even if the company has an overall structure in place that has been designed by operations, human resources, or corporate strategy specialists, each manager of an individual department or business unit is typically expected to determine the best substructure for that unit.

Typically, we do this best by beginning with the work that needs to be managed and the tasks required to achieve success. We identify partnerships between necessary roles and identify handoffs and dependencies with other departments. Then, once a basic structure of roles and responsibilities that includes lines of authority has been designed, the manager turns to look at the talent available and matches the available talent to the roles.

The Coaching Connection Among Organizations, Individuals, and Structures

Structure is an element of the Contextual Coaching model because organizational alignment is an essential element of the company. The structure of an organization provides a rich story for how your coaching client faces challenges, manages relationships, and uses influence to get things done. In many ways, this chapter argues the main thesis behind Contextual Coaching as a framework for coaching. Because coaching is not simply about the one-on-one relationship between the coach and the coaching client, the company, nonprofit, or public-sector organization provides the context for every step of the coaching process.

This underlying method for coaching requires that the coach comprehend the ways in which the organization operates, how power is shared, how people work together, and how alignment between roles and departments occurs. All of these topics affect how employees do their jobs. It tells us how they live an organizational life at work. Coaches do effective work when they coach in light of these realities, not in spite of them.

In our model, we partner structure with strategy to remind ourselves that organizational structure is not in place for its own sake. As we suggested earlier, the structure of the organization needs to serve the business strategy. This is not a chicken-and-egg dilemma. We know that strategy comes first and drives decisions, working relationships, and organizational design. The goal of any organization is to think critically about strategy and to determine how the people in the company can best meet the company's goals and objectives. This includes the way people are organized and assigned tasks.

Executive coaches hired from outside the organization are most effective if they are allowed to do a quick study of the organizational structure to determine key issues that are relevant to the coaching process. As a manager within an organization, you have an advantage in understanding what is important relative to the organizational structure and how to utilize that information within your coaching process. You know where the bones are buried and should be able to talk through issues such as required sign-offs and working partnerships and to identify executives to watch out for.

One of the things an executive coach often focuses on is the way the organization uses power in its day-to-day operations. In our politically correct society, "power" is a term we tend to avoid. The term has a negative dimension to it and often connotes one person's authority over another. This definition does not gel in organizations that claim to take more democratic or collaborative approaches to getting work done. Organizations that are more "top-down" in their orientation may also avoid the word since to use it would place additional emphasis on their authoritative and didactic structural model.

In truth, much of what takes place in an organization is all about power, and those who deny that fact limit their opportunities to be effective agents of positive change. As a coach, you should explore how power is used in your organization and discuss it with coaching clients whenever appropriate. It is important that you and your clients share a similar understanding of how people in the organization use power and influence to get things done. There are many coaching implications related to the use of power and influence, and opening up this conversation can accelerate the development of your client in serious and sustainable ways.

As a coach, your exposing your client to a broad view of organizational structure can provide a roadmap to new levels of success. Structure can be a way for your clients to better understand their everyday business experiences—managing direct reports; participating on cross-functional teams; managing up; working with other departments; responding to the requests of peers, direct reports, and internal and external customers; and identifying opportunities for themselves in jobs at the next level.

Why Structure Is Important to the Individual

The everyday anxieties of organizational life often include questions about managing relationships. Your clients might wonder:

- Am I getting recognition from my boss in a way that shows that I am valued?

- Does the interaction of my team demonstrate support and bonding?
- Do other departments make my life easy or difficult?
- Have I provided critical feedback to my subordinates in constructive ways?
- Can I manage the unhappy customer and turn around a difficult situation?
- Is there benefit for me to know leaders in other departments?
- Does participating in a cross-functional task force build my career potential?

Relationships provide many positive dimensions to the working experience. They also create complexities that require negotiation, capitulation, collaboration, delegation, and more. Structure within an organization is partly about creating systems and protocol for successfully managing multiple relationships. Structure can help decide which customers will work best with which account managers. Structure can help guide workflow, work sharing, and hand-offs between individuals and groups. Organizational structure is important to consider when designing how teams should be assembled and considering which teams might work best together on cross-functional assignments. Lines of authority are part and parcel of organizational structure and can be traced to how decisions are made and by whom. Organizational structure is a guide to managing relationships to ensure that both individual and organizational opportunities are maximized.

When you experience coaching as an individual, you will probably bring up relationship challenges. Because relationships are so essential to an effective work experience, we emphasize teaming as a unique element in coaching design and devote Chapter 10 to the dynamics of a team. However, structure is different from teaming in the way individuals experience it. While teams are about working together, structure is about working through channels of authority and between departments that are interlocked by workflow commitments. Whether you work in a matrix organization or in a more traditional structure, you interact with others around the organization knowing that lines of authority need to be acknowledged and managed and that you are in partnership with other individuals from other departments that call for flawless hand-offs and accountability between players.

As a coach, you should have a broad view of the organization as a backdrop for your coaching clients. This will help you consider the ways in which the organization puts pressures on your clients. Consider how cascading of the organizational strategy is important to your clients' working relationships. This is especially true when your clients have responsibility for determining the roles of others who report to them or in determining the workflow partnerships that are necessary to implement organizational strategy. The architecture of the organization is integral to the completion of this strategy at the global and local levels. The organizational structure must be synchronized with the goals and expectations set forth in the organization's strategic plan if you are to have any hope of flawless execution.

As a coach, you can help individuals think through the best ways to deploy staff to get work done. You can also aid your clients in identifying the important structure-driven, interdepartmental processes that must be successfully managed to maintain strategic direction. It is critical that the individual coaching process use organizational structure to illustrate and understand how the coaching clients' efforts will blend with (and enhance) the work of others.

When considering the structure of the organization, with your client, you should place special emphasis on the positive and negative implications of the relationship between your clients and the executives who manage them—even if that is you. The relationship with one's manager(s) is critical to success. The effective management of this important structural relationship in the work life of your client must be discussed and monitored throughout the process.

Involving Your Client's Manager

Let's assume that the manager in question is not you. In this case, you will treat the manager or executive as a constituent who is involved in the coaching process as a stakeholder. Managers can gain something from a successful coaching process and need to share goals and objectives with you, as well as your clients. The great coach interviews leaders not simply to learn about areas of growth and development for the coaching client but to get some sense of the manager's leadership style in order to help the client manage the relationship successfully. This includes looking at the way leaders use power in relationship to your coaching clients. Are they hands on? Hands off? Do they micromanage? Do they allow decision making at the next level? Do they provide critical feedback? Do they pay attention to stress levels in others? Are they able to empathize with their teams?

Researching and understanding the power dynamic between the leader and the direct report (who is your client) can help you provide effective empathy and guidance for managing the relationship, especially in times of stress. The 360-degree assessment process can help you gather additional information about the boss's style to help you in your coaching focus.

Coaching Your Own Direct Reports

If you are your client's direct manager, you have a different challenge: self-disclosure. It is time for you to open up about your own strengths and weaknesses and to discuss your understanding of decision-making authority, delegation, and how you manage up. You need to be transparent about your style and open when it comes to hearing feedback. You need to be open to the notion that some things you do as a leader may confuse, disappoint, or frustrate your direct report/coaching client. The coaching relationship works both ways as you receive important feedback and advice on how to do things differently.

This reciprocal relationship will be a positive demonstration of your own openness and acceptance that you are not perfect, which grants your clients permission to not be perfect. This will only strengthen the coaching process and relationship and opens up the possibility of deepening your working relationship as a coach and leader with your direct reports. In this part of the coaching process, consider yourself a player/coach and be willing to create a deep and effective bond.

Why Structure Is Important to the Organization

It is rare to find an organizational position that does not include interaction with other departments and other people. Some people work as individual contributors. But even working from home usually involves interaction with people in other departments, albeit from a distance. The tennis star stands on the court by herself and has to deliver. Yet, tennis stars need audiences, coaches, financial advisers, colleagues, and support systems to help them perform well. Most of the time, individuals within an organization cannot do their jobs effectively on their own. Success in their individual positions requires that they have productive working relationships.

As a contextual coach, you keep the coaching process organizationally focused by understanding and sharing how your clients' positions fit into the larger corporate structure. With this in mind, you help your clients understand all the structural strategies at play. By knowing the reporting relationships, the expectations for your clients and their teams, and how structural strategies can best be integrated and communicated, you are able to provide a powerful service to larger corporate constituencies that your clients serve.

Consider the sales department as an example. Sales representatives win deals because they are extremely persuasive and in tune with their clients' needs. They are driven by the excitement of the sales process, and the thrill of getting the "yes" from prospects provides a unique psychological motivation. The breakdown for many sales representatives comes when they fail to understand, appreciate, and collaborate with other parts of their own organizations, such as the customer service departments and the operations departments. This is especially true if they do not negotiate with profitability in mind or are overly focused on customized solutions that have no operational infrastructure or process support in place.

If sales managers are not able to successfully manage their relationships with their peers in other areas, all-out war can erupt between departments. Customers can sense these things, and they can eventually lead to the loss of business and/or unprofitable selling.

An effective organizational structure that enhances positive working relationships is not "nice to have"; it is a "must have." Relationships that work well and an effective organizational structure can be the difference between successfully realizing your organization's strategy and failing miserably.

To pick on our friends in the sales department again, let's consider the case of an individual sales representative who tends to irritate her partners in the service group. The organization would benefit tremendously if the sales representative could be coached to use the same sales skills she has mastered for use with clients with her partners in the service group. First, she should be as empathic with the internal resources as she is with her prospects. This means being able to consider the structural positions and situations of other individuals in order to negotiate positive terms that create win-win scenarios for all involved.

She should also attempt to be persuasive when she has a special need, instead of demonstrating frustration with the service department and exclaiming that they "don't get it." She could also consult with the service team *before* a contract is signed to ensure that she is not creating havoc within the organization. Helping ego-driven salespersons to slow down and consider structural implications of their behaviors is the responsibility of the sales manager as coach. As a contextual coach, you can help sales representatives use the skills they possess with "internal customers" as well as external clients and help them to consider the organizational and structural implications of the deals they close.

When the coaching process takes into account the multiple issues related to working relationships, decision making, hand-offs between departments, and cross-functionality-based partnerships, the organization can be more effective and efficient and can execute corporate strategy in ways that are more likely to meet organizational objectives.

The Objectives and Goals for Structure

As we have said, organizational structure is extremely important to the success of the individual and of the organization. Therefore, it is incumbent upon you, as a coach or a manager who coaches, to understand organizational structure and to be able to facilitate and guide your clients' understanding of structural issues. You know from your own experience that the better you understand structural issues of the organization, the better equipped you are to spot structural problems and help correct them.

The same is true of your clients. The more they understand about organizational structure, the less they will fall into the trap of believing that the cards are arbitrarily stacked against them when they encounter bottlenecks. They will begin to view organizational activities and transactions in the context of structure and work flow. Like you, they will be able to identify structural inefficiencies and/or dysfunction and make suggestions on how to restore previous structural efficiencies or even improve the situations through structural and process redesign.

Behaviors Related to Structure

As you continue to track the Contextual Coaching process, you will identify behaviors associated with both individual results and organizational results that you want to help achieve. As a contextual coach, you will pay attention to the ways your organization establishes and uses structure to help you provide practical and effective advice to your coaching clients.

In examining, tracking, and modifying your clients' habits, skills, and activities, you are looking to identify ways in which they can benefit from structural awareness. Depending on the number of your client's direct reports, you might also inquire as to how your client is using his or her knowledge of structure in team building. The following behaviors are part of the Contextual Coaching

360-degree assessment that measures your clients' proficiency in using structure as a tool for developing their own careers and/or the careers of their direct reports:

- Uses power for the benefit of the organization.
- Demonstrates political savvy in getting things done.
- Provides a framework for achieving organizational objectives.
- Creates relationships with managers to support initiatives and reach goals.
- Participates in cross-functional task forces that build organizational alliances.

> If you were to place these behaviors before a group of feedback providers and ask them to rank your client, what would they say? Would they say that the behaviors listed are overused, underused, or used optimally by your client? If you use the Contextual Coaching 360-degree assessment, you will get those answers. Although using the Contextual Coaching 360-degree assessment is a formal way to assess the over-, under-, or optimal use of each behavior in a survey format, you can also use these questions to conduct your own structured interviews with feedback providers, sitting down with them face to face and discussing each behavior. We provide specific questions for the coaching client and feedback providers later in the chapter.

Optimal Behavior for Structure

If your clients truly understand structure, they will be able to pull back for a wide shot of the organization and see for themselves how people and resources are arranged to maximize their benefit to the success of the organization. Structural awareness helps your clients be strategically savvy, as well. With a view from 35,000 feet, the structure of the organization becomes clearer and, thus, easier to navigate.

The optimal strength related to structure is the ability to make structural audits and assessments to determine whether the current structure is appropriate for achieving the stated goals and objectives and, if it is not, to know how structural modifications or redesign can bring the organization back to the optimal alignment of people and resources. If you have conversations on these subjects with your clients, you will be preparing them to be leaders of tomorrow.

Underuse of Structure

As you can see on the development approach chart for structure located on our Web site, www.WeMakeTalentWork.com (click on "The Coaching Connection" tab), remaining uninformed or unenlightened about the importance of structure in organizations can leave you and your clients standing on the outside looking in. No one can truly engage in strategic thinking without being able to see the big picture. When they do not adequately understand structure, people can relate to each other and organize themselves in bizarre ways that do nothing to promote the overarching goals of the organization.

Underuse of structure can lead to duplication of efforts and services. Your clients might not be aware of how their lack of structural awareness is causing them to work harder than necessary and work less quickly than they could and is costing the organization more money than needs to be spent. From a broad perspective, the underuse of structure and a lack of organizational awareness—resulting in misalignment between what people do best and what organizations need most—can cost the organization dearly in squandered money, resources, and human effort.

Overuse of Structure

As noted in greater detail in the development approach charts for structure, overuse of structure can cause problems for the individual and the organization. Continuing with the Goldilocks syndrome, we can see that the porridge that can be too cold can also be too hot. If the pendulum swings from a lack of knowledge and functional awareness regarding structure past the optimal zone and into the red or overused zone, the underuse problems change shape and become overuse problems.

Being too structured can mean being too rigid, too restricted, too constrained, too contained, too mundane, even. When an organization is locked down tight and the relationships between people and departments seem frozen in time or set in concrete, productivity can suffer. One of the chief reasons clients need to understand structure and organization is that this understanding can help them spot where organization for organization's sake might be hampering otherwise robust performance and productivity. Bureaucracy pleases only bureaucrats. As a coach, you can help your clients understand how flexible and adaptable structure can help keep things moving and grooving. (For examples of the underuse, overuse, and optimal use of structure behaviors, as well as for suggested additional reading on structure, visit www.WeMakeTalent Work.com and click on "The Coaching Connection.")

How Your Coaching Client Fits into Structure

As we have mentioned, many eyes can see a lot more than a few eyes. By coaching people to be aware of structural issues and how good organization can benefit everyone, you're adding to the number of eyes keeping a close watch for structural breakdowns and/or bottlenecks. The sooner people report organizational hiccups, the faster they can be remedied.

Helping your clients understand structure, organization, and all the subtleties and nuances that go with them is not enough. Your clients need to fully understand and appreciate how they fit into the structural and organizational picture. Only then will they have a strong sense of what their roles are and whether they are in the best possible alignment with the other people, resources, and processes that will help them be as efficient and as effective as possible.

How to Introduce Structure to Your Coaching Client

Introducing structure to your coaching clients can begin as simply as drawing diagrams. You can try these ideas:

- Draw how the organization looks from the customer's perspective.
- Draw how the organization looks from your CEO's perspective.
- Draw how the organization looks from your boss's perspective, and so on.

A great way for you and your clients to begin discussing structure and organization is to have your clients tell you what the organization looks like from *their* perspectives.

From that point forward, you can expand the discussion to explore how your clients interact with other individuals, groups, and departments in the organization. What do your clients truly understand about relationships and how the structured ways they deal with others determine their success and the success of the organization? From an individual or organizational perspective, it is not advisable for any of your clients to be restricted by what they don't know about any of the ten components in the Contextual Coaching model. That is why your role as a contextual coach is so critical to both individual and organizational success.

Connecting Structure to the Coaching Process

We've mentioned several times now specific ways that you can connect the topic of structure to the coaching process: (1) Use it as an illustration of how your clients need to be relationship-focused—and therefore structural—in their thinking; (2) raise your clients' collective consciousnesses about how structure is the positioning of people and resources in ways that help determine the success of individuals and the organization as a whole; and (3) make sure that structure is understood, acted upon, and discussed in the language of optimal, well-balanced use. To keep structure in perfect perspective, consider past, present, and future structural possibilities.

360-Degree Feedback Questions for Structure

All employees have a major stake in understanding their own roles in creating and maintaining the structure of the organization and must work to ensure that their individual efforts are aligned with the achievement of organizational goals and objectives.

Questions for the Coaching Client

As a means of further assessment, here are questions specific to structure to ask your coaching clients:

- Please provide examples of when you worked with people from multiple departments to solve a problem.
- Describe your role in the process of working with people from multiple departments to solve a problem.

If your coaching client has direct reports, you want to know how your client's management style supports structural integration and cross-functional teamwork. You might want to set up ways for your clients to demonstrate their understanding and savvy around structural issues. This is also a training opportunity for future management responsibilities. For those clients with direct reports, this is a good time to discuss what an important opportunity this can be to create a teachable moment for them regarding structure and structural relationships.

Even if your clients are individual contributors who do not

manage teams, this is a good exercise to illustrate that their being an organizationally savvy leader will have a positive influence on peers. It can be good practice in exercising in influence without authority. The earlier anyone in the organization starts talking structure, the better. Knowing who is tuned into organizational structure and who is not will ensure that your client's coaching engagement is aligned with your position in the organization's structure.

Questions for the Feedback Provider

If you are using the Contextual Coaching 360-degree assessment, these will be the questions that your feedback providers will need to answer as they regard your coaching client:

- What are some examples of times when the client worked with people from multiple departments to solve a problem?
- Can you describe the client's role in the process?
- How does the client demonstrate authority on the job and relate to others who hold authority over him or her?

You are looking for rich answers that will give you and your coaching clients material to work with in designing their coaching action plans. The answers you receive to these questions will spell out whether your clients have gaps in the area of structure and, if so, the type of remedy that is called for. It should be obvious that just exploring these topics with your clients and gathering data about them will heighten clients' awareness of the many hats a manager must wear—whether your client is a manager at present or aspires to become one. If your coaching client is on track to become a manager, this is a good opportunity for your client to learn about structure in the context of the organization.

Structure Summary

Structure is about how the organization, the people within the organization, and the relationships people have within the organization are organized. This is essential information for your coaching clients to understand. How they interact with others, as well as how their career paths are likely to unfold, is subject to the structural and organizational patterns in their organization. As a coach or a manager who coaches, you must make sure your clients are aware of what structure is—how it functions, and how it influences your clients' success—and the work and communications processes that determine the organization's ultimate success.

Your clients also need to know that everything they do has an impact on the structure of the organization. Perhaps their efforts day in and day out will resonate with organizational structure and thereby feel rewarding. Or perhaps their efforts will conflict with the structure of the organization and will always feel difficult, forced, and frustrating. You will help your clients learn to skillfully navigate organizational structure for their greatest benefit as individuals and for the greatest benefit of the organization as a whole. This requires advanced knowledge about organizational structure and appreciation of the importance of being able to maneuver deftly within it.

Armed with this information, your clients will be prepared to understand and apply principles concerning organizational culture, which are discussed in Chapter 5. Structure is part of an organization's culture, and it is important to include it in any sort of cultural audit. Your client's ability to think and act strategically is enhanced every time you introduce higher-level, enterprise-wide thinking and topics such as structure and culture.

CHAPTER 5

Area of Behavioral Focus: Culture

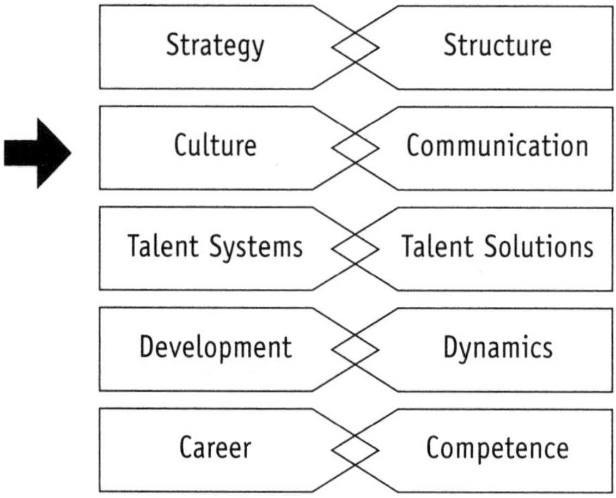

"Executive coaching enables our leaders to exercise behaviors that do not come easily for them, and receive feedback in a constructive manner. Where else do these leaders have the opportunity to practice the 'uncomfortable' and master a new way of doing things?"

—Jodi B. Rabinowitz
Head of Learning & Development
BNP Paribas

Culture is the third of the ten components in the Contextual Coaching model. For the purposes of Contextual Coaching, culture is defined as the quality in an organization that arises from what is regarded as excellent. Culture is reflected in the predominant behaviors, beliefs, and values most characteristic of a particular organization. It is the sum total of ways of living and working, built up by a group of human beings and transmitted from one generation to another.

Some organizations have cultures that are well thought-out, well crafted, sustained, and wonderful. Other organizations do not make any deliberate attempt to consciously craft a culture that will benefit individuals in the organization and the organization as an entity. As the organizational author James Belasco wrote in his 1991 book, *Teaching the Elephant to Dance,* every organization has a culture, whether it wants one or not. Whenever you get two or more people together, common beliefs, behaviors, and values will begin to emerge, congeal, and govern behavior.

If the culture in your organization is not intentionally designed and constantly reinforced and nurtured, the culture you are likely to end up with may be distinctly disagreeable. At best, it probably will not support or contribute to the achievement of the organization's stated goals or desired outcomes. At worst, it might sink the ship.

Organizational cultures either form naturally or are commanded to form by executives. Odd as it might sound, synthetic or unnatural cultural formation has the greatest chance to benefit the organization because it allows for the design, implementation, cultivation, and maintenance of a preferred culture—or culture of choice—such as the learning organization suggested by Peter Senge in his 1994 bestseller, *The Fifth Discipline.* The way to diagnose a culture, as in the way in which an organization behaves and how the values of an organization are realized, is to observe day-to-day organizational behavior as well as consistent actions over time. Not only do human beings create culture whenever they organize themselves, but those cultures can change shape, color, and intensity as individuals at various levels of an organization influence them. Culture is not a simple top-down phenomenon.

Cultural Markers

The markers of any culture can be both simple and complex. Some of the things that identify and define culture can be as obvious as the paint and/or pictures on the walls, the way a lobby is designed, or the way people in the organization dress. Other markers are more difficult to grasp, and it can require a great deal of investigation before you can interpret their meaning and level of profundity. These more nuanced aspects of an organization's culture can be easily overlooked when people study that culture only superficially; if ignored, they can create potential future problems for anyone who works inside the organization or for anyone who depends on the organization for anything.

For instance, individuals can derail initiatives and set off alarms when they engage in behaviors that are culturally unacceptable and run counter to the cultural expectations of an organization. Because of the conflict this type of dissonance can create, culture-averse behavior is not easily forgotten or forgiven.

Enter Politics

Managing culture can be a political process. While moral conflicts can arise when people feel that their personal ethical constructs have been challenged, managing the culture of an organization usually need not require individuals to betray their core values or to become manipulative. With rare exceptions, what is good for organizations is usually good for the individual team members. Supporting the organizational culture is politically consistent with supporting the needs of the organization.

Champions of the culture might be the very power brokers who have your coaching clients' best interests at heart. Then again, they might not. Sometimes the most powerful people in an organization are about as anticulture as you can imagine. When we say power brokers, we refer to people who have enormous influence over your future assignments and your clients' future assignments. There are people in any organization who want what they want and think that nothing should stop them from getting it.

Your political challenge is to decide whether to support the power brokers. If so, who? How? To which political cause are you going to subscribe? It may be enough just to remain aware that multiple political agendas are constantly churning within even the healthiest and most effective organizational cultures.

It is best if prospective employees are able to do some cultural analysis before joining a company to ensure that their personal moral and ethical convictions are not in conflict with the culture in a way that challenges their personal authenticity. Yet, no matter how well an employee interprets a culture before joining a firm, new and undisclosed aspects of the culture will reveal themselves over time and present new challenges. As a coach or a manager who coaches, you can help your clients remain flexible and adaptable in the face of shifts in culture or hidden booby traps.

Your coaching clients will benefit when you, as the coach, consider and pay attention to how different aspects of the organizational culture will bring success to your clients or present them with obstacles. This is especially true if your coaching client has joined a new team or is beginning a new position in the company where some risk is involved. This awareness and vigilance require you as the coach to do cultural analysis early on in the coaching engagement so that you become aware of the cultural factors that might be at play in any particular coaching engagement. You will need to work with your coaching clients to help them become "culture carriers" who champion and communicate the carefully crafted culture to others through their words and deeds.

Why Culture Is Important to the Individual

The culture of any organization constantly affects the success of any individual or team that operates within it. Culture is often unspoken and unheralded, especially if it is a natural-forming, organic organizational culture, meaning that most people do not even realize it exists, much less how it is affecting them.

Culture that people are not aware of exists all the same and can act like a strong undercurrent that will suck you down if you are not careful. Your coaching clients need to be aware that there are forces at work beneath the radar that are inaudible and invisible and vaporous in density. Despite how difficult the culture may be to detect, its gravitational pull affects everybody to one degree or another.

Make sure your clients are aware of this subtle culture. Help them to understand the subtle and insidious nature of undetected and undiscussed culture. It can adversely affect them and will. You can best serve your clients by helping them learn ways to detect the presence and influence of culture and how to align the existing culture with their personal and professional agendas. This is easy enough when cultural development is a big organizational initiative. If it is not acceptable to speak of culture in your organization, however, help your clients avoid swimming against a strong current that they don't even know is there. They can frequently feel the current but don't know how to explain it. That is where you, the coach, come to the rescue.

Why Culture Is Important to the Organization

Crews row their shells using long oars in a well-rehearsed and choreographed display of symmetry and precision movement. Think of Olympic rowing competitions where the shells are similar, the weight in the shells is similar, just about everything is equal—everything, that is, *except* the precision and symmetry of the rowing teams. "Everyone is pulling their oars in the same direction" is a tired old business colloquialism. Nevertheless, that is one way to explain what culture means to an organization.

An organization is, in some ways, a loosely knit confederation of individuals and groups of individuals. At some level, everyone in the organization shares common interests, motivations, rewards, beliefs, behaviors, and values. That is the flashpoint at which culture begins to form. If an organization wants to maximize the strengths, skills, abilities, knowledge, competencies, and full capacity of its organizational population, there must be a deliberate, methodical, systematic, and well-orchestrated effort to synchronize and align all that the organization population has to offer.

Anything less than full synchronization and alignment will waste some or even most of what the members of the organization bring to the table. If the culture of an organization forms naturally and has little, if anything, to do with stated organizational goals and objectives (except by coincidence—even a broken clock is right twice a day and a blind squirrel can stumble over an acorn now and then), it is practically a mathematical certainty that resources will be squandered, some if not most of the efforts of individuals and teams of individuals will be wasted, and opportunities will pass by undetected or will not be taken advantage of because the underlying culture is dragging too many people down and taking the organization with them.

As a coach or a manager who coaches, there are few things more important in which you should invest time and effort than helping your clients learn about culture, what it is, and what it means to every constituent inside and outside the organization. An intentionally designed positive and proactive culture can promote productivity, performance, and profitability through constant development, encouragement, and reward. A naturally forming culture of self-interest and avoidance can reinforce and encourage factionalism, isolation of business units, withholding of information, jealousy, unfair competition, and any number of nonproductive activities. Culture defines an organization and vice versa. You and your clients need to know that and to learn how to contribute to the design, implementation, and maintenance of a culture that reflects all that is best in your organizational intentions.

The Objectives and Goals for Culture

For the individual and for the organization, culture is in control. But is culture an independent power that influences us and takes us to places we never intended to go, or is culture merely a reflection of our own collective biases, behaviors, beliefs, and values? That debate will need to play out in another forum.

What we are looking at now, from a high-level perspective, is the fact that culture encompasses everything in the organization. If you think of an organization as a physical, carbon-based, biological body, culture would be the DNA. The good thing about culture, though, is the fact that, unlike DNA, it can be re-engineered.

Your clients' major goals and objectives around culture include understanding what it is, how it is formed, and how empowered they truly are to influence it and change it for the better. Culture is changeable. It takes consistent effort, but it can be done. If your clients are genuinely concerned with their own professional and career development, they will do well to become expert at reading culture, taking its temperature, measuring its pulse, and exerting an effective and positive influence on how it is shaped.

Behaviors Related to Culture

As you continue tracking the Contextual Coaching process, you will be identifying behaviors associated with the individual and organizational results you want to produce. As a Contextual Coach, you will pay attention to the ways your organization understands and crafts its own culture so that you can provide practical and effective guidance to your coaching clients. In examining, tracking, and modifying your clients' habits, skills, and activities, you will look to identify ways in which they can benefit from the forward-looking piece of culture as a powerful personal awareness, organizational awareness, and goal-setting exercise. You might also inquire as to how your clients are using culture in team building, depending on the number of their direct reports. The following behaviors are part of the Contextual Coaching 360-degree assessment that measures your clients' proficiency in using culture as a tool for developing their own careers and/or the careers of their direct reports:

- Values the differences of others
- Acts as a change agent at appropriate times
- Negotiates in a manner that builds consensus
- Exemplifies the norms and values of the organization

- Demonstrates concern for how the culture has an impact on the business

> If you were to place these behaviors before a group of feedback providers and ask them to rank your client, what would they say? Would they say that the behaviors listed are overused, underused, or used optimally by your client? If you use the Contextual Coaching 360-degree assessment, you will get those answers. Even though using the Contextual Coaching 360-degree assessment is a formal way to assess the overuse, underuse, or optimal use of each behavior in a survey format, you can also use these questions to conduct your own culture interviews with feedback providers, sitting down with them face to face and discussing each behavior.

Optimal Use of Cultural Behaviors

As we have been intimating all along, everyone in the organization needs to be a champion of cultural excellence. That is to say that everyone in the organization should play an active and enthusiastic role in building and sustaining a culture of excellence. It is in everybody's best interest—individually and organizationally— that cultural excellence be promoted at every opportunity.

No matter what specific culture-enhancing behavior you and your clients are discussing, if the net result is a stronger, more encouraging, more efficient, and more effective working environment, you have reached optimal behavior for culture. Like anything else worth having, a positive and productive culture is difficult to cultivate and even harder to sustain. The people who create a successful culture and keep it alive and thriving need to be continuously encouraged and rewarded. As a coach or a manager who coaches, you can provide such encouragement. This is one of the most valuable contributions you can make to the health and well-being of your organization.

Underuse of Cultural Behaviors

With culture, as with anything else, it is not a good idea to be willfully ignorant. Unfortunately, many people are oblivious to what culture is and how it controls organizational life and performance. How often do people in your organization talk about culture, either formally or informally? It is the rare organization indeed where people make a point of discussing culture and its current condition.

When people are not aware of culture's control over things, they are not making any conscious effort to positively shape and refine it. Even if people are aware of culture's influence on them and the organization, they often dismiss this influence as unimportant and therefore do not invest any effort or resources in refining, revising, or enriching culture. Underuse of behaviors related to culture is likely to result in wasted resources, wasted effort, missed opportunities, inefficiencies, inertia, and organizational entropy.

None of this is good for the individual or for the organization. Nevertheless, individuals and organizations too often plow ahead in spite of the incredible and unnecessary burdens that an undefined and unrefined culture places upon them. Whether from ignorance or complacency, failing to skillfully master and manage culture is to leave untold amounts of money on the table in everything your clients and the organization do.

Overuse of Cultural Behaviors

As a verb, culture means "to subject to culture or cultivate." In a perfect world, as a coach or a manager who coaches, you can help move an undercultured organization toward becoming an appropriately cultured organization by "culturing" it one client at a time. Your job, as far as culture is concerned, is to "culture" your clients.

The potential problem at the opposite end of the scale from the underused culture is the danger of *overculturing* the organization. In other words, an organization can be *cultured to death*. Your job at that point is to bring your client back into the optimal zone. You will find examples of how culture can be overused in the chart on the development approach for culture located at our Web site, www.WeMakeTalentWork.com. People can obsess over cultural issues to the point where it interferes with their productivity. If culture is the only thing that people think about, it will draw their focus away from other legitimate concerns. To the culturally obsessed, we say, "Your organization is probably not in business to manufacture, package, and market culture." But, culture is certainly all about *how* you manufacture, package, and market the goods and/or services you do provide. (For a chart of examples of the underuse, overuse, and optimal use of the culture behaviors, as well as for suggested reading on culture, visit www.WeMakeTalentWork.com and click on "The Coaching Connection.")

How Your Coaching Client Fits into Culture

If any of your clients are individual contributors, it might be more difficult for them to connect the dots between their individual roles and organizational culture. As a coach or a manager who coaches, you appreciate how every member of a system has an impact on every other part of the system. It is up to you to help your coaching clients understand and embrace the systems theory concept.

Everything your clients do—or leave undone—will enhance or encumber what others are doing elsewhere. Even if your clients manage an area or are members of departments filled with active people, their influence is felt by those closest to them, as well as by others in the organization who do not even know your client exists. Everybody exerts influence on the organization's culture in one of two ways:

1. Where there is no conscious and deliberate effort to establish and sustain a culture of excellence, individuals promote their own agendas, form coalitions with like-minded people, and unconsciously influence cultural construction in a zillion different ways—usually producing that unknown, unidentified, undefined,

unrefined, and unfriendly-to-change underground culture that chokes off productivity and performance.

2. In an organization that purposefully and skillfully designs, implements, and maintains a culture of excellence, people have the opportunities to champion that culture and to be involved in any number of programs or projects to keep cultural initiatives alive and well. The Disney Company is a stellar example of a company that set out to deliberately build a culture; in addition to establishing a corporate university that remains committed to sustaining a well-defined culture, management ensures that every aspect of organizational life is deliberately immersed in Disney culture.

How to Introduce Culture to Your Coaching Client

As a coach or a manager who coaches, you are an activist who falls into the second method of influence. You have a major and deliberate influence on your organization's culture every time you help a client. Are your organizational policymakers designing a culture of excellence and briefing you on how your efforts contribute to that overall objective? If not, maybe you should champion that effort with a grassroots campaign.

In the meantime, your role as a coach includes helping your clients find ways they can actively participate in establishing and sustaining cultural norms that contribute to the achievement of organizational goals and objectives. You will be surprised at how creative and inventive your clients can be once you introduce them to the fact that they play an important role in your organization's culture.

It can be a helpful exercise to have your clients observe cultural markers on their own and report back to you with a list of things they have identified. These markers can be anything from the ways the organization decorates its offices to the kinds of food served in the cafeteria. Dress codes, attendance policies, formality of meetings, and accessibility to senior management are all markers of the organization's culture. Nothing physical or behavioral in your organization exists outside its culture. Perhaps better said, everything physical or cultural in your organization is part of what constitutes your culture.

360-Degree Feedback Questions for Culture

All employees have a major stake in understanding their own roles in creating and maintaining the culture of the organization and must work to ensure that their individual efforts around culture are aligned with the organization's strategic plan. If your coaching client has direct reports, you want to know how your client's management style supports the strategic imperatives of the organization.

Questions for the Coaching Client

As a means of further assessment, here are questions specific to culture that you can ask your coaching clients:

- Can you describe any aspects of the culture that challenge your integrity?
- Can you provide examples of change processes in which you have participated?
- When the organization is facing change, what role do you take in the process?
- How do you reflect the cultural values of your organization in your day-to-day work?

Your clients will want to choose vivid examples to illustrate the depth of their own understanding of organizational culture issues in addition to examples of how they align personal and team efforts to build and sustain a culture of excellence. You might want to discuss ways that your clients might be able to demonstrate their understanding and savvy around cultural issues for key stakeholders to see. This is also a training opportunity for future management responsibilities. For those clients with direct reports, this is a good time to point out what an important opportunity this can be to elevate cultural awareness and support among those who report to your client.

Even if your clients do not manage teams, this is a good exercise to illustrate that being a champion of organizational culture will have a positive influence on both peers and internal and external constituents. It can provide good practice in exercising influence without authority. The earlier anyone in the organization starts talking culture, the better. Knowing who is tuned into organizational culture and who is not will ensure that your client's coaching engagement is aligned with the culture your organization wants to build.

Questions for the Feedback Provider

If you are using the Contextual Coaching 360-degree assessment, these will be the questions that your feedback providers will need to answer as they regard your coaching client:

- Does the client reflect the cultural values of the organization in day-to-day work?
- Are there aspects of the culture that challenge the client's integrity?
- When the organization is facing change, what role does the client take in the process?
- Can you provide examples of change processes in which the client has participated?

You are looking for rich answers that will give you and your coaching clients material to work with in designing their coaching action plans. The answers you receive to these questions will spell out whether your clients have gaps in the area of culture and, if so, the type of remedy that is called for. It should be obvious that just exploring these topics with your clients and gathering data about them will heighten clients' awareness of the many hats a manager must wear—whether your client is a manager at present or aspires to become one. If your coaching client is on track to become a manager, this is a good opportunity for your client to learn about culture in the context of the organization.

How to Use the Responses to the 360-Degree Assessment Questions for Culture

How perceptive do your clients seem to be about culture? Is it something that interests them? Do they get excited at the opportunity to talk culture and learn more about it? You will be able to tell from their answers to the questions and by the way others portray them through their answers. If the interest is not there, it could be because your clients "don't get it" and you need to be a better teacher. It could be because these types of human-centered issues don't really thrill them that much. It might be that you just need to put them on notice that issues of organizational culture are important and that they need to pay attention when they are discussed. Beyond that, they will go their own way.

More often than not, people get interested in a subject when the spotlight is on them. Even though the emphasis in Contextual Coaching is the balance between individual and organization, to get an individual's attention and help that person to learn, put the subject in a personal context. It can be as simple as delivering a compelling answer to "What's in it for me when it comes to this culture stuff?" Well, there is a lot in it for all coaching clients, if the information is presented in such a way that they see how their knowledge, capabilities, competencies, and capacities will be broadened—along with their vertical mobility.

Habits

Do your clients have habits that resonate with the kind of culture your organization is seeking to build? Is the kind of punctuality your client is known for consistent with the type of punctuality that is appropriate for the current or new culture? Do your clients communicate in ways that reflect the culture your organization is seeking? If not, then you will play a vital role in helping your clients shed destructive, counterproductive tasks and replace them with positive and productive habits. Coaches are particularly powerful teachers when it comes to new habit acquisition because the accountability is so direct.

Skills

What kind of skill sets do your clients bring to the game? The nice thing about skill sets is that they can be learned for the most part. If you have clients who are enthusiastic about supporting the organization's culture of choice but who lack certain skills that will make them much more effective in their support of cultural issues, they can be taught what they need to know. This is where training and development opportunities come in very handy. You, as coach, do not need to teach, necessarily, just ensure that the new skills are being acquired, practiced, and locked into place.

Activities

Even if your clients are naturally enthusiastic about cultural issues and possess good skill sets to support cultural initiatives, they may still not be engaged in the right kinds of activities. Are they aware of the kinds of activities they could be engaged in—management councils, community affairs, focus groups—that can make them major contributors to the cultural affairs of the organization? People need to be doing things about culture and cultural initiatives in order to maximize their learning. Activities, either directly related to their primary functions in the organization or ancillary to them, will help your clients master culture as a dynamic dimension of organizational life and their own future success.

Culture Summary

Culture controls the organization. If it is deliberately designed, implemented, and maintained, it will be your friend. The intentional development of a culture of choice or a culture of excellence puts all the power of the unspoken understandings about shared beliefs and values among your organizational population to work for the organization's best interests. Culture has tremendous power to shape the success of organizations and the individuals who depend on them.

Culture also has the potential to rip an organization apart if the culture is not intentionally designed, implemented, and maintained to be a culture of choice. If the culture just naturally forms as the residue from undefined and unspecified expectations among loosely confederated team members, the worst of people's habits, skills, activities, and attitudes can become the underlying, congealing force that dooms every attempt at positive change before it has a chance. Think of organizations that are best described as toxic and unhappy places to work.

Culture is a mighty force in organizations and is defined and perpetuated by communication. Communication is a primary definer of culture. It must be used deliberately, strategically, and, more than anything else, wisely. Communication, which is the topic of Chapter 6, has tremendous power, both obvious and insidious—above and below the radar. Communication can be used for good, or it can be used for evil. Communication carries messages that support and encourage your intentional agenda or sabotage it. Good or bad, right or wrong, messages circulate. In Chapter 6, we will explore why your clients need to become communication experts.

< C H A P T E R 6 >

Area of Behavioral Focus: Communication

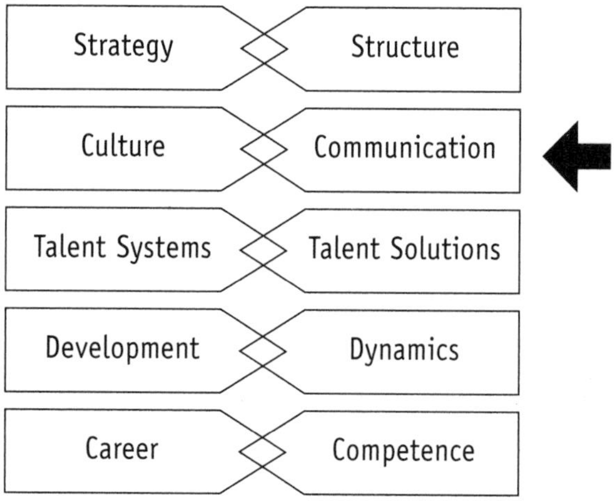

"Quality coaching can make the difference between a solid performer and an inspirational leader."

—**Jane C. Parker, CEO**
InterbrandHealth

Communication is the fourth component of the Contextual Coaching model and can be defined as the act or process of communicating. This sounds pretty vague. How about redefining it as the exchange of thoughts, messages, opinions, or information via speech, signals, writing, signs, or behavior? That's better.

Even at the molecular level, communication is sharing: Activity by one organism that changes or has the potential to change the behavior of other organisms through the transfer of information from one cell or molecule to another, as by chemical or electrical signals. That is not altogether different from how communications work in organizations.

Communication is serious business when it comes to individual and organizational success. Perhaps more than anything else, an organization expresses its culture by the way it communicates. Communication skills and practices affect every aspect of your effectiveness as a leader and team player. When dealing in the context of culture as a coach or a manager who coaches, you and your coaching client will carefully study and consider how communication is managed within the organization. The way individuals communicate within the organization provides telling information about how the company operates and how people are treated.

For example, if information is disseminated on a strict "need to know" basis, communication is being used as a command-and-control device to exert authority. Does your client experience that sort of communication in the organization? Is your client the victim of command-and-control tactics when it comes to communication? Do the people above, below, and at the same level as your client on the organization chart communicate openly and give access to data and information?

Do your clients share information openly or on a "need to know" basis with others above, below, and/or beside them on the organization chart? How open or closed your clients choose to be regarding communication says much about them personally, as well as about the communication style of the organization.

If your client and the organization are open about sharing information and even make it a priority to keep people informed, that also speaks volumes about the cultural context in the workplace. When it comes to communication, individuals (like organizations) can be "open" or "closed" or anywhere in between. Our 360-degree feedback assessment will help you to figure out where your clients fall on that continuum. As the coach, you should help your clients process and make good use of that information.

In any event, your clients need to find an authentic voice within this situation—a voice that will serve both your clients and their constituents well—especially if your clients' communication styles conflict with the communication style of the organization. The challenge for your clients is to balance personal and leadership communication styles with the larger imperatives of communication found in the everyday life of the organization. Unreliable or absent communication is often at the heart of workplace conflicts and frequently results in negative employee engagement. As a leader, your clients must compensate, within the relevant sphere of influence, for whatever the organization lacks in the way of good communication practices. Here, once again, you as coach will be an enormous help to your clients.

As the coach, you will also need to help your clients learn how to communicate effectively with individuals and groups at different levels in a way that complements and even compensates for the organization's style of communication. You should advise your clients when it is appropriate to go beyond the standard communication style of the organization and when such behavior might be problematic. Understanding how an organization communicates internally and externally will help your clients to create communication plans for team members and/or customers at critical times within the execution of coaching strategies. Remember, skilled communication is essential not only to your clients' success but also to the success of their constituents.

Why Communication Is Important to the Individual

There is probably no skill that is more critical to the success of an individual or an organization than the ability to communicate effectively. For individuals, it is essential that they be able to appropriately and properly represent their skills and capabilities to those with institutional authority over their career tracks. It is one thing to do a good job. It is something else to let the right people know.

Informing people of one's precise skills and capabilities, especially changes in those skills and capabilities, is a way of scripting conversations that take place outside your presence. As a coach, you need to help your clients understand that their career moves, both up and down the ladder, are determined during conversations between people who have the institutional authority to alter careers. These conversations, many of them informal and incidental, take place outside your clients' presence. What these institutional policymakers do not know about your clients' demonstrated abilities will not be talked about and, chances are, this failure will mean that your clients will not be considered for promotions.

The ability to communicate effectively with direct reports, peers, superiors, and customers of all kinds is pivotal to developing the legacy your clients need to succeed. This is an aspect of the type of career coaching you will be doing in element nine of the Contextual Coaching model. However, strengthening communication skills is always time well spent and an investment that will pay perpetual dividends.

The clearer, more consistently, and more concisely your clients can communicate with every one of their constituents, the more people will enjoy working with them. The more people enjoy working with them, the more favorably they will be considered for promotion and advancement. That might sound simple, but people truly value knowing what is going on and where they stand. The more you can help your clients execute on even these elementary communication outcomes, the more successful they will be.

Why Communication Is Important to the Organization

If it sounds self-serving to encourage your clients to toot their own horns regarding their skills, capabilities, and accomplishments, consider for a moment how much you and your clients might limit organization-wide capacity if that information is kept secret. Modesty is all well and good, but organizational designers, planners, and policymakers must know your client and the collective talents and abilities available within the organizational population.

Besides clear communication's career-enhancing benefits for individuals, the ability to write and speak clearly, to keep others informed of what is going on around them in a timely manner, to make expectations easily understood and outcomes measurable helps improve organization-wide performance. Think of it in the inverse. How many things can disrupt organizational performance and productivity more than poor or nonexistent communications? Not many.

When helping your clients improve their communication skills, it is important to do so in the context of the organization's mission. Sending individuals off to communication training classes can increase their awareness and skill sets around communication in general. However, unless the unique context in which your organization functions is considered, the skill enhancements will have a limited effect. Context differs from organization to organization, and you need to help your clients become proficient at identifying and developing communication styles, behaviors, expectations, and practices that will benefit them the most as individuals as well as the organization that employs you all.

The Objectives and Goals for Communication

As we have been pointing out, there are numerous reasons to focus on communication as an element of the Contextual Coaching model and to help your clients improve their skills and abilities around communication. It should be one of your goals to help your clients differentiate between the individual and the organizational benefits of good communications. This way, they can teach others how and why improved communication skills can help them as individuals and improve organizational performance—often in the form of highly functioning work groups.

Another goal is to give your clients more effective control of their career paths. Too many clients are frustrated, thinking the quality of their work and their years of service to the company are enough to warrant promotion and recognition. In the best of all possible worlds, career longevity and good work are good reasons for recognition and advancement. In the real world, advancement and, to a lesser degree, recognition are functions of how comfortable your clients make others in the organization feel.

Those "others" are first and foremost the people with institutional authority to promote your clients' careers. These are the folks who have the incidental and informal conversations outside your clients' presence that determine who gets promoted and who gets demoted. Another goal and objective for you as coach is to help your clients accept that these critical conversations are best influenced in your clients' favor by your clients' ability to communicate effectively—in the context of and consistent with the culture of the organization—with the ultimate result of making people comfortable. Nothing will move a career upward and create a positive and productive working environment faster than the ability to make people feel comfortable.

Other objectives and goals for your coaching engagements around communication issues can include:

- Creating and sustaining an open and lucid flow of information throughout the organization
- Eliminating blind spots that might cause individual and community-wide opportunities to be missed
- Ensuring that individuals on the line know, understand, and accept what is expected of them
- Keeping policymakers in senior management informed of the need for organizational change and redesign

Behaviors Related to Communication

As you have been tracking the Contextual Coaching process, you have been identifying behaviors associated with your client and the organizational results you want to produce. Communication is one of the most independently crucial components of Contextual Coaching. As a Contextual Coach, you pay attention to and study the ways your organization communicates. An examination of the formal and informal ways your organization communicates (how individuals officially and unofficially exchange information) will help you to guide your clients toward best communications practices that serve them well as individuals and that contribute to organizational success.

In examining, tracking, and modifying your clients' habits, skills, and activities, you are looking to identify ways in which they can benefit from the forward-looking piece of communication as a powerful personal awareness and goal-setting exercise. You might also inquire as to how your clients are using communication in team building, depending on the number of direct reports involved. The following behaviors are part of the Contextual Coaching 360-degree assessment that measures your clients' proficiency in using communication as a tool for developing their own careers and/or the careers of their direct reports:

- Persuades others to make commitments.
- Demonstrates empathy in communications.
- Consistently communicates essential information.
- Gives clear direction regarding roles and responsibilities.
- Fosters open communication throughout the organization.

> If you were to place these behaviors before a group of feedback providers and ask them to rank your client, what would they say? Would they say that the behaviors listed are overused, underused, or used optimally by your client? If you use the Contextual Coaching 360-degree assessment, you will get those answers. Even though using the Contextual Coaching 360-degree assessment is a formal way to assess the overuse, underuse, or optimal use of each behavior in a survey format, you can also use these questions to conduct your own communication interviews with feedback providers, sitting down with them face to face and discussing each behavior.

Optimal Behavior for Communication

Never leave a gap in the story. Just as nature abhors a vacuum, human beings will not tolerate a gap in the story, especially if the story involves their health, happiness, and/or well-being. Communication involves all of the things listed in the definition at the top of this chapter. However, it is much more. One of the most important functions of communication is to fill in gaps in narratives. What kinds of narratives? How about what's happening with your clients in their personal lives?

We are not suggesting that your clients become open books to the point of boring the people around them at work with color photos of their recent gall bladder surgery. But, if something is disrupting the flow of work or work patterns that will cause concern to others, it is best to offer some kind of plausible explanation so that people don't fill in the gap with stories conjured in their vivid imaginations—because they will. Count on it.

If something is going on with the organization, people need to know what it is. Coach your clients to help provide accurate and complete information as much as humanly possible to keep rumors and innuendo from slowing or even stopping your organization's progress. Where there are doubt and uncertainty, people will get themselves mired in conjuring explanations. Skilled communicators know this and keep people informed at all times.

Another optimal use of communication is to inform people of what they don't know. If there is new software being designed to expedite operations, let people know. If at all possible, solicit input and opinions from people whose jobs these new developments will affect. Coach your clients to use every opportunity to share new and exciting information to keep people feeling excited and hopeful. Hiding information and keeping secrets usually damages the organization and its stated goals and objectives more than information control freaks might imagine. Properly communicated, information should make people feel more a part of the big picture and more excited overall about their individual contributions to the big picture.

Underuse of Communication

As we just pointed out, withholding information rarely turns out well because people have a keen sense of when there is a gap in the story. If you fail to make a deliberate and concerted effort to be open with as many interested parties as possible, you might make matters worse, even when you're not withholding anything. As a coach or a manager who coaches, you must help your clients understand that people will suspect there is information being withheld from them—even if there is not—if they don't perceive any concerted effort on the part of their leaders to communicate with them.

Good leaders, peers, and even enlightened direct reports initiate and sustain ongoing conversations and dialogues with every critical constituency. If you are an open and intentional communicator, people will not have cause to become suspicious. If your clients' opportunities to communicate are underused, you will need to help them avoid secrecy. If they are perceived as withholding, for every inaccurate story that imaginative team members invent, you and your clients will need to invest significant time, effort, and sometimes substantial resources to straighten out what would have never been misunderstood to begin with if their behavior had been more open.

Overuse of Communication

How can there be too much information? How can people be too informed? At first blush, it may be hard to imagine that people could overuse communication. Perhaps a better way to describe the potential overuse of communication would be to suggest a possible *misuse* of information.

There are many ways to describe the misuse of communication. A particularly pernicious example is the dissemination of information that is incomplete, partial, and/or intentionally misleading and intended to deceive others. This kind of behavior has obvious ethical implications and does not demonstrate effective leadership or an open culture.

Less intentionally damaging but just as potentially dangerous is the problem of "loose lips." While we do not want to encourage the withholding of information in an organization, some degree of prudence is helpful when it comes to the timing, style, and content of information that is shared. In fact, there are appropriate times to withhold information because of its negative effect on others and because it would be unhelpful to share the information at that time. For instance, we might not let individuals know that a downsizing is coming until we are prepared to effectively communicate the information and set up systems to handle things like release processes and outplacement packages with our employees. We may also want to be careful with the information we communicate when we are committed to holding to an oath of confidentiality. If judicious distribution of information serves the greatest good for the greatest number of people, it is worth considering.

We should also discuss the individual who talks too much and fails to allow the input and ideas of others to surface. Sometimes, the most effective leaders stay quiet and listen to others communicate. Such active listening speaks volumes. Salespeople face a similar problem when they speak past the close and wind up losing a sale by overtalking in the sales presentation. To avoid overcommunicating by talking too much, make sure that whatever you are about to say is an improvement on silence. (For examples of the underuse, overuse, and optimal use of communication, as well as for suggested reading on communication, visit www.WeMakeTalentWork.com and click on "The Coaching Connection.")

How Your Coaching Client Fits into Communication

As a coach or a manager who coaches, help your clients to understand how communication and the free flow of information are the lifeblood of a successful organization. Often, clients don't realize that information they possess or come across on a regular basis can be vitally helpful to others in the organization. You can help your clients see the big picture and how communications and the free flow of information keep people informed and thereby become more effective, efficient, and productive.

The old maxim "There's never enough time to do something right the first time, but there is always enough time to go back and do it again" reminds us that errors occur often because we don't have sufficient or accurate information (or both) when we need it. Coach your clients to share information whenever possible, in appropriate quantities, to the appropriate people, through appropriate channels. To invoke the Goldilocks imperative once again, there is just the right amount of information, delivered at just the right time, to just the right audience, to help produce the outcome that is "just right."

At the risk of overcommunicating, we feel it is important to point out that communication should not be left to chance. If an organization simply allows people to communicate when they feel it is necessary, in ways that are determined by each person individually, vast amounts of important data are never going to make it to the people who need them. Organizations must reward and otherwise incentivize good communication practices. Coach your clients to the point that, if they must err, they err on the side of overcommunicating rather than undercommunicating. You can always dial back, edit, consolidate, or collapse more information than necessary. But it is impossible to learn from something you do not know. When the film editor brags that she "saved" a poorly directed film, the director retorts, "You didn't edit anything that I didn't shoot." Ten minutes of raw footage for every minute in the final production is not a bad ratio.

How to Introduce Communication to Your Coaching Client

You must introduce the concept of communication to your clients at a level they can understand. Then you can ramp up their knowledge from there. We explain to our clients what Paul Watzlawick, Janet Beavin, and Don Jackson, in *The Pragmatics of Human Com-*

munication (Norton, 1967), meant when they said that "One can never not communicate." People who claim that they do not have time to communicate need to understand that they are communicating constantly.

The way people dress, the way they groom themselves, the way they accessorize themselves, the cars they choose to drive, how they decorate their workspace, how well they speak and write, the vocabulary they choose to use, the expressions they choose to use, whom they choose to associate with, their punctuality, their attendance, whether they meet deadlines, whether their work is complete and accurate or incomplete and poorly done, plus many, many other choices people make every minute of every day—all of these scream messages about who they are and what they value.

Most people are not aware of how much they are communicating to everyone around them. As their coach, help them understand that the difference between being a constant communicator (which we all are) and a constructive communicator is how deliberately we pay attention to what we are communicating. Introduce your clients to subtle yet consistent ways they can share what is going on with their peers and with the people to whom they report. If your clients have direct reports of their own, how thoughtful and structured are their communications with them? Do your clients make a habit of keeping people informed all of the time? Never assume that someone knows something. Never assume that people do not want or need to know. Help your clients become "know and tell" people. Others will let them know if they are overcommunicating.

360-Degree Feedback Questions for Communication

Whether your clients are individual contributors or lead a sizable team, you can use questions to launch a fruitful discussion about their own understanding of communication as a strategic leadership tool. Employees all have a major stake in understanding their own roles in effective communication throughout the organization and must work hard to ensure that their individual efforts are aligned with the organization's overall need for effective communication. If your client has direct reports, you want to know how his or her communication style models, supports, and encourages effective communication to everyone.

Questions for the Coaching Client

As a means of further assessment, here are questions specific to communication for you to ask your clients:

- What are some examples of your communication style when essential information is necessary for completing work?
- How do you acquire a sense of where others stand on important matters?

Questions for the Feedback Providers

If you are using the Contextual Coaching 360-degree assessment, these will be the questions that your feedback providers will need to answer as they regard your clients:

- What are some examples of the client's communication style when essential information is necessary for completing work?
- Does the client have a sense of where others stand on important matters?

Individual contributors will choose examples to illustrate the depth of their own understanding of communication issues in addition to examples of how they communicate, all of which will give you fertile material to address how your clients' communication skills are helping or hindering their immediate effectiveness and career progression. For individual or team leader contributors, communication skills have everything to do with influence—gaining it, maintaining it, expanding it, and using it to benefit the individual and the organization. If your client lacks influence, discussing these questions and analyzing the answers you receive can reveal why. You can then set up methods and techniques that clients might be able to use to demonstrate their understanding and savvy around communication issues. This is a training opportunity for future, high-level management responsibilities. For those clients with a few or many direct reports, this is a good opportunity to discuss what an important opportunity coaching can present to achieve strategic alignment throughout your client's staff through improved and enhanced communications practices.

How to Use the Responses to the 360-Degree Questions for Communication

Even if your clients do not manage teams, this is a good exercise to use to illustrate that being an effective communicator improves one's influence among one's peers and superiors. It can be good practice for exercising influence without authority. The earlier people in the organization start sharpening their communication skills, the better. Knowing who is tuned into organizational communication dynamics and who is not will ensure that your client's coaching engagement is aligned with your organization's communication needs.

As always, these questions are not flip or shallow. You are looking for rich answers that will give you and your clients material to work with in designing their coaching action plans. You don't have time to waste, and neither do they. The answers you receive to your questions will spell out whether your clients have gaps in the area of communication and, if so, the type of remedy that is called for. It should be obvious that just exploring these topics with your clients and gathering data about them will heighten clients' awareness of the many hats a manager must wear—whether your client is a manager at present or aspires to become one. If your client is on track to become a manager, this is a good opportunity for your client to learn about communication in the context of the organization.

Identify the Gaps

Where exactly do your clients' communication skills fall short? Are they failing to listen to others? Do they think they have all the answers and feel that they do not need to pay attention to anything anybody else has to say? Do they give the appearance of listening but fail to really understand what they are hearing? This last can truly frustrate others who think they have effectively expressed themselves, only to have your clients proceed as if they weren't paying attention. Listening, or, better yet, not listening is a problem; not comprehending is a problem, as well. As a contextual coach, you need to detect the difference.

Do your clients talk too much? We all have two ears and one mouth; the old maxim urges us to use them in that proportion. Twice as much listening as talking is a good rule of thumb—as a minimum. Talking too much can indicate that the talker assumes the listener does not yet grasp the message. As a coach or a manager who coaches, you can help your clients learn that asking smart questions on a regular basis will reveal how much their listeners do or do not understand. Once they are aware of the degree to which the listener has understood their point, your clients can make a better assessment of how soon they can stop talking and let people get on with the task at hand.

Gaps in listening, gaps in knowing how much to talk, and gaps in comprehension are all fixable problems. As a coach, your assignment is to make your clients aware that these issues exist. It is virtually impossible for any human being to objectively assess how effectively he or she communicates. Coaches and 360-degree feedback providers are critical to that task. As the Scottish poet and author Robert Burns put it: "O would some Power the gift to give us—to see ourselves as others see us!"

Habits

Is your clients' reluctance to listen or tendency to talk too much a habit formed over a lifetime and never corrected? If so, then you can help correct it. Many people do things that are harmful or, more innocuously, not helpful because they simply do not know any better. Perhaps they are modeling poor communication habits that their parents or their former bosses modeled. In any case, such habits can and should be addressed. As a coach, it will be hard to look into a mirror knowing that you let bad habits bring down your clients or diminish their effectiveness in the organization.

We often mention helping your clients become aware of the issues they need to address to enhance their effectiveness or to correct a problem. Becoming aware that a habit exists is a good example. Nothing can be done to correct or modify the habit until your clients realize that it exists.

Following close on the tail of the awareness is acceptance. What if your client tells you, "Yeah, I know I do that. So what?" Beyond making your clients aware that potentially harmful habits exist, you must help them understand that they must accept that the habit is causing a problem and that it is in their best interest to seek a remedy.

The more time you spend coaching, the more you will be faced with clients who deny they have real issues that scream for improvement and who are not all that interested in promoting their own best interests and the best interests of the organization. You will encounter lethargy sooner or later.

Moving your clients to action completes the awareness–acceptance–action trilogy. Finding your clients' flashpoints can be challenging, but, at some level, in some way, everybody has a trigger. Is your client motivated by promotion? How about more money and benefits? Does your client shun money and seek only recognition? Perhaps your client most craves acceptance and inclusion in the process or the social network within the organization.

Whatever your clients' motivations are, you will need to identify them to move the clients forward. This brings us back to communication. How effectively do your clients express their desires? How good are you at ferreting them out? You and your clients need a solid grip on the concept of effective communication and the demonstrated ability to identify helpful and nonhelpful communication habits before anyone moves on to the next step.

Skills

Whereas changing habits takes deliberate, consistent, incremental efforts, improving skills is more a question of education and practice. Practice is very similar to the consistent, incremental behaviors that change habits but includes a learning component. You have no doubt heard someone referred to as a skilled communicator. As natural as that person might sound when you listen to him or her talk, the smoothness of delivery and captivating nature of the presentation are probably learned.

Some people acquire good communication skills by mimicking what good role models have demonstrated. They might not know why they are effective communicators, at least in some areas, until someone like you makes some objective observations. As a coach, you play a critical role in observing not only communication habits and behaviors that can be problematic, but also to observe what your clients do well.

By identifying good communication habits like active listening, clear and concise writing, and expressing oneself succinctly and clearly and without ambiguity, you identify a platform for your clients to build on. Part of your job as a coach is to encourage people in things they do well and to encourage them to do them even better—in this case, to communicate effectively.

Activities

Improving communication skills can also be a function of engaging in the correct communication activities. Do your clients write down their thoughts and instructions for others on a regular and disciplined basis? Do your clients write too much? Is the writing activity optimal but the face time suboptimal?

In communications, as in all things, engaging in the appropriate activities to maximize effectiveness as a communicator is essential if you are going to coach the whole person in the context of the organization. The activities must be balanced. The appropriate and most effective amount and frequency of written communication must be balanced with the optimal amount of face-to-face dialogue and other conversations, such as telephone and teleconference. Speaking must be balanced with true listening. Writing must be balanced with reading what has been written in response.

It is in the planning and tracking of activities that you and your clients will be able to see how effectively they communicate. As a coach, you might recommend tweaking existing practices. A little more written instruction here, faster responses to written or verbal inquiries there, more face time and physical presence everywhere are all examples of possible changes to activities.

How to Discuss the Communication Gaps with Your Coaching Client

Everything we have just described is part of your coaching conversation on communications. Looking at all the communications issues your clients face can be overwhelming for you and your clients if you don't break them down. Begin with a conversation about the Contextual Coaching model and how important it is to be aware of and effective in dealing with all ten components. Your clients will surely agree that effective communication is one of the most important of the ten. Your clients might even have a preexisting and real appreciation for how important it is for them to improve their communication skills. They might be the victims of the poor communication skills their bosses, direct reports, or peers engage in.

In any event, regardless of how they became aware of the power of communication, people usually have an idea of what constitutes quality communication. As a coach or a manager who coaches, you are a first-line model of effective communication. By actively questioning and listening, you quickly gauge the degree of your clients' knowledge and feelings about communication. By soliciting feedback from 360-degree feedback providers, you can help your clients come to grips with the potential gaps between how they perceive themselves as communicators and how others see them.

That is when you go to work. Your entry point for discussing communications with your client will be to identify and encourage existing good communication behaviors and practices. The gap analysis will provide you a blueprint for helping your clients to significantly enhance their effectiveness as leaders, not to mention their career potential. If your clients are not aware of how becoming more effective communicators will make them more valuable in every aspect of their careers, that must be your opening conversation.

Connecting Communication to the Coaching Process

You and you clients are the first line of communication in their futures. The communication that takes place between you and your clients is a laboratory for gauging how effective your clients will be in their everyday activities. Your effectiveness as a coach will invariably depend upon identifying and helping your clients alter their habits, skills, and activities.

Staying in the moment with your clients, pay attention to the communication dynamics between you. Are your clients demonstrating good communication technique? Are you? Talk about it. As a coach or a manager who coaches, you will need to initiate this dialogue and keep it positive and productive. But the coach-client relationship is the perfect forum for giving traction to the topic of communication.

Communication Summary

From the beginning, we have maintained that communication is a technical process of encoding and decoding messages. More specifically, it is the exchange of thoughts, messages, opinions, or information via speech, signals, writing, signs, or behavior. As a contextual coach, you help your clients become aware of, accept, and take action on closing the gaps between their current communications skill level and an improved and enhanced skill level that will both make them much more effective in their current jobs and prepare them for expanded responsibilities in the future. As one of the most critical components of the Contextual Coaching model, communication is a candidate for perpetual improvement.

We communicate all the time—either poorly or skillfully, but at all times and in all places. We communicate in the way we've learned from childhood and that we replicate through *habits* until we deliberately examine our communication skills and make a conscious and deliberate choice to improve them. Then we choose to engage in the proper communication *activities* to make the most of our learned way of interacting with others.

These enhanced communication skills will become extremely important as you venture deeper into the Contextual Coaching model in Chapter 7 and deal with talent systems. A sophisticated component in the craft of leadership, talent systems help the organization measure talent levels and identify unique skill sets in the organizational population. As a coach or a manager who coaches, you will help your clients discover how talent systems are essential to managing the organizational population's collective capabilities and capacity.

CHAPTER 7

Area of Behavioral Focus: Talent Systems

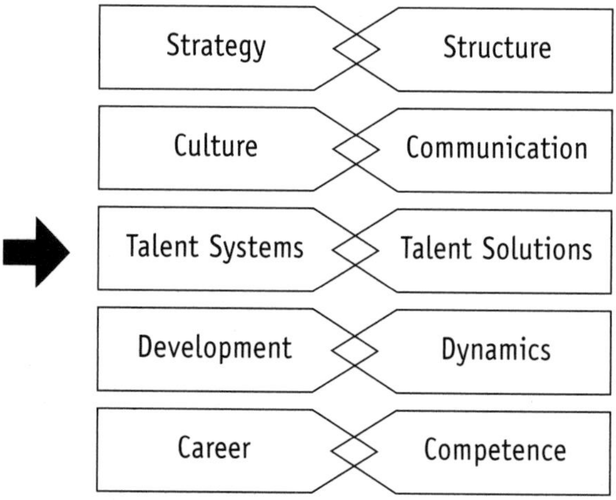

"Coaching helps leaders to develop new methods to address old problems. This one-on-one interaction with an objective third party is focused on enhancing performance."

—Michael Mimnaugh
Vice President, Human Resources
Sony Corporation of America

A talent system is any structured process that helps organizations manage their people. Talent systems form a bridge between the individual and the organization, and much in the way of technology, tools, and products has been developed to assist in that effort. Talent systems provide organized structures that marry the corporate brand of the organization and the personal brand of the individual. Through talent systems, employers of choice meet and manage employees of choice. This is another way that Contextual Coaching embraces organizational and individual needs in the same model.

Managing people is not something to be left to chance or happenstance. At least we hope it is not. Talent is too valuable and the lost efficiencies and profits that result from poorly managed talent are too costly for organizations not to take talent systems seriously and use them wisely. If managing talent is not a deliberate, systematic, and strategic practice in your organization, do not be surprised if productivity begins to diminish or languish.

The Difference Between Talent Systems and the Technology That Supports Them

People often confuse talent systems and the technological tools that support them. Talent systems represent the overall process of systematically managing talent across an organization to meet specific goals like talent acquisition, retention, career management, and succession. There are many technological tools available that provide elegant solutions for carrying out a wide variety of targeted talent strategies and managing day-to-day execution.

Talent systems are sometimes known as performance management systems. Performance management gets a lot of attention in training and development circles because it deals with performance, productivity, and profitability—areas where there is constant pressure to improve. However, talent systems include many additional processes that complement performance management and expand the horizons of talent acquisition and development. These are some examples of generalized talent systems processes:

- Talent acquisition
- Career management
- Performance management
- Potential management
- Succession planning

- Rewards and recognition
- Compensation
- Health and well-being

The Contextual Coaching process requires an understanding of the basic principles associated with managing talent, whether one is speaking of talent systems or of its companion, talent solutions (described in Chapter 8). As a function within talent systems, performance management systems capture, collect, categorize, and store data on individuals and groups of individuals. Team members' performance can be evaluated by talent-management software systems and their performance can be analyzed and rated against predetermined performance standards.

Analyzed performance data, collected as part of a talent systems process, is extremely useful in your coaching experience. Just remember that performance is only part of the talent systems equation. The critical balance you are seeking in the individual you are coaching is between performance and *potential.* As a coach of your direct reports and others, it is important that you determine the potential that individuals have to perform in new roles and new tasks as they grow and develop.

People Make the Difference

Just as performance management fits inside the overall concept of talent systems, talent systems fit inside the overarching umbrella of talent management. Talent management is an organizational concept anchored by the premise that people are the key competitive differentiators among organizations. A fundamental premise of talent management is that people are primary assets of organizations and must be managed strategically in light of the organization's current and future needs. An enterprise-wide initiative, talent management seeks to increase the competitive advantage of an organization and to raise the credibility of an organization's brand as an employer.

Because talent management is a system, foundational aspects are required for building an approach with sustainable effect. This includes the need to clarify what we mean by the present and future talent needs of an organization. Determining talent requirements includes the process of creating competency models that identify appropriate behaviors for talent at multiple levels.

Competencies are knowledge, skills, and behaviors that are organized in logical clusters (i.e., communication, leadership, problem solving) corresponding to an organization's talent strategy. When these competencies are written as observable behaviors, they become easier to identify and discuss with your clients. Some competencies are considered "core" because they apply to all functions and all members of your organization no matter what their level. Others are specific to critical workforce groups and job functions and keep a keen eye on the alignment between roles to ensure that they reflect working relationships and potential career ladders.

As the foundation of a talent planning process, competencies set the benchmark for behavior and create the opportunities to describe an individual's value proposition to the organization. Once in place and corporately recognized as philosophical descriptions of talent at multiple levels, competencies drive the content for the ten components of Contextual Coaching.

Why Talent Systems Are Important to the Individual

As we have stressed repeatedly, Contextual Coaching is meant to produce well-balanced managers of people or, at the very least, higher-performing individuals. Yet, even people in premanagerial roles need to be schooled in the depth and breadth of organizational life. We find far too many executives who should be *experts* in the depth and breadth of organizational life but who lack in the most fundamental understanding of some, if not most, of the ten components of Contextual Coaching. If team members are exposed to all the components of Contextual Coaching early on, they develop a balanced awareness and understanding of organizational life over time and evolve into well-balanced and effective executives. That is when you will know whether the Coaching Connection is really working.

Great managers not only have well-developed strengths across the ten dimensions of the Contextual Coaching model but optimize the use of each strength in relation to talent systems and resist over- or underusing them. As a coach or a manager who coaches, you need to help your clients continuously seek optimal balance in their emerging leadership styles and delivery. Mastering talent systems is part of their complete balance as leaders and effective team members.

As we often say, nothing can be managed well unless it can first be measured. If job expectations have been clearly articulated by managers and documented and signed off on by clients, the stage is set for evaluating the ways clients fulfill the expectations associated with their jobs. Assuming that the expectations are established up front, the ability to meet performance goals should be a major criterion for career advancement and will matter more to managers approving promotions than any other individual development issue.

The following descriptions of talent systems as they apply to the individual form a partial road map for you to use when coaching your clients. The more aware your clients are of these talent systems and how the systems apply directly to them, the better prepared they will be to prepare themselves for expanded responsibilities and even promotion. In the upcoming section on talent systems and the organization, you will learn how to build a bridge between the individual context of your coaching client and the greater context of the organization.

Talent Acquisition and the Individual

A talent plan is a great way to ensure that you have the right people on the bus, as Jim Collins, author of *Good to Great,* would say. There are two fundamental challenges in the process of acquiring talent that your clients should be aware of; after all, they too are acquired talent. The first challenge is finding the talent, and the second is determining the right fit. Have your clients considered how they came to the organization and discussed with you how they feel about the fit?

Recruiting talent has multiple challenges today because of the dearth of available talent and the competitive nature of organizations, which are all going after the best talent. Individuals often see themselves as "employees of choice," and they feel a high level of confidence in the individual value they bring to the organization. This not only provides them with leverage for negotiation; it creates a sense of personal value that can keep individuals cool and composed as other organizations reach out to them. Many employees are contacted by recruiters on a regular basis.

Because it can be difficult to recruit talent away from another organization, some recruiters cast a wide net, hoping to catch something or someone. This approach carries a risk of wasted time and energy because individuals recruited in desperation may not be the best fit. Help your clients understand the big picture of how they fit into the competition for talent and how highly they are valued in your organization.

Your client might be running a department and need to become better versed in the ways of hiring and recruitment as part of his or her talent scheme. Expose your client to the systems and tools that can help determine whether a potential hire is a good fit and thereby prevent hiring mistakes and miscues. Help your client understand what constitutes a hiring mistake or miscue in your organization.

Can your client play a role in attracting new talent? Sending people to a seminar on interviewing skills does not make them talented acquirers of talent. Such training should be a supplement to coaching, not the other way around. It is important to advise on the hiring process and to point out to direct reports who have hiring responsibilities that there is a difference between *recruiting* talent and *selecting* talent. Recruiting is the exercise of increasing the potential pool of talent and being a magnet to individuals seeking new roles. Selecting talent is about having the skills to identify the right people for specific roles. Coach your people about how to manage the interview, not only in light of best practices for interviewing but in light of your own individual management style. Do not be frustrated when your clients don't hire good people; coach them on how to do it. Refer to the Behaviors section of this chapter for tips.

Talent Acquisition and the Organization

Like every other aspect of talent management, assembling the most talented and enthusiastic team possible is a vital step in any talent systems scheme. It is vital because the organization, not the individual members of the organizational population, needs to be competitive in the global marketplace. That requires the best possible talent, trained and developed to the peak of their capabilities.

Not only must the organization be populated with the best talent available, but the talent needs to "fit" the organization's overall strategy. That is another way that talent systems serve the needs of the organization. Finding the best fit relies on systems and tools that can help prevent mistakes and that highlight the best-qualified individuals. Many organizations screen individuals through Applicant Tracking Software (ATS), which can eliminate individuals who do not meet specific requirements in areas like education or years of experience. Wise use of ATS also incorporates surveys around competencies that can isolate the potential fit of individual to job, culture, and future opportunities for the individual down the road—all in the context of organizational strategy.

Once individuals are part of a potential pool for joining an organization, behavioral interviews based on the competency models should be used to achieve more precise matching, avoiding "gut" decisions based on comfort with the individual. An individual interviewer's emotional connection to an interviewee may be totally unconnected to the true needs of the organization. If the emotional response to an applicant matches the organization's needs, bravo. If not, the organization's needs must override the influence of the recruiter's or hiring manager's comfort zone.

Using personality tests or assessment centers that have been validated for the hiring process in order to meet legal requirements protects the organization from litigation. The assessment licensor can inform you if the instrument has been sufficiently validated to meet rigorous reliability standards sufficient for hiring. If the instrument has not been validated for use in hiring, you leave your organization vulnerable to litigation should the hire not work out. These validated tools can be mapped to competency models and show very precise and objective data that can be used in the hiring process. The journey to organizational excellence begins with the acquisition of top talent.

Career Management and the Individual

There is a great deal of focus in organizations on developing high-potential (HiPo) talent. But we wonder, "What about the rest?" Not everybody can be a rapidly ascending star, glowing brightly against the corporate skyline. Organizations are made up of many different types of people, many of them duller and less astonishing than high-potential meteors but nevertheless sources of tremendous value and producers of significant results. Where is your client on the spectrum of stars, from dimly lit to dazzling?

In the June 1, 2003, issue of the *Harvard Business Review*, Thomas J. DeLong and Vineeta Vijayaraghavan claimed the "B" players (those who form the backbone of an organization) are often found in the middle of the talent pool. Without the "B" players, a great deal of productivity would be lost. Just because they are not considered HiPo material—performing well and on track for bigger and more influential roles—does not mean they don't wish for development to help them advance their career potential. As a coach, how actively do you seek out solid, non-HiPo talent to develop? Do you look over your ranks and identify the steady contributors who carry much of the burden in your department? Do you engage those people in conversations about their career potential?

Without active solicitation by you, your steady contributors may feel that they have little hope for career enhancement or advancement. It is not enough to wait for these people to come to you. You must be proactive about engaging your clients in conversations about their career paths and ambitions.

Career management is a major component in a holistic talent-management system. Career management offers three distinct elements as part of one solution. First, career management offers programs and processes that enable individuals to *create career plans* and to fine-tune essential skills for the process of career development itself. Some of these skills include networking, developing a personal value proposition that becomes the "elevator pitch" for one's career, and managing up. The career-planning process helps individuals to identify their goals and to lay out a course of action to close any gaps that might be inhibiting their advancement. Some of these gaps may be in the areas of experience, education, or networking relationships.

The second career-management element offers programs for managers to advance their coaching and mentoring skills to help them *become competent coaches* for the career-development process—much as you're doing now. Managers may recognize that there are opportunities to provide feedback in the midst of a subordinate's everyday job performance but may be less comfortable and less schooled in the art of holding more formal conversations about career aspirations and career development. They may also avoid these conversations if they believe that coaching someone toward career advancement could cause them to lose valuable talent.

The third element in this career-management process is *a technological platform* that typically provides career advancement data and research information. The platform provides easy access for individuals who want to plan their careers, for managers who want to provide mentoring for their direct reports, and for organization development (OD) professionals in the HR department who want to monitor aggregate career data across the organization. Technology can provide the experience of individuality inside an organizational context.

Career Management and the Organization

From an organizational perspective, recruitment and hiring of top talent are only the beginning of the process. Tuning the talent to the organization's pitch pipe will ensure harmonious activity rather than dissonance. Who will be the "B" players who form the mainstream of the organizational population? Who will be the HiPos? How will those distinctions be determined to best serve the organization?

Managing careers from the organization's perspective means testing and retesting people's habits, skills, and activities to ensure that they are not drifting from their optimal career tracks. "Optimal" is the operative word because the organization will benefit most from having the right people doing the right things in the most productive and profitable way. Internal mobility is great as long as there is a role in the organization that is both well suited to the individual's natural interests and a critical function to the organization's strategy. One without the other means that the organization loses. You wind up with either someone doing something the organization needs but the individual does not enjoy (in which case it will get done poorly) or someone doing what he or she loves but without helping the organization, at least not in the sense of providing a return on investment to the organization.

Inasmuch as career management helps retain top talent, it serves the organization. As the organization's needs change, so must the contributions of the organizational population. This requires constant career examination and rethinking. As the organization's needs continue to evolve, so does the career development challenge that keeps jobs and job functions aligned with organizational strategy.

As part of a larger career-management solution, organizations rely on coaches like you to proactively manage the career progression of your clients and to keep that progression in alignment with organizational strategy. Commitment to career development is essential for the strength and longevity of the organization's brand both as an employer and as a provider of goods and/or services to the public. As we mentioned before, this process is best managed by the use of a technological platform that provides individuals with easy access to plan their careers and supports managers who want to provide mentoring for their direct reports and OD professionals in the HR department who want to monitor aggregate data across the organization. Technology not only provides the experience of individuality within an organizational context but also allows these data to be used to keep career development precisely tuned to the organization's evolving needs.

Performance Management and the Individual

Managing performance includes taking advantage of systems and processes that offer the opportunity to collect information used to assess performance over a specific period of time. These systems make it possible to look backward to assess and analyze the success of an individual's performance measured against predetermined goals and expectations and to look forward in setting new performance goals.

The looking-back piece includes an assessment of the individual based on the competencies that are both core to the organization and specific to the particular job. This ensures standardization in the way talent is evaluated and reflects the importance of focusing on the right things when considering individual performance. Managers are responsible for performing this assessment, since they are close to the work and talk with their direct reports about their performance over time.

We recommend that organizations also provide an opportunity for managers and coaches to get feedback from others about their client's performance. However, this performance feedback should not be gathered through 360-degree tools since the results are often invalid when in connection with a performance appraisal. Instead, searching out feedback from others should be done through interviews with key stakeholders. In the end, the manager is responsible for the final assessment.

The goal-setting process for individuals typically involves very specific strategies relevant to upcoming work, projects, or initiatives that contain key performance indicators for the individual's performance. It is essential that individuals understand how their goals are connected to larger organizational or team strategies. This demonstrates the importance of their work and the power of working together as a corporate entity in pursuit of specific goals. The future-oriented aspect of performance appraisals should also include developmental goal setting that relates back to performance data. Performance appraisals that include developmental goal setting that relates back to performance data challenge individuals to identify ways in which they plan to grow their own capabilities to ensure future success.

Performance Management and the Organization

From the organization's perspective, continued assessment and tracking of individual competencies is part of fine-tuning the individual through the refinement process that began with talent acquisition. If managing something or someone requires the ability to measure performance, then performance management is essential to managing. As a coach or a manager who coaches, you need to impress upon your client that current performance might or might not (probably will not) conform to future performance standards, given the evolving needs of the organization.

The individual goal-setting process must reflect and be a support base for organizational goals. Both the major indicators for performance monitoring and the appraisal process must line up with the larger organizational strategy. The future-oriented aspect of performance appraisals that includes developmental goal setting is linked to the competency data *and* to the corporate strategy. Performance appraisals must always be conducted in the context of the organization's needs.

This means that managers should be continually providing coaching to their team members who are engaged in tactical work that supports the strategic agenda. A performance culture, if you can successfully create one, links individual performance even more directly to organizational performance. The more your clients are aware of how their efforts serve the greater organization, the more they will be energized by the heightened sense of purpose, inclusion, and contribution.

Potential Management and the Individual

Present performance means a lot to an organization and its operations. Part of the Coaching Connection is helping employees understand that they must reach their individual goals if the organization they work for is to reach its corporate goals. Managing individual performance requires managing individual responsibilities. This is why successful organizations pay so much attention to the management of employee *potential.* Nothing gets senior executives more excited about the future of their organizations than identifying up-and-comers who demonstrate good leadership capabilities.

Coaching these future stars helps accelerate their growth and development and prepares them for the future success of the organization as well as their own individual success. The faster these high-potentials can step up and contribute as strong leaders, the faster the organization will benefit from the increased efficiencies, accountability, performance, productivity, and profitability that strong leadership makes possible.

Coaching high-potential leaders also helps the organization retain them. When organizations make an investment in the growth and development of young leaders, it is hard for the recipients of these efforts to feel uninvolved, unengaged, or unimportant in the life of the organization. This, of course, is true of all employees, not only high-potentials. The more plugged into the organization individuals feel, the less likely they are to leave to pursue opportunities elsewhere. If employees are fully engaged, they will:

- Feel content with their roles and responsibilities (i.e., their jobs).
- Feel supported socially within the organization (i.e., their relationships).
- Feel they are compensated fairly for the contributions they make.
- Feel there is a good future for them in the organization.

It is easy to see how the Coaching Connection you make between your client and the organization will point your client up the ladder or out the door. At the very least, you want your clients to feel actively engaged right where they are. For high-potentials, that look up the ladder is important. They must feel that the higher positions will be there for them eventually if they work hard and prepare.

Preparation for expanded responsibility is at the very heart of Contextual Coaching. More important, following the Contextual Coaching model will instill a palpable belief in high-potentials that their future success is assured if they can just become the balanced executives the model is designed to produce. What organization is not hungry to identify bright and well-prepared leaders, barring the influence of office politics or nepotism? Did we say "hungry"? Let us upgrade that to "desperate."

Management of high-potentials is a key element to a successful talent management system. The competency models we discussed earlier help the organization define what competent leadership looks like in the organization so that the competency models can be used to assess employee potential. It can be tricky to evaluate leadership potential in people who do not yet have explicit leadership responsibilities. This kind of assessment takes careful thought and partnership between people who design talent-management systems and the managers who use the systems in their employee assessments.

Managers are often asked to assess both performance and potential on a regular basis, and talent-management leaders gather information from across the organization to determine which individuals have both strong performance in their current roles and the potential to take on leadership roles in the future. As a designated coach or a manager who coaches, your input into this process is invaluable. This information is the database upon which succession planning can be designed.

Potential Management and the Organization

The potential of an organization will not exceed the potential of its organizational population, period. The Coaching Connection helps employees understand why they must reach their individual potential in order for the organization they work for to reach its corporate potential. Successful organizations pay attention to the management of employee potential because embedded in the collective potential of the organizational population is the potential of the organization. That is no small consideration.

The coaching of future leaders of the organization must include emphasis on the organizational perspective. In its simplest form, there is no "I" in "T-E-A-M," but there are two in "O-R-G-A-N-I-Z-A-T-I-O-N." The more advanced lesson your clients need to learn is that every person in the organizational system (although on an individual level a valuable contributor) is either helping move the entire organization toward successful completion of its predetermined agenda or imposing a burden on the system, slowing it down and making it more cumbersome. Nobody is in neutral. Doing nothing causes a drag on the compensation component. Future leaders with high potential must become systems thinkers invested in the growth and success of the organization as soon as possible, or their individual talent will be wasted. That reality imposes a major responsibility on you as a coach or a manager who coaches.

Once the organization has invested in the growth and development of high-potential leaders, the last thing you want to do is have them lured away to another organization. You will lose the institutional memory you have built up in the high-potential person. You will lose all of the new knowledge that you have implanted. Worst of all, you will be sending all of that expensive knowledge, refined talent, and potential to someone else. If you can't retain your talent, you're paying to develop another organization's potential. As we noted before, "What organization is not desperate for bright and well-prepared leaders to emerge?" Other organizations will be more than happy to take yours.

Succession Planning and the Individual

Once a pool of high-potential leadership candidates has been identified, it is hard to think of them as anything *but* the future leaders of the organization. Identifying a pool of future leaders is one thing; identifying replacements for top positions in the company is something else. The succession planning process focuses in part on who can step into critical placeholder positions as they become vacant. But there is much more to it. This pool of HiPos is indeed a rich resource for filling future openings in the organization—but not simply to plug holes. HiPos are the building blocks of a larger and more targeted growth strategy.

More than just a career path for high-potential talent, succession planning is an effective tool for managing talent. It is vital that all employees know and understand how their roles fit into the strategy of the organization. As a coach, you need to focus part of your attention and your client's attention on the future needs of the organization, whether or not your client is a high potential. This adds perspective, context, and meaning to the current work.

By helping your client identify high-potential individuals who can fill critical roles, including the role your client currently occupies, you are helping your client build a platform upon which to move up. You are also helping your client to look ahead to the evolving needs of the organization over time, which is what strategic leaders do. If your clients are not managers with direct reports, this is preparation for the day when they will.

Typically, the succession planning process involves a partnership that includes human resources managers, other managers in the business, and specialists in organization development. It is important to discuss with your clients how they currently partner with human resources professionals, other managers in the business, and specialists in organization development. If their exposure to these resources is minimal and/or they have not engaged in true succession planning, the time is right to get them thinking about this future-focused activity.

Succession Planning and the Organization

When we were focusing on the individual, we mentioned that organizations use other important talent systems, such as succession planning, as effective tools for managing talent. As a coach or a manager who coaches, you need to understand what succession planning means from the organization's perspective. You need to help your client identify HiPos as well as fully test out their potential. Does your client have high potential? You and your organization need to know as you and your client look ahead to the evolving needs of the organization over time.

The reason that the succession planning process involves a partnership among human resources professionals, other managers in the business, and specialists in organization development is to ensure that the mapping of future leadership is consistent across the organization. It is essential for organizational designers to strategically position their top talent in complementary ways. This is also why you discuss with your clients how they currently partner with human resources managers, other managers in the business, and specialists in organization development. You need to get your client up to speed as quickly as possible on the organizational implications of succession planning.

Rewards and Recognition and the Individual

There is an old saying: "Rewarded behavior is repeated behavior." This is essentially what B. F. Skinner taught us with rats and pigeons in his Skinner Box and what Ivan Pavlov taught us with food, bells, and salivating dogs. It is behavior modification—or classical conditioning, if you prefer. It is about planned behavior. At the top of this chapter we said that managing people is not something to be left to chance. In organizational life, human behavior (in the form of relational skills, personal performance and productivity, habits, skills, and activities) is one of the elements of success to which we must allocate sufficient resources, time, and energy.

As organizational behavior specialists, we know that most people are motivated by internal reward systems through which they derive a sense of accomplishment, job satisfaction, and pride in association. External reward systems, including opportunities to pursue meaningful and enjoyable work, inclusion in supportive social networks, fair compensation, and a promising future, are extremely powerful motivators. As coaches, we know that we can have a great deal of influence on how people experience internal and external reward systems.

Recognizing individuals and groups for their contributions costs organizations little if anything. Adding a reward to the recognition is a little more (perhaps a lot more) expensive, depending on the type and size of the reward. As coaches, one of the most valuable and effective tools we can hand to our clients is our willingness to intentionally, systematically, and consistently identify the behaviors we want to see repeated.

More than identifying the behaviors we want to reinforce and distinguishing between the behaviors we want repeated and the ones we want to go away, we must give our clients the tools to provide recognition and reinforcement. There is no better preparation to move up in the organization. Read any book by Bob Nelson on rewarding employees and you will have more than enough techniques at your disposal (1,001 to be exact) to recognize and reward your employees. The biggest hurdle is the commitment to provide reinforcement and to do it with regularity.

Since talent management is a total system that represents the life cycle of an employee, it is important to connect reward systems to talent management strategically. We want to reward the right things and to provide incentives that help to inspire future positive behavior. One way to think about rewards and recognition is as a celebration of the behaviors that serve the overarching organizational strategy. If rewards and recognition are mainstays of the coaching culture you have helped build in your organization, you and your clients are never far away from a celebration.

Rewards and Recognition and the Organization

Organizations need to encourage collaborative and collegial behavior on a large scale. This requires rewarding and recognizing outstanding individual performance, but only in the context of how the individual is contributing to the needs of the organization. As a coach or a manager who coaches, you must know what success looks like from the organizational side, not just from what your client is doing.

How do internal and external reward systems tie into organizational performance expectations? How does a sense of accomplishment, job satisfaction, and pride in association at the individual level translate into organizational excellence? As coaches, we have a great deal of influence on how people experience internal and external reward systems. Plugging your clients' efforts and contributions into the organization's success story is one of the best external rewards possible and brings with it an unmistakable internal sense of accomplishment and belonging.

It is up to organizational designers to extol the virtues of a coaching culture. It is up to coaches like you to implement it. It is at your level that coaching gains its traction and that the organization's agenda is truly carried out. Senior organizational leaders take an astonishingly large amount of credit for making decisions they do not have the hands and feet to make happen.

Make sure, as an advocate for the organization, that you set up rewards and recognition that reinforce what the organization needs most out of your clients. Among his many accomplishments, Jack Welch made sure that every employee at GE knew the company's mission statement, right through to the custodians. Can all the people within your sphere of influence as a coach eloquently describe how their efforts and contributions help move the organization forward? If you are recognizing and rewarding people properly and frequently enough, they will know and be able to recite the mission statement without a hitch.

Compensation and the Individual

Money and benefits are not the only incentives for employees to be loyal and hard working. The employee engagement issues of job satisfaction, social support (which includes reward and recognition), and hope for future growth potential are present, as well. Through the years, security (concern for the future) has consistently ranked as a major issue among workers. Money is important, of course. People need to live, and they want to live well. That is natural. We hope your organization offers competitive salaries and benefits because, as a coach or manager who coaches, you might not be able to do much to change things if it doesn't.

The June 2004 issue of *CPA Journal* reported on a survey conducted by Ajilon Office, a national specialty staffing and recruiting services firm, that identified the top five reasons people leave their jobs and the five top reasons they remain. The top five reasons people stay at their jobs are these:

1. Being paid well
2. Liking their coworkers
3. Having job security or building equity/seniority
4. Having good benefits, such as medical/dental insurance and pension plans
5. Being used to the job

According to the Ajilon study, the top five reasons people leave their jobs are these:

1. More money
2. Better benefits
3. More opportunity for career growth
4. Less stress or pressure
5. Desire for a change of pace

The themes we described as important to successful employee engagement are all there: job satisfaction, social network support, compensation, and a promising future. We suspect that "getting along with your boss" was not one of the options available in the Ajilon survey because, unlike the Ajilon study, we have found, over decades of coaching and human capital management, and a preponderance of research supports, that management practices, more than any other single factor, determine whether a person stays with or leaves an organization. After conducting an employee retention study called "The Top Ten Reasons People Quit Their Jobs," the Atlanta-based author and international business consultant Gregory P. Smith concluded that "People don't quit their companies, they quit their bosses."

We have seen people stay in organizations that paid them poorly in order to stay with a boss they like. We have seen them turn down bigger-money opportunities for the same reason. We have seen people leave incredibly high-paying positions because the relationship with their boss, and the organization as it was passed through the boss, was too broken.

As you coach your clients, be aware that money might not be the most powerful magnet to keep them onboard. Obviously, the higher the stakes are for leaving, the more a person will hesitate and tolerate. As you work with a blend of cash and benefits packages, we highly recommend that you consult your human resources professional and seek his or her expert assistance.

In the end, your clients are going to look at compensation as a complex and layered issue. They might not say that in so many words, but to them the question will be "Is this worth it?" The decision whether to stay on the job is the result of a potentially mysterious and inexplicable combination of factors, including salary, job satisfaction, social network, and future prospects. Quite possibly the most important factor among all of these is the quality of the supervisor-employee component of the social relationship dimension.

Compensation and the Organization

From an organizational perspective, there must be a balance between optimal compensation and optimal performance. Too often people are paid far too much or far too little for what they contribute. Either way, the organization suffers. If people are overpaid, there is an unreasonable burden on organizational resources.

If people are underpaid, they burn out quickly and the organization loses good talent.

If Vilfredo Pareto's principle of economics holds here, then 20 percent of an organization's population is overpaid, while 80 percent is underpaid. The 20 percent of the organizational population that does 80 percent of the work is most likely the underpaid population. Fair and equitable compensation goes a long way to moving an organization's agenda forward. Good, hard-working people are less stressed and overworked, and the workload is better matched and distributed across the talents and abilities of the organizational population.

Are the people you coach asking themselves if it is worth it? Is your compensation structure set up in such a way that it promotes the organizational agenda and the ideal attitude? If not, you might need to coach around these issues to keep people interested and on board. Remember, what makes people stay is quality relationships. Do not invite people to quit the company by failing them in compensation. Compensation must be set in the context of organizational realities. As a coach or a manager who coaches, coach to the full engagement of your clients: job satisfaction, social support, compensation, and a promising future.

Health and Well-Being and the Individual

As a coach or a manager who coaches, you will need to be aware of how your clients' general health and state of mind influence their success in the organization. As you are already aware, strengths can be underused or overused. Coaches often deal with workaholism that negatively impacts clients' health and places unnecessary pressure on their peers and direct reports and with people who are allowing personal issues to contaminate their working environment and work relationships.

Coaching is often not easy and not always pleasant. Human beings have a habit of bringing unresolved emotional issues into the workplace and acting them out on their fellow workers. In the effort to plan and execute the best talent systems possible, you will need to deal from time to time with highly personal issues related to an individual's health and well-being. For this you might want to partner once again with professionals in the human resources area. If they are not credentialed to assist with some of the more challenging health and well-being issues, they are authorized to refer you to someone who is.

You need to be sensitive to how an individual's health and well-being can enhance or negate the other good work you are doing as a coach. Don't dismiss any aspect of talent systems. By definition, a system is an interconnected network in which whatever happens to any element of the system has an impact on every other element of the system.

If you are a runner and in perfect health, you have a magnificent physical system working for you. Break one of your big toes on a coffee table leg and see what happens. The entire system is still magnificent, save for that broken big toe—which cripples the entire system's ability to function to its full capacity. Do not let your client's health and well-being or any other talent management issue cripple your coaching accomplishments.

Health and Well-Being and the Organization

If it is true that an organization cannot be any physically or emotionally healthier than its population, then what is the organization's role in keeping its employees physically and emotionally healthy? Most HR departments in organizations of any appreciable size offer blood pressure monitoring and various types of health screenings and refer employees to resources for emotional counseling services and a variety of other interventions for the purpose of promoting employee health and well-being. Organizations sponsor sports leagues and other recreational activities because it has been known for a long time that a proper work-life balance results in greater personal performance, productivity, and profitability than burned-out workers can produce.

In a labor-rich market, employees can be easily (and relatively inexpensively) replaced. In a labor-rich or labor-poor market, organizations are best served by keeping their organizational populations emotionally and physically healthy in order to produce better work. The investment in health and well-being plays particularly well with a younger, health-conscious population. The investment organizations make in the health and well-being of their employees plays an increasingly important role in employee recruitment and retention. Organizational health and well-being programs are important factors in attracting and retaining talent. As such, they are an increasingly important part of talent systems.

Now that organizations have such a high-stakes interest in the physical and emotional health and well-being of their organizational populations, you, as a coach or a manager who coaches, need to encourage your clients to take full advantage of the services available to them. By working hard to promote the physical and emotional health and well-being of your clients you are promoting the health and well-being of the organization.

Behaviors Related to Talent Systems

As you have been tracking the Contextual Coaching process, you have been identifying behaviors associated with the individual and organizational results you want to produce. Talent systems are no different. As a contextual coach, you pay attention to the ways your organization sets expectations, manages performance, and measures results in order to provide practical and effective advice to the individual receiving your coaching.

In examining, tracking, and modifying your clients' habits, skills, and activities, you are looking to identify ways in which they can benefit from the forward-looking piece of performance management (i.e., the development planning aspect) as a powerful personal awareness and goal-setting exercise. You might also inquire as to how your clients are using talent systems in team building, depending on the number of their direct reports. The following behaviors are part of the Contextual Coaching 360-degree assessment that measures your clients' proficiency in using talent systems as a tool for developing their own careers and/or the careers of their direct reports:

- Sets standards for performance.
- Rewards performance appropriately.

- Gives specific and accurate feedback.
- Identifies top talent against succession plan.
- Uses effective hiring process to engage top talent.
- Uses performance management systems to monitor performance of individuals.

These are management behaviors for those responsible for managing the performance of others and for utilizing the talent systems within an organization. When coaching individual contributors, it will be important to see these competencies from the perspective of the individual's potential to become a manager in the future.

> If you were to place these behaviors before a group of feedback providers and ask them to rank your client, what would they say? Would they say that the behaviors listed are overused, underused, or used optimally by your client? If you use the Contextual Coaching 360-degree assessment, you will get those answers. Even though using the Contextual Coaching 360-degree assessment is a formal way to assess the overuse, underuse, or optimal use of each behavior in a survey format, you can also use these questions to conduct your own structured interviews with feedback providers, sitting down with them face to face and discussing each behavior. (For examples of the underuse, overuse, and optimal use of the talent systems structure behaviors, as well as for suggested reading on talent systems, visit www.WeMakeTalentWork.com and click on "The Coaching Connection.")

360-Degree Feedback Questions for Talent Systems

As with all ten areas of the Coaching Connection model, it is a good idea to elicit responses to the 360-degree feedback questions to get an idea of where your client stands in working with talent systems.

Questions for the Coaching Client

As a means of further assessment, here are questions specific to talent systems to ask your clients:

- Can you give examples of how the management of talent is a major investment of time, energy, and focus for you?
- How do you acquire a sense of where others stand on important matters?
- How do you give people the feedback on their performance that will help them do a better job?

If your client is an individual contributor, the first question relates to his or her own talent management. All employees have a major investment in their own development and must work to ensure that their efforts on their own behalf interface with the organization's talent systems. The second question works for both individual contributors and those with teams to manage. For individual contributors, the third question relates to peers and is a training opportunity for future management responsibilities. Even if your clients manage teams, it is a good exercise to make sure the client is providing feedback to peers, as well. It is equally important that the client solicit feedback from peers and superiors in a welcoming and collaborative manner.

Questions for the Feedback Providers

If you are using the Contextual Coaching 360-degree assessment, these will be the questions that your feedback providers will need to answer as they regard your client:

- How can you see whether the management of talent is a major investment of time, energy, and focus for the client?
- How does the client demonstrate a sense of where others stand on important matters?
- In what ways, how often, and to what extent do people get the feedback on performance from the client that will help them do a better job?

You are looking for rich answers that will give you and your clients material to work with in designing their coaching action plans. The answers you receive to these questions will spell out whether your clients have gaps in the area of talent systems and, if so, the type of remedy that is called for. The very act of exploring these topics with your clients and gathering data about them will heighten your clients' awareness of the many hats a manager must wear. If your client is on track to become a manager, this is a good opportunity for your client to learn about talent systems in the context of the organization.

Connecting Talent Management Systems to the Coaching Process

Being good at the one-on-one coaching process does not necessarily mean that an individual is a talent management expert. Many coaches or managers who coach are not well trained in the basics of talent management and need deeper education on the importance and particulars of these systems for managing performance and potential within their organizations. It is extremely important that coaches or managers who coach become familiar with the specific talent management system of the organization in which they coach.

In the Contextual Coaching model, talent systems are included in the process to promote the talent agenda for the organization *in the context of the organization.* Even though the coaching process is a one-to-one relationship, the performance and productivity increases your client will achieve are a significant contribution to the organization's talent equation. This is yet another way that the coaching you provide serves both the individual and the organization.

Talent Systems Summary

From the beginning, we have maintained that talent systems are structured processes that help an organization manage its people, and that talent systems form a bridge between the individual and the organization. Because talent systems encompass so many different aspects of individual and organization development, it is best to approach them like a true systems thinker. Every aspect of talent systems affects every other aspect of talent systems. Compensation affects retention and vice versa. Employees' health and well-being affect career management and vice versa. Potential management affects succession planning and vice versa.

Organizational talent defines the unique selling proposition of an enterprise as much as or more than any other factor. A superior product will eventually fade and fail if it is not supported and continually reinvented by the best people, positioned in the most strategic manner. The talent factor in an organization is nothing less than huge in establishing and maintaining the competitive supremacy of the enterprise or agency.

Because everything affects everything else, which is the core principle of systems theory, every aspect of talent systems is part of the *talent solution.* In Chapter 8, we highlight talent solutions and explain how they are the operational manifestation of talent systems. Talent solutions are where talent systems truly find traction. Talent solutions are where the rubber of talent systems meets the road.

< CHAPTER 8 >

Area of Behavioral Focus: Talent Solutions

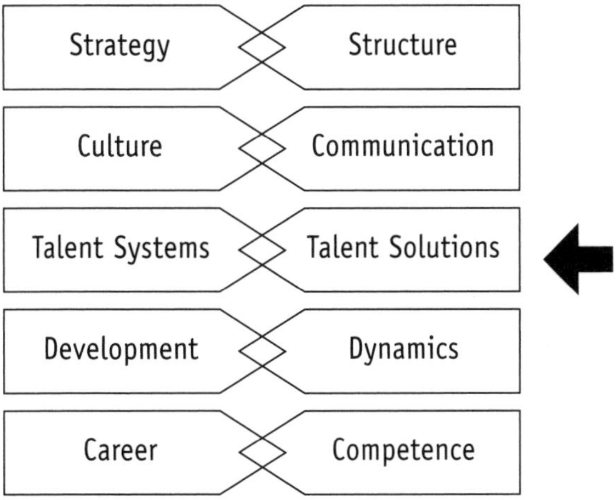

"Coaching serves as a critical tool to help senior succession candidates and leaders change how they view themselves; this in turn gives them the power to get the most out of everyone who works for them."

—**Hy Pomerance**
Global Head, Talent Management
Human Resources
UBS Investment Bank

The dictionary tells us that a "solution" is a method of solving a problem or answering a question. A *talent solution* is how a talent problem or challenge is solved. We'll go on record saying that providing an answer to a talent *question,* as important as that can be, is only *part* of a solution, not the solution itself. Answering a question about talent is more a talent systems measurement and/or assessment issue. Nevertheless, answering questions related to talent solutions marries talent systems and talent solutions in a systemic way. That means the two are operating as parts of the same system.

This chapter on talent solutions covers the sixth of the ten components in the Contextual Coaching model. Talent solutions and talent systems continuously circle each other in a spiraling symbiosis. One feeds the other, after which the other returns the favor. Talent *systems* define, measure, and monitor the raw and experienced talent that talent *solutions* develop and optimize. More and better talent *solutions* based on ever-evolving definitions of needs, new measurements, and feedback provided by talent systems can be applied to keep individual and organizational learning alive and growing.

Solving a talent problem or challenge (our preferred term) requires more than studying, researching, discussing, and/or pondering. Solving a talent challenge requires action, and lots of it—before, during, and even after the solution has been achieved. Only action can transform talent systems information into a true talent solution, and only action can make the solution sustainable. In a nutshell, we believe that solving a talent challenge means resolving, repairing, fixing, tuning up, and/or generally making something better than it is or, better yet, the best it can be—with an eye to making it better yet at every opportunity. Therein can be found the three prongs of the talent solutions fork:

1. Teaching something that has never been learned before (new knowledge)
2. Repairing something that is broken or bogged down (restorative knowledge)
3. Making something good even better (expanding and enhancing knowledge)

At the risk of getting cute with semantics, talent solutions are rarely singular. "One-size-fits-all" and "universal wrench" are not terms commonly associated with talent solutions. Talent challenges tend to be layered and complex in nature, requiring multifaceted solutions. Put another way, a true and lasting talent solution is a carefully concocted blend of different individual solutions, which becomes a complex and unique chemical-type "solution" of its own.

Talent Solutions in Perspective

It helps to put the topic of talent solutions into some context that many can relate to or, at least, understand—like sales. How universally corporate can you get? Customer service is a good metaphor for illustrating the type of positive attitude you should be wearing when approaching a coaching engagement.

You can think about selling in a lot of different ways. If you look at the job description for a sales position today, you will probably read that the applicant needs to have expertise in solution selling. The term "solution selling" is used to describe a shift in focus from selling a product to convincing customers or prospective customers that it is in their best interest to buy into a complete solution. Combining the notion of "solution" with sales also marks a shift in focus from product-based competitive advantage to people-based competitive advantage. The solution, of course, features the products and services the sales person represents. Solution selling is based on hearing your clients' perspective, understanding the gaps in their satisfaction, and crafting a solution that uses the stuff your organization offers.

Solution selling is dominant in the world of consulting, financial services, and technology. It is rapidly becoming the standard for sales programs in many different industries. Food distributors, transportation companies, and automobile dealers (among others) are sending their salespeople to training programs on solution selling in the belief that sales representatives will do a better job pushing product if they sell that product as part of a solution to the customers' problems.

Selling Talent Solutions

Solutions create satisfaction. That is why sales professionals emphasize them. Human resources and training and development professionals inside and outside organizations have been "selling" talent solutions for a long, long time. Just because a talent solution is good for the organization does not mean that people are eager to pay for it. Payers must be convinced that they will receive satisfaction for the investment. Coaching—as beneficial as it can be to individual and organizational performance, productivity, and profitability—is often a tough sell to department heads and other sponsors because of the costs involved.

Solutions make sense. They are not imposed on the end user. Even if they are more "off the shelf" than the prospect knows, they are ultimately responsive to known information about gaps, wants, concerns, and shortfalls. People want to buy solutions because they feel part of the design process. They feel heard.

Discussing and positioning solutions based on clients' needs or concerns requires a different skill set than that required to persuade people to buy. The persuasion is successful when customers (1) believe they will be truly satisfied with the solution, and (2) actually *make the purchase.* The art of bundling products and services into a solution is to make it feel "customized" to your clients. Satisfaction with bundled solutions is a direct result of how quickly and comprehensively you respond to the way your customers communicate their needs. The sales representative must be skilled at:

- Eliciting input from potential clients
- Crafting a solution in front of your client that becomes the basis for a proposal
- Negotiating with the sales representative's own organization to bundle the services and products in a manner acceptable to the prospect

Organizations that have talent management groups often focus on the things we discussed in Chapter 7, on talent systems. They create effective talent systems that provide them with the opportunity to effectively gather, organize, and slice data in order to identify specific gaps and plan for the future. The systems provide the necessary insight and structure for the hiring process, identifying high-potential people, success planning, and performance management.

Your message to those who are current and potential customers of your talent solutions, as well as to your coaching clients who must master talent solutions as part of their balanced management development, is this: Great talent management does not stop at talent systems. Talent solutions go farther by creating opportunities to close the gaps that analytical systems reveal. For instance, if an organization has a competency model that is seen as important for managing the talent pool, the organization should be able to measure the specific behavioral competencies that are weakest in the organization. Once talent systems identify this challenge, they can create multiple opportunities to develop individuals within the organization to strengthen these areas of weakness.

Just as salespeople are shifting from selling products to selling solutions, learning professionals and coaches like you need to operate in the realm of bundled solutions, not hit-and-miss products. Coaches and other learning professionals need to think and act more like consultants than trainers. They need to forge a bond with the business, understand the changing concerns, operate with an appreciation for complexity, and be artistic in the way they respond with services. Serving solutions is less black and white than buying products and never allows providers to rest on their laurels. Your Contextual Coaching clients also need to be more solutions-focused in their consumption of learning and development services. This adds to their balance as managers or executives.

As one who coaches in your organization, you will most likely be partnering with learning and development professionals on a regular basis. You need to push to get the solutions that are going to bring the most impact for your individual clients and team. As the primary person responsible for the talent management of your team, you should work with your learning and development partners to understand the talent gaps that influence your team and identify the potential solutions that can produce sustainable positive impact. These solutions should form another layer of context for your coaching and be integrated into the coaching process to create one systematic approach toward improving the capabilities of your team.

Why Talent Solutions Are Important to the Individual

Learning and development are critical ingredients in any talent management system. While the buzzword "continuous learning" has become somewhat tired, it still speaks to the core sense that individuals are more engaged in their work if they are able to find opportunities to develop their skills. Knowing that an organization is investing in their individual growth and development makes employees feel more connected to the organization, more engaged and enthusiastic about working there, and more positive in relationships with other team members. This is especially true when the investment in growth is focused on the individual and is not a cookie cutter solution but one that understands individual gaps that could get in the way of individuals' future career success.

Great learning and development organizations typically provide tiered opportunities for individuals based on employees' current needs, often as revealed in performance management data. Multiple approaches to developing people are best. Organizations often offer training in both individual and group settings. Either way, the most effective training programs include a coaching component. We call this a *hybrid* approach to employee development. A study sponsored by the International Personnel Management Association found that training alone can produce a 22 percent improvement in productivity. When coaching is added to the training process, the productivity increase reached 88 percent. The opportunity to reflect on training content with a coach and to map the content to an individual's everyday work provides sustainable growth for the coaching client.

Most often, as your client's coach, you will be the one who maps the coaching process to the training programs. There is clear payoff for doing this in terms of performance and engagement. As a manager, your people will be in different kinds of training programs that can help them perform their jobs more effectively and also help their future potential. As their coach, you need to know the content of these programs and to incorporate the major topics in your coaching. This way, you can offer all the relevant teachings for your clients and maximize their impact.

For coaching to have the markers of an organizational process, it must be mapped to the talent solutions made available to the employee. For instance, if coaching clients need to learn to be more strategic and the organization sends them to advanced seminars in strategic planning, the coach can help the coaching clients relate the content of the course to their own particular situation.

The coaching process does not provide all the elements that the coaching client needs in closing talent gaps. Therefore, coaches create more opportunity for success when they connect the one-on-one work with other talent solutions provided within the organization. This enables the coaching client to tap into a broad spectrum of organizational training and development services that promote growth.

One role of the coaching manager is to include learning and development in every workday for every individual. This is more than simply identifying programs that may help employees. This mandate is not satisfied by simply buying into an existing corporate program. It is about giving feedback on a regular basis that helps your clients to grow and develop. The benefit to individuals within an organization can be huge. Such feedback helps them in their current jobs and helps them prepare them for future jobs with more responsibility.

Why Talent Solutions Are Important to the Organization

The challenges associated with the shortage of available talent have taught organizations that to acquire and keep the best talent, they need to invest in talent development. An organization can no longer present itself as a premier brand in the marketplace without establishing itself as a premier employer. Serving up talent solutions requires an organizational commitment to move past transactional approaches to learning and development.

This costs money. Yet, organizations are increasingly willing to spend dollars to improve organizational capabilities. To maximize the performance, productivity, and profit potential of employees, organizations like yours allocate financial resources for specific kinds of talent programs that help to develop individuals, groups, and teams. While there can still be, and too often is, knee-jerk cutting of these budgets during economic downturns, organizations are nevertheless demonstrating more and more commitment to developing talent. If a company wants to honestly claim that its talent is its key differentiator, then it must obviously invest in talent development.

In a solutions world, the customary investment in product development should be matched with a corresponding investment in staff development. You and your coaching activities are part of that investment. You are part of that emerging parity between people and product. The talent solutions in which you participate are not gratuitous. In a people-centric marketplace, the talent development that you're engaged in as a manager who coaches is as much about competitive advantage as it is any other aspect of your enterprise.

In providing organizationally focused solutions, it is wise for organizations to attack talent gap issues using multiple methods, processes, and deliverables. Great talent solutions are crafted with:

- Consultation with business leaders to fully understand the current demands that create pressure for them and raise fears about performance and future potential
- Analysis of talent system data to create focused solutions that target the right things
- Multipronged approaches to talent development that populate a catalogue of opportunities for your clients
- Effective internal marketing of the programs that engages the interest of employees, demonstrating a value proposition for their participation
- Elegant solutions that provide rich content, integrated elements, and user-friendly processes
- Ongoing measurement of successes and continuing challenges

Implicit in this list is an organization that is first and foremost committed to the development of talent and a culture that creates the conditions necessary for growth and development. The fine work of the management guru and author Peter Senge (*The Dance of Change,* 2000) on the learning organization is still a rich model for understanding how a for-profit, nonprofit, public-sector, or private-sector organization can make an ongoing commitment to real learning day in and day out in order to expand capacity for everyone, especially high performers. This involves collaboration among the business units, the learning organization, and people like you, who have the ability to give and receive feedback and to reach agreement on common and unique tools and methods for promoting growth and who are never satisfied with the status quo.

An investment in talent solutions implies that the organization is promoting a culture of continuous learning. In each and every thing we do, there is an opportunity to learn something about ourselves, about others, and/or about some content with which we are not familiar. The Jack Welch legacy culture at GE is legendary for its commitment to learning and development, to which Welch dedicated a budget of more than $1 billion per year. On its Web site, GE boldly claims that people at GE never stop learning. A commitment to continuous learning not only verifies the value placed on learning but is an admission that learning is essential for long-term success.

We *need* learning. No one knows everything there is to know. We can all benefit from striving to improve. Although the abundance and the availability of coaching wax and wane with budget worries, the need for coaching will never diminish until 100 percent of the organization is putting out 100 percent of its performance, productivity, and profitability capacity.

Creating a culture of continuous learning is the responsibility of leaders within an organization. This means that it is your responsibility. We expect that you already know this or you would not be committed to coaching. While learning and development professionals can help articulate the value proposition of learning programs and provide excellent solutions that help the organization live up to its commitment, leaders in the organization must set the tone for continuous learning. This is done by demonstrating curiosity, humility, passion for growth, and a commitment to the development of each individual within the organization.

You can measure an organization's commitment to continuous learning through the proportion of its budget that it dedicates to learning and development. You can also see it through interactions between managers and direct reports. It is in the conversations about the real work people are involved in that the best kinds of continuous learning can occur. Cascading learning into the organization is not done effectively through programmatic responses. Learning needs to permeate the air. It requires an investment of time and energy—not just for the learner but also for the learner's sponsors, peers, mentors, and coaches. This is why developing your coaching skills is an organizational imperative.

The Objectives and Goals for Talent Solutions

Organizations also benefit tremendously from talent solutions as they endeavor to build bench strength for the future. This can mean positioning people in a succession sequence so that one day they can replace retiring executives or other key players. Merely placing people in a succession sequence doesn't give them the training or preparation to fill the role or, more important, to succeed in the role. That is where training, especially a coaching program, can ensure that the organization gets the greatest return possible on its investment in human capital.

In other scenarios, talent solutions increase enterprise-wide capacity and capability. Many development programs focus on high-potential (HiPo) individuals who are seen as future leaders because of their current success and their likelihood of future success. When individuals are selected for the HiPo pool for future roles, they are often placed in accelerated leadership programs. These programs are designed to increase their capacity for taking on responsibility within an organization. Accelerated programs and other learning and development opportunities are among the most exciting and dynamic talent solutions.

Once individuals are identified as HiPos and/or replacements for major position holders, it is time for their development program to go on steroids. This hyped-up leadership preparation positions them for the future, demonstrates commitment to their growth, and builds organizational talent in a proactive way. Organizations that can promote from within instead of looking outside can create better and highly motivating opportunities and synergies for individuals within the company and express a powerful message heralding the value of their talent to stakeholders and potential stakeholders outside the organization. With HiPos, we find it is best to identify the gaps across the HiPo group and create customized solutions based on those gaps. The solutions should include both group-based and individual opportunities.

Coaching is a highly effective engagement for HiPos because it helps them to focus on potential gaps in their competencies without creating an intense development experience. While managers who can coach on performance provide specific value in the here and now to individuals and the organizations, managers who can coach on potential provide lasting benefit to the organization and their coaching clients. This kind of coaching accelerates leadership potential, providing added benefits to the organization.

Action learning programs (real-time problem solving with groups that incorporates coaching feedback) also help create just-in-time development experiences that bring deeper awareness of leadership responsibilities to the HiPo population. Too often, star performers who also have the potential to take on major roles in the future do not fully understand what higher-level leadership in an organization actually entails. Providing them an experience where they can have an impact on a current problem in the organization can help them to experience leadership responsibility while receiving feedback on their style, behaviors, and ways of communicating. Providing a mentoring element with senior people who have already "arrived" can add an extra and extremely powerful dimension to an action learning experience.

Behaviors Related to Talent Solutions

As you continue through the Contextual Coaching process, you will pay attention to the ways your organization establishes and uses talent solutions to help you provide practical and effective advice to your coaching clients.

Optimal Behaviors for Talent Solutions

As you have been tracking the Contextual Coaching process, you have been identifying behaviors associated with your client and organizational results you want to achieve. As a contextual coach, you pay attention to the ways your organization establishes and executes talent solutions in order to provide practical and effective advice to your client receiving your coaching.

In examining, tracking, and modifying your clients' habits, skills, and activities, you are looking to identify ways in which they can benefit from the forward-looking piece of talent solutions as a powerful personal awareness and goal-setting exercise. You might also inquire as to how your clients are using talent solutions in team building, depending on the number of their direct reports. The following behaviors are part of the Contextual Coaching 360-degree assessment that measures your clients' proficiencies in using talent solutions as a tool for developing their own careers and/or the careers of their direct reports:

- Encourages others to learn.
- Utilizes company resources to develop others.
- Invests time and energy in the development planning process.
- Understands strengths and weaknesses of self and direct reports.
- Offers praise when individuals and groups take appropriate risks.

If you were to place these behaviors before a group of feedback providers and ask them to rank your client, what would they say? Would they say that the behaviors listed are overused, underused, or used optimally by your client? If you use the Contextual Coaching 360-degree assessment, you will get those answers. Even though using the Contextual Coaching 360-degree assessment is a formal way to assess the overuse, underuse, or optimal use of each behavior in a survey format, you can also use these questions to conduct your own talent solutions interviews with feedback providers, sitting down with them face to face and discussing each behavior.

Underuse of Talent Solutions

In an organization that is not dedicated to learning and development, it is common for the working population to be underschooled in many important skills and competencies. Organizations that don't understand or value talent solutions may attempt to increase productivity and improve performance through positive incentives, like bonuses or performance overrides. They might also try to use aversion therapy and lay heavy consequences on people who fail to improve, to the point of termination. One thing is sure: If the appropriate talent solution is not being applied to the performance gap, no amount of incentives—positive or negative—will matter much. Incentives in combination with appropriate and effective talent solutions will go much farther and produce superior results.

Overuse of Talent Solutions

Just as talent solutions can be underused by some organizations, other organizations (but more likely individual department heads) can overuse talent solutions. The focus on training and development can become so intense that there is hardly any time or energy left over to do any work. Naturally, if there is only limited time to focus on the real work, productivity and performance will suffer.

This overuse of talent solutions can be an attempt by certain managers and executives to look good and have their people engaged in good activities (who can complain about learning and development?) when what these managers and/or executives are really doing is avoiding their leadership responsibilities in the face of difficult management and/or marketplace challenges. (For examples of the underuse, overuse, and optimal use of the talent solutions behaviors, as well as for suggested reading on talent solutions, visit www.We Make TalentWork.com and click on "The Coaching Connection.")

How Your Coaching Client Fits into Talent Solutions

As we have been discussing throughout this chapter, just because an individual is a sole contributor or otherwise has no direct reports, he or she can still acquire the right attitude about learning and development. One of the things that a Contextual Coaching approach brings to developing new managers is a focus on problem solving. Whether working in isolation or on identified small teams or department-wide, your client should be able to advocate for talent solutions and how they can correct for deficiencies in knowledge and competencies—regardless of who is involved and on what level.

How to Introduce Talent Solutions to Your Coaching Client

There is no better way to learn about the many benefits of talent solutions than to be directly involved in some aspect of organizational learning and development. If you have been assigned a coaching client who is fighting to get back to a positive and productive attitude through a lot of cynicism and disappointment brought on by bad experiences, learning new skills and techniques may help your client adopt a fresh, new view of his or her job.

Whether the knowledge of talent solutions is primarily for your clients' consumption or for their team members, learning how to advocate and facilitate organizational learning will be a career-enhancing move for them. Explain to your clients how expanding their skill sets, capabilities, and/or capacities makes them more valuable commodities to the organization. Explain and illustrate how they need to pass that same awareness on to their reports and even peers with whom they work on teams and special projects.

Make sure that when you are promoting talent solutions to your clients, you connect the positive organizational and individual outcomes to the learning and development activities you are advocating. Many people see learning and development activities as disruptive to doing the real work at hand. That can be a legitimate complaint if the talent solutions are not thoughtfully and judiciously applied. So don't argue with their points of view. Coach them toward using and advocating talent solutions that make sense and provide practical value. We doubt that your clients will disagree that it is best to thoroughly train athletes before sending them into a contest. Your clients' best performance depends just as much on training and practice.

360-Degree Feedback Questions for Talent Solutions

All employees can benefit from understanding the talent solutions preferred by the organization and must work to ensure that their individual efforts are aligned with the achievement of organizational goals and objectives.

Questions for the Coaching Client

As a means of further assessment, here are questions specific to talent solutions to ask your coaching clients:

- Can you give examples of times when you have provided learning opportunities for members of your team?

- How have you assigned job responsibilities that might have caused difficulties or dissensions within your team?

If your client is an individual contributor, rephrase these questions:

- Can you give examples of times when you have sought out learning opportunities for yourself or advocated for learning opportunities for other members of your team?
- How have you discussed job responsibilities with your manager or others in order to avoid or prevent difficulties or dissensions?

The first question relates to how well your clients understand the importance of organizational learning and how actively they pursue it. If your client is an individual contributor or has no direct reports, he or she can still proactively engage in talent solutions that benefit your client as well as the organization. The second question also works for both individual contributors and those with teams to manage. Individual contributors can answer in terms of how they experience being assigned job responsibilities and, in a future-focused way, how they would assign job responsibilities in order to avoid causing difficulties or dissensions on a team. The examples your clients give will illustrate the depth of their own understanding of learning strategies in addition to examples of how they align (or plan to align) personal and team learning efforts with strategic objectives.

Questions for the Feedback Providers

If you are using the Contextual Coaching 360-degree assessment, these will be the questions that your feedback providers will need to answer as they regard your coaching client:

- Can you give examples of times when the client has provided learning opportunities for other members of his or her team?
- Can you give examples of times when the client assigned job responsibilities that caused difficulties or dissensions within his or her team?

If your client is an individual contributor, rephrase these questions for 360-degree feedback providers:

- Can you give examples of times when the client has sought out learning opportunities him- or herself, or for other members of his or her team?
- Can you give examples of times when the client discussed job responsibilities in an effort to minimize or avert difficulties or dissensions?

The answers you receive to these questions will spell out whether your clients have gaps in the area of talent solutions and, if so, the type of remedy that is called for. It should be obvious that just exploring these topics with your clients and gathering data about them will heighten clients' awareness of the many hats a manager must wear—whether your client is presently a manager or aspires to become one. If your client is on track to become a manager, this is a good opportunity for your client to learn about talent solutions in the context of the organization.

How to Use the Responses to the 360-Degree Assessment Questions for Talent Solutions

As with every other component of the Contextual Coaching model, you want your clients to be aware of talent solutions. You want them to understand what talent solutions are and why they are important to the organization and to the individual. As a coach, you help your clients look into their blind spots and decide what aspect they need to become more familiar with.

You will use the answers your clients provide to assess their level of knowledge and comfort around talent solutions. You will use your clients' answers to see how well their understanding and perspectives on talent solutions align with yours. Then you will use the answers your clients' feedback providers provide to see how the three perspectives align and where the gaps exist.

Identify the Gaps

As the contextual coach, you represent the organization. You are, of course, in contact and work in conjunction with your clients' supervisors. However, you represent the macro perspective for the collective. As such, you can monitor how the individual's perspective needs to better align with the organization's needs.

The gap may be closed by not only modifying the individual's thinking and behavior but also seeking concessions or improvements in service delivery from the organization. Your coaching clients might have a healthier and more robust approach to organizational learning than does the organization. Between the two of you, along with whatever foot soldiers you can muster, you can use the gap analysis to launch a campaign for a new and improved, more comprehensive talent solutions agenda in your organization.

Habits

Back within the individual working relationship you have with your coaching clients, you might discover that they have never developed good habits around identifying and pursuing teaching and learning opportunities. That wouldn't surprise us. How many organizations model a truly advanced and sophisticated approach to continuous learning to accompany their imperative for continuous improvement?

Organizations committed to quality improvements such as International Organization for Standardization (ISO) and Six Sigma make continuous learning an integral part of the overarching, enterprise-wide effort to improve quality across the board. Sadly, most organizations don't make a direct and immutable linkage among their product quality, customer support, and organizational learning activities. If learning is a way of life in your organization, it will be much easier to encourage the development of good habits around routinely identifying and acting on learning opportunities.

Skills

Skills improvement is precisely why talent solutions exist. Talent solutions are all about helping people to get better at what they do and to help the organization thrive because of that improvement. Part of the gap analysis described earlier involves identifying gaps in skills. What do people need to learn in order to be able to apply more of what they know?

In addition to developing the habit of identifying learning opportunities and ensuring that there will be learning activities to meet the opportunities, a strategic approach to talent solutions also ensures that the talent solutions are aligned with the operational, growth, and development needs of the organization. The contextual approach to skill building benefits the individual's career development and serves the greater needs of the organization and everyone the organization serves at the same time.

Activities

Beyond predetermined learning activities, there are the day-in and day-out activities of the job. As we pointed out earlier, those routine activities can be carried out without regard to—or acknowledgment of—the ongoing learning needs of the individual or the organization. Unless there is a fully comprehensive program in place, such as ISO or Six Sigma, that blends continuous learning with operational activities, the two are likely to support each other only tangentially and/or coincidentally.

Taking a contextual approach to coaching your clients to initiate and engage in more learning activities will result in the creation of more activities that promote individual learning and get practical things done that build and strengthen the organization at the same time. When we talked about communication, we reminded you of what the author and communication scholar Paul Watzlawick said: "One can never not communicate." In the spirit of Watzlawick's statement, organizations are full of people who are busy doing things. Invoking a comprehensive talent solutions agenda and making continuous learning a way of life in your organization will transform people who are busy doing things into people who are busy *getting things done.*

How to Discuss the Development Gaps with Your Coaching Client

As a coach or a manager who coaches, you need to take everything we have talked about regarding talent solutions and make sure your coaching client "gets it." As you are no doubt aware, "talent solutions" is not a phrase that crosses your lips or anybody else's lips outside HR or training and development very often. In our experience, it does not get talked about in HR or T&D as much as it should.

That means that you have some explaining to do. More appropriately stated, you have a teachable moment at hand. You need to make the case for why talent solutions are important, how they dovetail with talent systems, and what exactly that all means to your clients. As a coach, it is incumbent on you to help your clients put themselves in the organizational learning picture and understand why that is so critical to their career success as well as to the success of the organization. It is sometimes as simple as asking whether your clients have more faith in a smart organization or a dumb organization. Help them accept that they play a vital role in making a dumb organization smart or making a smart organization brilliant.

Connecting Talent Solutions to the Coaching Process

As the sixth component of the Contextual Coaching model, talent solutions is something your clients need to embrace, and that requires that the organization do more than just send them to a seminar on the subject. As we have maintained, if training is a topical application of developing talent or modifying behavior, then coaching is a concentrated dosage. It works faster, lasts longer, and won't stain your shirt.

Coaching is learning. Coaching is therefore a type of talent solution. It is the most intense and effective form of talent solution we know of. If you and your clients have a solid and mutually acceptable definition of what coaching is and how it brings great value to individuals and organizations, then it will become a role model for what a talent solution should be.

Talent Solutions Summary

In order to maximize the potential of employees, companies allocate budgets for specific kinds of learning and development programs that help to develop individuals. These talent solutions are best designed to help meet the strategic needs of the organization and to fill real gaps in employee performance and/or potential. It is best to have multiple approaches to developing staff, including training in both individual and group settings.

For coaching to become a true organizational process, it must be mapped to the talent solutions made available to the employee. If a coaching client needs to learn to be more strategic and the organization sends individuals for advanced seminars in strategic planning, you as the coach might suggest that your client enroll in such a program. The coaching process does not provide all the elements your clients need to close talent gaps. Therefore, you create more opportunities for success for your coaching clients when you connect the one-on-one work you are doing with other talent solutions provided within the organization. This enables your clients to tap into a broad spectrum of organizational learning opportunities that will help them grow and develop.

In Chapter 9, you will be introduced to the concept of development as an overarching methodology that guides the overall growth journey of your clients and the people for whose growth and development they are responsible—if not now, in the future. Development, like its counterpart, team dynamics, is about discovering what is best in individuals and teams and cultivating that unique talent to the best advantage of the individual and the organization.

CHAPTER 9

Area of Behavioral Focus: Development

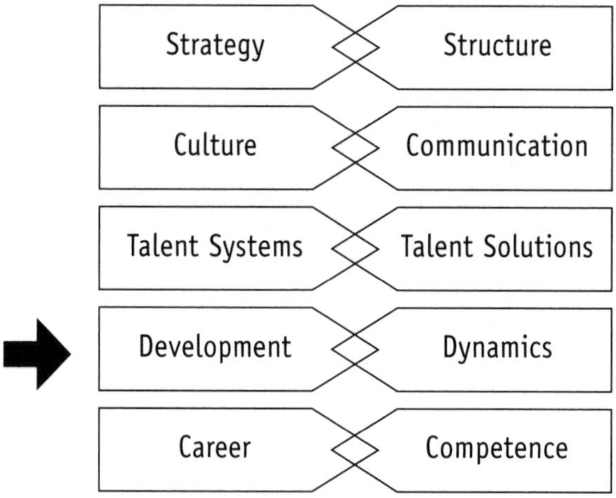

"The true differentiator between strong managers and great leaders is the ability to make a distinction between the short-term benefits of effective performance management and the lasting increase in organizational capacity achieved through developmental coaching."

—Scott McElhone
SVP Human Resources
Home Box Office, Inc.

Development is the seventh component in the Contextual Coaching model and is generally defined as the act or process of developing, the act of growing, or making progress. Training and development, or learning and development, as it is often referred to, encompasses three main activities: training, education, and development. For our Contextual Coaching purposes, we use the term "development" to capture all three. If training, education, and development are not synonymous in a business or organizational environment, they are certainly interrelated.

Here are some of the nuanced distinctions between the terms: Training is usually focused upon, and evaluated against, the job that an individual currently holds. Education is usually focused upon the jobs that an individual may potentially hold in the future. Development is a holistic approach to improve and enhance everything professional about your clients for current and future benefit of your clients and the organization.

If we were life coaches, we would say similar things about developing everything about your clients that will enhance their personal lives. For our purposes, we focus on professional development, which, coincidentally, can never be fully disengaged from personal development, as so many aspects of human behavior are interrelated. People who establish and maintain good habits in their personal lives tend to do the same in their professional lives. There are exceptions to everything. But successful living and successful working often go hand in hand.

Companies employ contextual coaches to work with individuals for many reasons. Through this investment, organizations demonstrate their commitment to their human capital. This is a strategic choice, made in response to intense pressure to retain existing talent and to compete for new talent in the most competitive recruiting environment in recent memory.

The Contextual Coaching process does not erase your clients' development work that can be achieved through a rich and focused coaching experience. Your clients' development processes embedded in traditional executive coaching are still essential to the Contextual Coaching process and are not meant to be replaced by our shared focus on your clients and the organizations they work for.

Individual development creates the opportunity for heightened self-awareness through the coaching process. When your clients become more aware of their modes of behavior, they will be better able to understand how they engage, empower, and energize others. All individuals are blind to certain aspects of their behavior and have some patterns of behavior that may fail to motivate other members of their teams. Deepening self-awareness helps your clients better anticipate the perceptions and reactions of others and to avoid falling into patterns that have a negative impact on others.

Managing personal tendencies and coping with individual personality styles in a way that maximizes human potential take some deep personal work. It is not easy to adjust behaviors that relate to the deepest aspects of our personalities. As we review our histories, each of us can see evidence of repeated behaviors that get us into trouble. Identifying those behaviors and creating strategies to manage and even improve them is a major aspect of developmental coaching.

As the coach, you will lead your coaching clients through their development by helping identify systems and strategies that encourage the developmental practice of addressing issues instead of the destructive practice of repeatedly creating, then avoiding issues. Fundamentally, you will have the opportunity to open up new worlds to your coaching clients by providing the insight and understanding that personal and professional changes are necessary for unlocking potential. Once they achieve this level of enhanced consciousness, your clients will be able to more effectively and more consistently captivate the hearts and minds of others and encourage development in everyone they encounter.

Developmental Change Is Simple—Not Easy

It is often assumed that, as a rule, people do not like change. True, people often resist and even sabotage change efforts in organizations. However, the assumption that people do not like change is misleading. There are many times when people embrace change wholeheartedly. People like change when it benefits them, taps into their curiosity, and offers us positive opportunities. Who would not want an increase in salary? That is a change. Most people would embrace new responsibilities and the opportunity for independent decision making—especially if that is a change from where they are now.

Losing weight is a change. Losing weight is simple. It is not easy. It is simple. An important lesson you can help your clients to embrace is that simple concepts are not always easy to execute. Two things are essential for a weight-loss program to succeed: Eat less and exercise more. Simple. Burn more calories than you consume. It is not easy for most people. But anyone doing those two things consistently, over time, will lose weight.

There are two things required before people will change and develop. People will participate in change, support change, and even champion change if they think they (1) will be happier with the new outcome than they are with the present situation, and (2) believe the change is possible. Potential happiness and likely success drive the acceptance of change. Your clients will probably agree that achieving much higher levels of proficiency, productivity, and performance will benefit them as individuals and the organization as a whole. If they do not think such improvements are attainable, however, they will not try.

As a coach or a manager who coaches, you must accept that the statement about people resisting change as a rule is wrong. The real rule is that people do not like challenges they do not feel they can rise to meet. They do not want to engage in activities that burden their hearts and minds, not to mention their backs, with no palpable promise of happiness and success at the other end. People do not like to waste their time and effort on something that will (1) not make them happier than they are now and (2) leave them with that familiar feeling of failure.

If your clients look upon their own development as if it is going to hurt, do not expect much enthusiasm or success. Many people associate pain with change. Organizational change, for instance, requires learning to negotiate new circumstances, navigate a new landscape, and learn a new power structure. It creates anxiety and exacerbates fear of the unknown.

Yet, we cannot forget that change is a constant in our lives. As a coach, you need to entertain conversation with your clients about how we are continually moving forward in time with a world that is evolving around us. Today is not the same as yesterday. Tomorrow will not be the same as today. Change is part of the human experience. Help your clients become aware that, like most things in life, change can be their friend or their enemy, depending upon how they decide to deal with it. Do your clients look upon change as danger or opportunity?

Development requires a willingness to change qualities about ourselves that would otherwise get in the way of present and future success. When your clients enter into a spirit of development and its associated activities, they take the lead in bringing about change. They are no longer passive and reactive to change around them. Under your guidance, they purposely address their strengths and weaknesses—creating and executing an action plan to confront change head on.

Think of the many times a manager or organization has encouraged you to complete an individual development plan (IDP). The plan probably included some self-assessment of strengths and weaknesses against some kind of criteria such as a competency model. Then you identified areas of strengths that could be better leveraged. You noted talent gaps that needed to be filled in order to get to the next level of performance.

In the IDP, we are making a commitment to change ourselves. We are promising to work on those qualities that prevent us from being as successful as possible. We may also be willing to grow in areas that will help us to accelerate our own position in the organization. For instance, if we need financial acumen to get to a vice president position, we may take a course on finance for nonfinance managers.

Coaching is known to be the most successful individual development activity. It focuses on development like a laser beam, creating tremendous opportunities for your coaching clients. It also becomes the chance to address any negative behaviors that your clients engage in that create negative stories in everyday work experiences. Coaching is a development activity that holds out developmental change as a shared responsibility of the coach and the coaching client.

Why Development Is Important to the Individual

The Contextual Coaching model takes your clients' development process to the next level by positioning their development processes inside an organization development system. We never lose sight of your clients' development goal of being coached and deriving all the many benefits of coaching. Your clients remain central in our process because managing their own need to change is difficult. Your clients will forever drive their own process, as you advise from the sideline. This shared-responsibility process gives them the emotional support they need to tackle the development process.

Coaching is a rare experience in business. Participants are provided the opportunity to discuss their challenges, receive assessment information that provides self-insight, build an action plan for change with a trained partner, and reflect on behaviors, relationships, and specific work challenges that impede success. Coaching is a highly intensive process that builds on the potential of your coaching clients, one individual at a time.

Depending upon your clients' focus of this work, there is good reason that many coaches have background or training in counseling skills. Counseling skills provide a foundation that helps create client-coach rapport and ongoing partnership for change. While coaching is not therapy, it has some similar dynamics when it comes to active listening, accurate assessment, and personal growth. The organizational context is always there as a backdrop for the coaching process, but your clients stand squarely in the foreground. Your clients are your primary focus, and your ability to diagnose the best course of developmental action for them is eclipsed only by how you can best apply your talents, skills, and abilities to help them succeed.

There are clear benefits for your coaching clients in having this intense opportunity to focus on personal development. Not only will they be able to address specific changes needed to move their careers forward; they will also design a plan for how to maximize the benefit of those changes, all with the support and guidance of a trusted adviser—you.

Why Development Is Important to the Organization

When standing back and examining a globe or a wall map of the world, most people can easily identify at least one or two countries or regions that could be classified as "undeveloped" when compared to more prosperous and industrially and/or agriculturally productive countries or regions. An undeveloped country is typically characterized by an undeveloped population. A country where the general population falls short of world norms in education, industriousness, or productivity is usually labeled part of the third world.

The same is true of organizations. An organization that is characterized by a poorly educated, poorly trained, poorly led organizational population—in short, an underdeveloped population—could be considered a third-tier organization. An organization, like a country on the world map, is only as effective, resourceful, productive, and talented as its population. The approach that global assistance agencies take, in concert with the governments of underdeveloped countries, is not unlike the approach taken by underdeveloped organizations.

To start, companies must train, educate, and otherwise develop their organizational populations. Organizations, like underdeveloped countries, are going to become only as functional as their populations. Progress through training and education can take place on a macro level. But even more rapid and intense improvements can be made on the micro, or individual, level. That's why you, as a coach or a manager who coaches, play such a vital role.

As you help identify individuals with high leadership potential and then coach them to excellence in their abilities to work and lead others, you are providing the organization with what it most desperately needs. Emerging leaders, not simply individual contributors, help develop an organization exponentially faster than enterprise-wide training and education initiatives and activities. The tensile strength of an organization is directly proportionate to the tensile strength of its organizational population.

We have already discussed in Chapters 7 and 8 the importance of focusing attention on and committing resources to developing talent. We connected talent solutions to the competition for talent in the marketplace and the necessity of acquiring and retaining top talent. When it comes to coaching, the organization benefits enormously when key individuals embrace the process of personal and professional development. These people stand out as role models. They become the highly visible embodiment of what others in the organization can aspire to be. When talented people scrutinize your organization, trying to determine if they should join your ranks, a vigorous and rigorous program of coaching high-potential workers will enhance your organization's appeal.

The Objectives and Goals for Development

Emergent leaders, the products of quality coaching, well balanced in the context of the organization's needs, shape and define the culture and the cultural expectations of the organization. Coaching not only provides the organization with increased performance in the present; it also provides a platform for ongoing leadership development into the future. Without the coaching process, things will remain the same or at best improve at the speed of molasses. Your goal and the goal of the organization through the contextual coaching process is simple: Key talent becomes better faster.

Begin building your coaching platform with the engagement benefit. While some clients resist coaching at first, especially if there is some confusion about the goals of the process, most coaching clients appreciate the individual attention that coaching provides when it comes to career development. They see the clear commitment to their growth from their managers and the organization. They appreciate the magnitude of the investment and connect the dots between why an organization makes an investment and the expectation for a positive return on that investment. This energizes participation in your clients' day-to-day work and instills a deeper loyalty and commitment when recruiters call with job offers from a competitor.

Next, consider performance improvements as your clients experience developmental progress through coaching. There is true and immediate benefit to the coaching process. Individuals are encouraged to try new behaviors in their work and to manage their gaps more effectively. Skillful guidance by the coach produces incremental improvements in performance over time. The quality of work being done by your coaching client improves faster and in ways that would have not occurred without commitment to the coaching process.

Third, the organization is preparing people for the future by building bench strength. Often, your coaching process will include helping your clients target their future path. Some of the strengths that they possess will be terrific when they take on new roles and will benefit them greatly. But they will probably require some strengths in the future that they have not yet developed. By engaging in the coaching process, your clients can build their own potential for long-term success. When it's time for the organization to tap your clients on the shoulder for a higher-level job, they will be better prepared for success and better set up to achieve the goals of the job.

Your coaching objectives where development is concerned include establishing benefits, performance improvements, and bench strength. Combined advantages for the individual client and the organization make up the coaching platform. As a manager who is committed to coaching your people, you are one of the greatest assets to your organization as you develop your clients in the context of the organization. You have formed a strategic partnership with your organization to work on an initiative that provides both immediate and ongoing benefit at the same time. And you are treating a precious organizational asset—its talent—with the proper care and respect it deserves. There is no more worthwhile goal than that. All of this will enhance your own job satisfaction, your bond with your team, and your potential for expanded leadership roles in the future.

Behaviors Related to Development

As you coach your clients to prepare them for future roles in the organization, you can help them to develop the necessary skills and attitudes that will serve them and the organization well later on.

Optimal Behavior for Development

Ideally, your clients will be enthusiastically engaged in their own development activities and the development activities of the people in their spheres of influence. When people are genuinely interested in their own long-term development and the long-term development of their direct reports and colleagues, they consider what they do and what the organization does in future terms. Because development is so future focused, conversations tend to be conducted in the future tense.

"When our people reach this waypoint in their development, our organizational capacity to do XYZ will be significantly increased." Such visionary references prove that people are focused on development, rather than on survival. They are looking down the road, not at the road. As a coach or a manager who coaches, you want to encourage your clients to think of their futures and the future of the organization.

When people are future focused, they tend to adopt a fresh perspective on things like talent systems and talent management. Measuring and enhancing knowledge, skills, abilities, and capacities takes on new meaning when the overall developmental plan of the individual and the organization are considered. The optimal behavior for development is to always keep the big picture in mind—to always look at the developmental arc of the individual in the context of the organization's future. This will be energizing, as your clients cannot wait to hit their next developmental milestone.

Underuse of Development

People who cannot see the light at the end of the tunnel become cynical because they feel as if their cumbersome journey will go on forever. They feel as if the burden they carry will never be lifted from their shoulders. Their frustration turns to hopelessness. Their cynicism, that feeling that "This will never end," saps their energy, and it becomes a gargantuan effort just to get through the day, much less the week, the month, the quarter.

As a coach or a manager who coaches, you need to identify this cynicism when you see it and to diagnose its cause. You must develop the ability to detect the absence of developmental focus and then to consult with your clients, the appropriate human resources professionals, and your clients' superiors to assess the reasons why this gap in development exists. That blank look in your clients' eyes, the slumped shoulders, the downcast gaze, the dragging feet, and the general lethargy in the workplace all point to the underuse of development.

Overuse of Development

If your clients are obsessed with their developmental plans at the expense of their ongoing responsibilities, you have a problem on your hands. Preparing for future responsibilities and broader areas of focus is all well and good, but there are things that need to be tended to today. Achieving the optimal focus on development, as we just described, and building that platform for personal and professional growth, requires that people balance a vision for the future and attentiveness to their current roles and responsibilities.

Overuse of development can cost a great deal in neglected current needs. One factor you must be aware of as a coach is a tendency for people to escape their current situations by projecting themselves into the future. Particularly if people are not happy with their current roles and responsibilities, they might ride their developmental bandwagon too far, too fast. Your job as a contextual coach is to help stabilize your clients' developmental activities and help your clients achieve that all-important balance between current responsibilities and continuous expansion of their habits, skills, and attitudes. (For examples of the underuse, overuse, and optimal use of development behaviors, as well as for suggested reading on development, visit www.WeMakeTalentWork.com and click on "The Coaching Connection.")

How Your Coaching Client Fits into Development

A 360-degree assessment is an effective way to plot where your coaching client is in the view of others: subordinates, superiors, colleagues, and customers. Under the umbrella of engineering their own developmental formulas, your clients are requesting assistance in the form of feedback from their various constituencies. Your clients have many opportunities to assist in other employees' development, just as they request assistance from others in their own development.

Accepting where exactly they are positioned in the organization is a major part of your clients' developmental success. That can be determined only with the objective assistance of others. But then your clients need to craft the plan, draw the blueprint, and create the roadmap for their own developmental journey.

With your expert guidance as their coach, your clients must establish their own developmental trajectory. They need to take ownership of those training and educational activities required to move forward with their developmental agenda. Your clients fit into the developmental picture by becoming the authors of their own future and negotiating each and every element of their developmental architecture. The most successful developmental plans are drafted in the context of the organization. As we often say, it is the alignment between what people do best and what the organization needs most that produces wins for everyone.

How to Introduce Development to Your Coaching Client

As a coach or a manager who coaches, it is incumbent upon you to bring all of this enlightenment to your clients. Perhaps it would be better to say that you should skillfully lead them to the point where they can achieve and experience their own epiphanies. How do you ask your clients if they have considered their futures? Have you initiated dialogues about how your clients are going to progress from where they are now to where they want to be in five years?

As the coach, you might need to help your clients raise their sights, optimally so, to gaze into their own futures and develop a meaningful and realistic vision. You do not want to lead them to overuse development. Neither do you want to discourage them. Help your clients understand all that is required to make the moves they hope to make.

Your constant frame of reference as you introduce your clients to the developmental process is the context of the organization. Talk to your clients about where the organization is headed. What is the organization's short-, mid-, and long-term plan for growth and expansion? How do your clients fit in to that emerging picture? These types of conversations get your clients' minds focused properly and realistically on what is available to them and what they should be setting as developmental objectives.

Development Behaviors

As you have been tracking the Contextual Coaching process, you have been identifying behaviors associated with your clients and organizational results you want to produce. Development encompasses all of the other elements as your clients engineer a comprehensive developmental approach to their future responsibilities. As a contextual coach, you pay particular attention to the ways your organization encourages and supports development in order to provide practical and effective advice to your clients.

In examining, tracking, and modifying your clients' habits, skills, and activities, you are looking to identify ways in which they can benefit from the forward-looking nature of development as a powerful personal awareness and goal-setting exercise. You might also inquire as to how your clients are using development in team building, depending on the number of direct reports they supervise. The following behaviors are part of the Contextual Coaching 360-degree assessment that measures your clients' proficiency in using development as a tool for developing their own careers and/or the careers of their direct reports.

- Demonstrates self-awareness.
- Is open to feedback from others.
- Accepts responsibility for mistakes.
- Seeks out mentors and key advisers.
- Commits to the process of growing and developing.

If you were to place these behaviors before a group of feedback providers and ask them to rank your client, what would they say? Would they say that the behaviors listed are overused, underused, or used optimally by your client? If you use the Contextual Coaching 360-degree assessment, you will get those answers. Even though using the Contextual Coaching 360-degree assessment is a formal way to assess the overuse, underuse, or optimal use of each behavior in a survey format, you can also use these questions to conduct your own development interviews with feedback providers, sitting down with them face to face and discussing each behavior.

360-Degree Feedback Questions for Development

A thorough assessment of your client's understanding of the importance of development in furthering your client's career and those of his or her direct reports is an important part of the Contextual Coaching process.

Questions for the Coaching Client

As a means of further assessment, here are questions specific to development to ask your coaching clients:

- What areas of individual development are most important for you in this process?
- How open are you to feedback from others in the organization when individuals communicate concerns, feedback, and/or advice.

Whether your clients are individual contributors or lead large departments, the first question probes how tuned in they are to their own developmental aspirations. If they are not ready to clearly articulate what they want professionally, you will need to work with them to achieve that clarity. No one can engage in a meaningful development process without being able to plainly state what he or she is hoping for.

The second question also works for both individual contributors and those with teams to manage. The key issue here is how receptive your clients are to receiving and accepting objective feedback about their demonstrated abilities and overall performance. Feedback will also deal with how well your clients manage relationships and expectations with subordinates, colleagues, and superiors. If your clients lead teams, they need to be good role models for accepting feedback. If they are individual contributors, their ability to accept and make good use of feedback will go a long way toward the success of their developmental plan.

Questions for the Feedback Provider

If you are using the Contextual Coaching 360-degree assessment, these will be the questions that your feedback providers will need to answer regarding your coaching client:

- What areas of individual development are most important through this process for the client?
- Does the client accept feedback from others in the organization when individuals communicate concerns, feedback, and/or advice?

Once again, you are looking for rich answers that will give you and your coaching clients material to work with in designing their developmental action plans. The answers you receive to these questions will spell out whether your clients have gaps in the area of development and, if so, the type of remedy that is called for. It should be obvious that just exploring the topic of development with your clients and gathering data about them will heighten your clients' awareness of the many hats a manager must wear—whether your client is a manager at present or aspires to become one. If your coaching client is on track to become a manager, this is a good opportunity for your client to learn about development in the context of the organization.

How to Use the Responses to the 360-Degree Assessment Questions for Development

Development encompasses the process of crafting and executing an action plan. Development is the doing part of the Contextual Coaching model. This fact makes responses to the 360-degree assessment questions extremely important to your clients' futures. How good are your clients at getting in touch with what they want and need from a developmental perspective? How receptive are they to the suggestions or observations of others?

This information is the substance of intense and meaningful conversations that you need to initiate with your coaching clients. This is how you, as a coach or a manager who coaches, find out what kind of work you will be doing with your clients. This is where your road map comes from. Since coaching is a client-driven process, your clients need to learn how to drive their own development.

Identify the Gaps

Where do your clients struggle with the concept of development? Where do they stumble when trying to execute the activities associated with developmental growth? Many clients have difficulty talking openly about what they want out of their professional careers. Others have unreasonable expectations, at least in the timelines they associate with attaining their goals.

Do your clients' development plans track with the goals and objectives of the organization? Do they resonate nicely? Where do your clients' self-described career ambitions diverge from the organization's needs? Where do your clients' career ambitions cross wires with their managers' expectations of them?

Your gap analysis of your clients' development issues will identify where there are disconnects between your clients' perceptions of their developmental paths and the perceptions held by their bosses and organizational designers. That is when you, the coach, jump into the gap. Your job is to guide your clients through the process of negotiating with their managers and organizational designers and to find the point of convergence and the optimal plan to get there.

Habits

Development should be a habit for your clients. Unfortunately, most people do not pay regular attention to what they should be doing now to ensure their future success. One of the most difficult transitions for workers is to shift focus from the operational and tactical tasks of the moment to what will be needed in the future. Moving from mission thinking to vision thinking is tough for many people. We teach entire training courses around how to move from operational manager to strategic thinker.

How does one make a habit of strategic thinking? The same way any habit is formed—by deliberate, consistent, redundant, and incremental application. As a coach or a manager who coaches, you will provide critical guidance and encouragement through this difficult transition. People too often just want to give up and lapse into old habits of transactional thinking. Knowing that a gap exists between a developmental perspective and how your clients think in the moment, you will have to keep that momentum going until you can sit back and watch your clients routinely consider their long-term prospects and plans.

Skills

Besides developing the habit of thinking in multiple dimensions—present and future—your clients must also develop new skill sets around developmental activities. With your help, they will develop the ability to connect what they are doing in the moment to its implications for the future. Your clients will become skilled at finding economies of scale in what they do and at spreading costs over time as they consider the future and the forward-looking derivatives of their efforts.

If your clients begin thinking of everything they now do as part of the process of building a platform for where they want to be in five years, they will become more adept at working at a high level as much as possible. As the long-term benefits of what they do kick in over time, the organization will benefit in cost savings and earning enhancements. Any executive will appreciate acquiring the skill to have such an impact.

Activities

Spreading the word about development will become a new activity for your clients. As they master a developmental perspective and work their developmental plans, your clients will share the good news with subordinates and colleagues, even becoming skilled and competent mentors who can help others as you helped them.

The sooner you can encourage your clients to become mentors and advisers, the better. We are not advising you to push them on unsuspecting subordinates and colleagues before they are ready and properly vetted. However, as soon as they are, urge them to get involved with teaching others. Teaching others is the best and fastest way for them to improve themselves. Encourage your clients to teach classes, conduct workshops, or just mentor one on one.

How to Discuss the Development Gaps with Your Coaching Client

Since most clients are not familiar with and perhaps are not comfortable talking about their futures, be patient. It might be best to back into the conversation by talking about where the organization is headed over the next five years. By discussing the organizational context of your clients' development, you dilute the focus, so your clients will not feel that they are under the interrogation light down at the police precinct.

Another good way to begin a conversation with your clients about development is to help them position themselves to mentor and/or advise others. Again, when the harsh spotlight is not on them, your clients will not feel so singled out for the development discussion. They will put two and two together and become increasingly comfortable with the concept of development; in all likelihood, they will begin quizzing you about how they should go about it.

Regardless of what attitudes your clients come in with, they need to become comfortable with development-speak as soon as possible. Remember that people are always interested in their futures and what is going to happen to them. They just might not be aware that they have a stronger hand to play than they might have originally thought in determining their own destiny. The final piece of the puzzle that you need to make clear is that planning their own development and then executing their plan is a large part of what they're getting paid for. Development is not decadent, self-serving, or vain. It is an organizational necessity. The organization needs to plan its future and to know who can be counted on to move up and accept more leadership responsibility.

Connecting Development to the Coaching Process

As we mentioned, development is the comprehensive category of the Contextual Coaching model where future plans are made, aspirations are mapped, and strategies are devised. It is an exercise in strategic thinking. As a coach or a manager who coaches, you can help your clients in numerous ways to become familiar and comfortable with this new way of thinking and behaving.

Development conversations between coaches and clients are the planning sessions for career success as far as the individual is concerned. They are also essential for organizational success, because a strong, well-developed leadership team is essential for the organization's future. Your goal as a coach is to facilitate and accelerate the growth and development of your clients. Development planning is at the heart of that. As a contextual coach, you help your clients to master the development category, which connects the development of the individual with the current and future needs of the organization, aligning what people do best with what the organization needs most.

Development Summary

Development is a forward-looking, future-focused concept. It is not mission focused but vision focused. The development process helps your clients to lift their vision from the transactional task at hand and to redirect it to the strategic considerations that will affect your clients both individually and as part of the organizational population.

Development of the individual is a parallel activity that takes place alongside organization development. As a coach or a manager who coaches, you need to make sure that your clients develop the ability to discuss their own developmental plans as freely and objectively as they discuss the developmental scheme for the organization. Your clients must also endeavor to become mentors and advisers to others as quickly as possible to fortify their understanding of and proficiency with the concept and execution of development. As your clients' knowledge and skill level around development increase, the more valuable your clients will become to the organization. This value will be realized in the way that your clients lead others and prepare them to assume leadership roles in the future.

Because none of us in organizational life work in isolation, the discussion in Chapter 10 shifts gears from development to the dynamics of working in teams. As with all of the concepts embedded in the Contextual Coaching model, development is a preamble to the complexities and possibilities of teamwork—all in the context of the organization.

CHAPTER 10

Area of Behavioral Focus: Team Dynamics

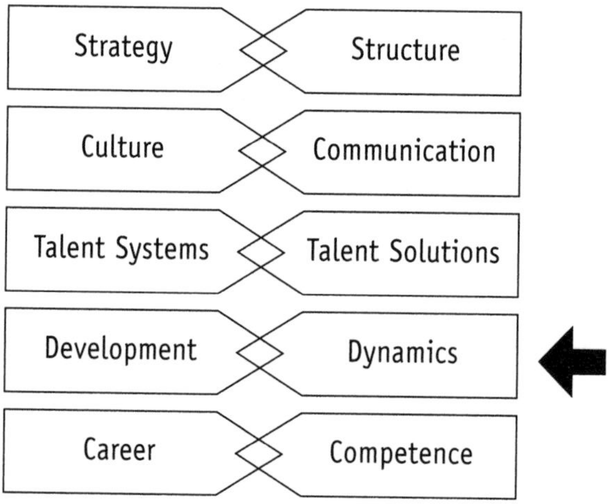

"Well-placed support from an executive coach can unlock the full potential of leaders while enabling the teams they lead to more fully and rapidly achieve the intended benefits of learning opportunities, which emerge during times of change in order to get immediate results and build leadership capability for the long term."

—**Mark Mula**
Vice President, Leader Capability & Learning
Pfizer, Inc.

Team dynamics are the eighth component in the Contextual Coaching model, and we define dynamics as motion or a driving force, an equilibrium of systems, or under the action of forces from outside the system. Obviously, the study of team dynamics is the study of how teams influence the environment in which they exist and how teams are influenced by their environments, thus establishing an equilibrium in their environments as shaped by the forces inside and outside the system. In the case of organizations, teams are mightily influenced by the organizational culture and, on rare occasions, return the favor. Although all teams have dynamics, some teams are more dynamic than others. Any executive will tell you that teams should be in motion and driving forward.

We have argued within this book that coaching involves situating an individual within the context of his or her work—aligning what individuals do best with what organizations need most. The context of the work involves many factors embedded in the seven prior components of the Contextual Coaching model we have already discussed. We understand a team to be a group of people who find themselves united by a common cause, a goal, or an objective, which may be short term or long term in nature, official or unofficial, naturally forming or synthetic.

A team under this definition can be a generic, unofficial group in the sense that voters may see themselves as being on a presidential candidate's "team" even though there is no official affiliation between them and the candidate and even though they never have any direct contact whatsoever with the campaign. All the people who support that candidate are part of the "team," which, by definition, is naturally forming. That is, nobody forced them to come together. Churches are naturally forming groups. Bridge clubs are naturally forming groups. Political parties are naturally forming groups.

By contrast, groups that come together involuntarily are artificially formed groups. Juries are artificially formed groups placed together to take on a public service that is mandatory for all citizens—but not something people naturally gather together to do. Most of these jurors would rather spend their time another way with better earning potential. But they are commanded to form a team that needs to make crucial decisions in a consensus format. The team may be artificially formed, but its decisions have huge implications for the individuals on trial.

People who choose to work for or otherwise join an organization are assembling voluntarily. Yet, once part of the organizational population, they might not choose to join a work group or team that they find themselves compelled to join by their boss or someone else higher on the organizational food chain. The vast majority of formally organized work teams in organizations are also synthetically, or artificially, organized.

Enter Dynamics

Regardless of how a team is formed, team dynamics is a complex notion that includes the working style of the group, interrelationships of team members, group knowledge and experience, and the level of clarity in understanding roles and responsibilities within the team. As a coach or a manager who coaches, you will need to break down this definition for your clients and discuss each element.

Working Style. Team dynamics comprise those elements of a team's style that relate directly to both the innate personality traits of team members and the ways individuals on the team exhibit their personal behavioral styles. In other words, the working style of a team is driven by the working style of individuals on the team. When these styles come together in the team setting, they form a group approach to doing work and an approach to how individuals work with others when responsibilities are shared.

For instance, if the individuals on a team tend to have a psychological interest in controlling their work closely in order to ensure perfection, they may have some issues with trusting one another and delegating responsibilities across the team. The individual styles of team members create a force that is unseen but completely real. The working style of the team ends up playing itself out in the progress of the work the team is doing.

You can calculate the composite personality of the team and get a sense of the collective personality—the phantom personality, if you will—that takes over when two or more people come together to accomplish anything. The composite personality of a team always overrides the individual personalities. On a macro level, organizational culture is the composite personality of the entire organizational population. You can find the method for calculating the composite personality of a team in *Unleashing Leadership,* by John Hoover and Angelo Valenti (Career Press, 2005).

Another way to describe this team dynamic is to consider all of the individual personalities on the team. That's easy enough. You can give everyone a personality assessment, such as the commonly used DISC (for Dominance, Influence, Steadiness, Conscientiousness), a behavioral model based on the work of the late William Moulton Marston. They then plot their personality preferences on a scattergram. By examining the scattergram you can draw conclusions about how the various personality styles will interact.

Interrelationships of Team Members. The dynamics of a team also include the relationships between individual team members beyond the personality assessment scattergrams we mentioned before. These relationships include histories of positive work experiences and not-so-positive work experiences. The underlying dynamics of the team include the ways in which the team understands its internal connections, how members experience one another in the past and in the present, and alliances that form between team members.

In some ways, the dynamics of a team mirror the dynamics in a family system, where unwritten and often unspoken rules apply to internal relationships and progress can be diminished or enhanced by team members' past and current experiences with one another. It is natural for humans to seek alliances and to create partnerships. New teams brought together with no histories can form interrelationships quickly. These miniteams, subgroups, or teams-within-the-team can be the pathway to overall team success or the undermining element that causes team dysfunction.

Group Knowledge and Experience. Team dynamics include all the competencies that the team possesses. If managed correctly, the aggregate knowledge and experience the team possesses can create a powerful resource for solving problems and facing challenging projects. However, the group knowledge and experience sometimes do not "add up" in a simple way. If the group members' combined experience and knowledge are concentrated within a small subgroup of individuals or in one individual, it can create tension within the team and a power dynamic that places decision making in the hands of a few. The way a team uses its competencies and balances the power dynamics against the competencies can determine the level of success that the team realizes. As a contextual coach, it is up to you to observe your clients in action leading teams and to assess where the gaps are between what your clients are capable of inspiring in the teams and what can be reasonably expected in team performance.

Level of Clarity in Roles and Responsibilities. A team's dynamics are often driven by the individual members through the roles they play, how well they understand their individual roles, and the degree of clarity in the roles of all the members of the team. Dysfunctional teams often fail to identify the roles of individual team members and fail to communicate those roles in a coherent way.

As a coach or a manager who coaches, you must conduct critical conversations with your clients about how important it is for a team's effectiveness that it make the fullest use of the skills individuals bring to the team process and create an equitable balance in the work expected of individual team members. The roles within a team can be interpreted in many different ways. They may relate to essential activities within an organizational environment. We can also talk about team member roles in more generalized ways and apply this information to work groups.

The work of Meredith Belbin on roles within teams (see Suggested Reading list for "Dynamics of a Team" under "The Coaching Connection" tab at www.WeMakeTalentWork.com) provides an excellent model for understanding how team roles are balanced. She divides nine roles into three sections: (1) people who take action, (2) people who create social bonds within the team, and (3) people who provide effective thinking. Teams can benefit from identifying these roles and discussing how to empower team members to maximize the benefit derived from their capabilities, energies, and styles.

People in organizations do not work in isolation. The work your clients engage in involves hand-offs to others, partnerships that require sharing of information and capabilities, and group work that calls for facilitated problem solving and planning. The people we coach work in multiple simultaneous team settings, and our coaching needs to reflect this reality. As a coach, you must help your clients avoid settling into a relationship with you that excludes a focus on their broader and more significant relationships. Work hard on your clients' individual stuff—but always in the context of the organization.

Why Team Dynamics Are Important to the Individual

With this in mind, we can see that development of the individual needs to be balanced with the intricacies and issues related to the dynamics of the teams in which they are involved. Many years ago, Aristotle was insightful in saying that the person is a social animal. The individual's behavior consistently interacts with the modes of behavior of other individuals. In group settings, this interaction is more layered and complex and can stimulate significant team synergy and group success. It can also lead to infighting, stress, lack of engagement, and distrust—ultimately derailing an opportunity for high team performance.

The development process for your clients should involve individuals with whom your clients work on a regular basis as fellow team members. Whether the teams your clients work with act as working groups, cross-functional task forces, or clans of direct reports, their team dynamics must be considered within the coaching engagement for the development process to have sustainable impact as your clients grow into leadership. By focusing on the teams that surround your clients, you ensure that the coaching engagement is an organizational development process instead of a "one-off" and isolated experience.

Focusing on team dynamics that surround the coaching client provides benefits for identifying the appropriate areas of development. You can gather helpful information about your clients by speaking with other team members about their perceptions of your clients. Even if you do not conduct a formal 360-degree assessment, you can still use the interview questions for each of the ten Contextual Coaching categories to help you keep your interactions with team members on track toward the ultimate growth and development of your coaching client.

The objective observations of others are extremely powerful and help you to identify blind spots that your clients possess when it comes to their interactions with others. The teams your clients lead, work as members of, and generally interact with, provide insight into your clients' developmental needs and can help both flesh out the developmental plan and drive it forward. Information gathered from a team or a group of teams can be the "aha" that your client needs when it comes to identifying thinking and behavior that needs to change.

Once an individual coaching client begins to adopt change, teams are often the focus once again—but for a different reason. Change within the individual can affect the relationships within this team and influence the way individuals work together. It is basic systems theory at work. If one element of the system changes, that change affects every other element of the system.

There is also the additional challenge to others on the team, who must decide to either embrace the change or fight it. Helping your coaching client to change and grow can create new opportunities or threats for everyone else on the team. Too often, team members hang on to the legacy they have created and decide to resist the change your coaching client brings to the team. This is especially true if the surrounding culture includes negativity and triangulation.

As a coach, you are often called upon to help your clients communicate their willingness to change and, more important, to make a case for why the change is helpful for everyone. People need to be sold on why the results of someone else's 360-degree assessment process have implications for them and how they can create opportunities for everyone surrounding your client. This calls for you, as a contextual coach, to have a keen sense of the big picture, your clients, and how they fit into the organizational landscape.

Why Team Dynamics Are Important to the Organization

As the coach, you will become involved in understanding the dynamics of the many teams that your clients interact with, especially the ones that they manage. Your advanced understanding of the dynamics of the various teams will help your clients to see how changes in their behavior affect others and change the team dynamics everywhere they are involved. You will help them see the big picture, appreciate that the teams are just subpopulations of the aggregate organizational population, and appreciate, most of all, how their growth and development as leaders help every team with which they interact and help the organization as a whole.

One way to map an organization is to sketch out the corporate collection of teams. As we have mentioned, teams are like suborganizations that, when considered together, make up the larger corporate reality. That makes the success and functionality of teams within an organization essential to the overall success of the organization. Your organization is investing in coaching for your clients so that they can be:

- More effective in directing teams
- Able to identify team roles to ensure the successful completion of assignments
- Able to set strategies and game plans for future-focused teamwork
- Able to persuade people to work together in positive and fruitful ways

By coaching your clients to become dynamic team leaders and key team members, you help to build effective team processes within your organization and help achieve new levels of work group success. Often, leaders become leaders because they have experienced individual success as a subject-matter expert. This does not mean they are necessarily good at generating l'esprit de corps (devotion to a cause) and identifying roles and responsibilities that ensure the positive completion of assignments.

The more you can help your clients comprehend and appreciate how effective teams provide a positive platform for positive business outcomes, the more they will be eager to drive business results, employee engagement, and a culture of bonding between team members and teams. By helping clients build teams and manage team dynamics, you are contributing to organizational results. Never assume that, because your clients have been around a while and served on many teams, they are truly knowledgeable and skilled at being effective team members and/or team leaders. Team dynamics may be one of the shadow areas of growth and development where you make a truly significant difference in the lives and working capacities of those you coach.

The Objectives and Goals for Team Dynamics

As with any of the coaching you do on any of the ten components of the Contextual Coaching model, your ultimate objective is to help your clients grow and develop into highly skilled and well-balanced leaders. Because people work in groups more than in isolation in most organizations, the understanding of what makes groups tick and the ability to lead work groups toward realizing their greatest potential are profound goals for you and your clients to work toward. As a coach, you may have more specific outcomes in your crosshairs, depending upon what your clients' unique challenges are.

You might have been brought in to coach because your clients are challenged in leading work teams, departments, or entire divisions. Regardless of the size of the work group, there will be scalable application of the team dynamics we have been discussing. Your ultimate goal is to help your clients acquire the knowledge, skill, and capacity to transform the work teams they are responsible for into highly effective, enthusiastic, and productive subpopulations.

Behaviors Related to Team Dynamics

For your clients to truly succeed in this area, they must master the skills necessary to assemble a team that will be naturally suited for the tasks ahead of them (see the CompposiTEAM description in John Hoover and Angelo Valenti's book, *Unleashing Leadership: Aligning What People Do Best With What Organizations Need*). Beyond assembling the right team, which Jim Collins, author of *Good to Great,* would describe as getting the right people on the bus, those team members, no matter how talented and motivated they are, need to be skillfully led.

Optimal Behavior for Team Dynamics

Your clients might be tremendously talented individual contributors. Yet, that is no predictor of whether or not they can migrate those highly effective work habits, skills, or productive work activities into a team scenario. Too often, policymakers and others higher on the organizational food chain than your clients assume that a person who can make highly effective contributions as an individual can apply a multiplier effect and spread the productivity. This is a classic mistake in executive judgment that, despite being disproved, preached about, and preached about some more, we continue to encounter time and time again.

The optimal behavior you are shooting for is to transform your clients from sole contributors to masterful facilitators of work teams. They will not be able to clone themselves, but they can set the stage and act as catalysts for teams of others to perform to their full potential. You cannot ask for more than that.

Underuse of Team Dynamics

If you and/or your clients fail to "get it" when it comes to team dynamics and how the most highly functioning teams work, the team's results may be disappointing at best and disastrous at worst. If your clients do not have the knowledge and the skill to lead a team effectively, their teams will be lackluster. There will be role confusion, lack of focus, lack of mission clarity, and frustration mixed with cynicism and lethargy.

Sound familiar? We could not help throwing in that little barb because anyone who tells you he or she has not worked on or at least been familiar with lackluster teams (1) is lying for some reason, (2) has not been in business very long, or (3) is in complete denial. Underuse of team dynamics results in an underperforming work group that simply cannot get out of its own way long enough to get anything done or that, through negligence, allows huge, expensive, and potentially catastrophic mistakes to be made that stand a good chance of costing the organization big time in goodwill, human capital, resources, and market share.

Overuse of Team Dynamics

In the early stages of the Civil War, President Abraham Lincoln was getting increasingly frustrated with George Brinton McClellan, Supreme Commander of the U.S. Army. Lincoln and others in Washington, D.C., had good reason to be concerned that Robert E. Lee and his Army of Northern Virginia might launch a concerted assault on the nation's capital. The Confederates were a bold and brash bunch with the capability and derring to pull it off if they had a mind to.

It seems McClellan, however, was busy drilling his Army of the Potomac in Maryland and not engaging the Confederates in a decisive battle to drive them away. Lincoln's frustrations and anxiety grew by the day. Finally, in a note that reflected his signature Illinois folk humor and wisdom, he sent a communiqué to McClellan that reflected brilliant understatement that would not be seen in the White House again until Ronald Reagan:

> "If you are not using the army, I should like to borrow it for a while."
>
> Yours respectfully, Abraham Lincoln

If your clients are too hung up on team dynamics, they may spend altogether too much time in team-building exercises. Not that team-building exercises are not a valuable tool at some level and in appropriate proportion for getting actual work done, but, if all the team does is sing *Kumbaya,* ponder whom they would throw out of a lifeboat or what they would need to pack for a trip to the moon, or shoot each other with paint balls, your organization is coming up the big loser.

As we have previously mentioned, you do not want your clients to lead groups of people who are busy doing things. Your clients will be considered successful only if they lead groups of people who are *getting things done.* This is precisely why they cannot afford to underuse or overuse team dynamics. If everybody is busy checking in with everybody else and deliberating process, how is anything going to get accomplished? (For examples of the underuse, overuse, and optimal use examples of the dynamics behaviors, as well as for suggested reading on dynamics, visit www.WeMakeTalentWork.com and click on "The Coaching Connection.")

How Your Coaching Client Fits into Team Dynamics

Your clients have some relationships to teams. They are leading teams or serving on teams, usually both. As such, they have many opportunities to use team dynamics to their career growth advantage. They can become better and more effective team members, thus building equity for themselves for future leadership assignments. In addition to adding value to the team, if they are already in team leader positions, they can show demonstrable improvement in their team leadership capabilities, thereby inviting promotion to higher-level assignments.

As a coach or a manager who coaches, you have the opportunity to help your clients become higher-contributing team members, earning the trust and respect of colleagues on the team and impressing leaders who are invested in the team's performance. Somebody out there put the team together to accomplish something that is important to someone. Everything the team does, including—but not limited to—achieving stated goals, creating new and better ways of conducting business or the affairs of the organization, and innovating to improve processes, practices, and protocols that will move the organization upward and onward, will be closely monitored.

How to Introduce Team Dynamics to Your Coaching Client

Taking much of what we have just described and breaking it down for your clients will help them see themselves in the sometimes dim and murky picture of team dynamics. More than dim and murky, team dynamics are often too subtle and, at the same time, too complex for the average employee to see opportunities in them. Yet mastering team dynamics is a major credential for moving up in any organization.

Your conversation with your coaching clients should include what they will get from being more than just loyal contributors to the work of the team. We are not suggesting that your clients immediately buck for team leader if they are not presently in that position. That could create a lot of resentment, pushback, and disconnect from other team members—none of which would put your clients' team leadership credentials in a glowing light.

Your job as a contextual coach, however, involves helping your clients connect the dots between how their enhanced knowledge of team dynamics and their demonstrated ability to function on and/or lead a team is a harbinger of opportunities in the organization. This is a must conversation. Between you and your clients, under the cone of confidentiality, you can point out that the ability to contribute to successful team and organizational outcomes, either as a member of the team or a leader of it, will open up opportunities at other organizations. Demonstrated expertise in team dynamics is simply a tremendous career advancement credential.

Team Dynamics Behaviors

As you have been tracking the Contextual Coaching process, you have been identifying behaviors associated with the individual and organizational results and outcomes you want to produce through improvements in your clients' habits, skills, and behaviors. Team dynamics are the eighth of ten areas of behavioral focus. As a contextual coach, you pay attention to the ways team dynamics affect the success of both your clients as individuals and the organization as a whole. As a coach, you can make practical and effective interventions to substantially improve your clients' capabilities as team members and team leaders, as well as their capacity to take on an additional workload.

In examining, tracking, and modifying your clients' habits, skills, and activities, you are looking to identify ways in which they can benefit from the forward-looking and strategic dimensions of team dynamics as a powerful personal awareness and goal-setting exercise. You might also inquire as to how your client is using dynamics in team building, depending on the number of his or her direct reports. The following behaviors are part of the Contextual Coaching 360-degree assessment that measures your clients' proficiency in using team dynamics as a tool for developing their own careers and/or the careers of their direct reports:

- Delegates appropriately.
- Celebrates team success.
- Manages team meetings effectively.
- Resolves conflicts between colleagues.
- Values the ideas and opinions of others.
- Encourages collaboration with problem-solving initiatives.

If you were to place these behaviors before a group of feedback providers and ask them to rank your client, what would they say? Would they say that the behaviors listed are overused, underused, or used optimally by your client? If you use the Contextual Coaching 360-degree assessment, you will get those answers. Even though using the Contextual Coaching 360-degree assessment is a formal way to assess the overuse, underuse, or optimal use of each behavior in a survey format, you can also use these questions to conduct your own team dynamics interviews with feedback providers, sitting down with them face to face and discussing each behavior.

360-Degree Feedback Questions for Team Dynamics

All employees can benefit from an evaluation of their understanding of the importance of team dynamics for themselves and for the organization.

Questions for the Coaching Client

As a means of further assessment, here are questions specific to team dynamics to ask your clients:

- Can you provide examples of how you engage the team that reports to you?
- Can you describe the best and worst team meeting that you have attended in the last year?

If your client is an individual contributor, alter the first question to relate to his or her own experience as an active member of some team. Each employee has a major stake in understanding his or her own role in team dynamics, since everyone is involved in teamwork at one time or another. All team members engage the team in their own unique ways, and organizations must work to ensure that everyone's efforts are aligned with the organization's strategic needs. If your coaching client has direct reports, you want to know how his or her management style supports the strategic imperatives of the organization through the way he or she manages teams.

The second question also works for both individual contributors and those with teams to manage. Individual contributors will choose examples to illustrate the depth of their own understanding of team dynamics, in addition to examples of how they align personal and team efforts with organizational strategic objectives. You might want to set up ways that your clients might be able to demonstrate their understanding and savvy around team dynamics. This is also a training opportunity for those hoping to take on management responsibilities in the future. For those clients with direct reports, this is a good opportunity to discuss what an important opportunity this can be to achieve strategic alignment among team members reporting to your client.

Even if your clients do not manage teams, this is a good exercise to illustrate that being a strategic team member will have a positive influence on peers with whom your client shares team membership. It can be good practice in exercising influence without authority. The earlier anyone in the organization starts talking about team dynamics, the better. Because teams are such a part of organizational life, team dynamics are a critical skill set for everyone.

Questions for the Feedback Providers

If you are using the Contextual Coaching 360-degree assessment, these will be the questions that your feedback providers will need to answer as they regard your coaching client:

- How would you describe the engagement of the team that reports to the client? Can you provide examples?
- Can you describe the best and worst team meeting that the client has facilitated in the last year?

You are looking for rich answers that will give you and your clients material to work with in designing their coaching action plans. The answers you receive to these questions will spell out whether your clients have gaps in the area of team dynamics and, if so, the type of remedy that is called for. It should be obvious that just exploring these topics with your clients and gathering data about them will heighten your clients' awareness of the many hats a manager must wear—including becoming a dynamic leader of teams—whether your client is a manager at present or aspires to become one. If your client is on track to become a manager, this is a good opportunity for your client to learn about team dynamics in the context of the organization.

How to Use the Responses to the 360-Degree Assessment Questions for Team Dynamics

When feedback providers have the chance to rate clients on their performance as team members or team leaders, you are bound to gather some comprehensive, if not spirited, feedback. People are very tuned into how teams they are involved in are working and have strong opinions of how teams should function. At least they have strong opinions about how they *think* teams should function.

The feedback your clients will receive on their 360-degree assessments will provide vital information about whether they are perceived as effective at participating in or leading teams. Since the ability to lead teams or to be seen as a team player is critical to career success, this information will be invaluable. Regardless of how well your clients think they are doing when participating in or leading teams, it is the opinion of the team members (the feedback providers) that will have a major impact on organizational decision makers. The judgments about your clients' team savvy that leak out in incidental conversations or are spoken directly to organizational decision makers will significantly influence your clients' career potential.

Identify the Gaps

Where are your clients running afoul of their fellow team members' or team leaders' expectations? This is the most salient information. We mention what your clients think of their performance because so often they cling to that perception, even when it is directly contradicted by the 360-degree feedback. In some of the worst cases, the worse the feedback, the more desperately your clients may cling to their positive impressions of themselves.

As a coach or a manager who coaches, you must penetrate that denial and help your clients not take negative (even mildly critical) feedback personally. The gaps that the feedback exposes are gaps between how your clients present themselves in team situations and other people's expectations. Filling these gaps is about managing expectations, aligning your clients' performance with expectations, convincing your clients of all the benefits of meeting expectations, and building an action plan to get those behaviors started.

Habits

What things does your client habitually do that cause disconnects with other team members? What is in your client's essential nature that impedes collaboration? People are rarely aware, fully aware anyway, of things they do habitually. That is why they so often push back at critical feedback and cannot understand who would say such things and why. As their coach, you can help your clients connect the dots between their unconscious behaviors and the impressions they are making on their fellow team members—and these are not always bad.

Do your clients possess natural tendencies that actually enhance teamwork and a collaborative environment? These are strengths that you can build on to expand and enhance their effectiveness as team players and team leaders. As a coach or a manager who coaches, you are sometimes the only real link between what other people perceive about your clients and your clients' self-perceptions. You might represent one of the only work relationships that can connect the perceptions of feedback providers and your clients' realities, especially as they relate to habitual behavior.

Skills

If the feedback you receive on your clients indicates that the issues they have around team participation and leadership are simply developmental, you can effectively address them through training, organizational education, and practice. Team dynamics can be complex to understand, much less deal with. You can help your clients learn more about how teams function and what can be reasonably expected from them.

By blending your coaching and encouragement with classroom or online learning that your clients participate in, you can help your clients make rapid improvements in the value they add to teams, both through participation as members and through their leadership. Skill development is relatively easy to discuss and promote with your clients because it does not imply that there is a gap in their performance. It implies that they can start from where they are and improve not only their skill level around team dynamics but also their reputation for being team savvy. Your clients want this latter information to be part of the conversations people of influence have about them when they are not present.

Activities

Besides the training and organizational education we described, practice is where your clients will achieve traction with their expanding knowledge of and abilities regarding team dynamics. Paying heightened attention to how team members interact with one another, how the team interacts with the environment in which it operates, and how the team takes on a composite personality of its own will position your clients for maximum participation and collaboration in a team environment.

Actual application of communication techniques, conflict deescalation techniques, methods of finding consensus and convergence among team members, and many other interventions will make your clients increasingly effective in achieving desired team outcomes. Your clients can and will learn about such methods and techniques in their reading, self-studies, and formal classroom and online learning activities. But you will coach the practice. You will help your clients set out a plan to try certain things and then quickly debrief and refine what they do until you see demonstrable progress.

Then, budget allowing, you will continue to guide your clients toward greater success using team dynamics as long as you are engaged. If all is done well, your clients should become true subject-matter experts in team dynamics. Well-planned activities can result in significantly enhanced subject-matter expertise in all ten components of the Contextual Coaching model.

How to Discuss the Team Dynamics Gaps with Your Coaching Client

Do not get caught in your clients' defensiveness. We are not implying that all of your clients will defend themselves unreasonably against critical feedback. However, some will. Be prepared. It is perfectly natural for human beings to be at the very least nervous about receiving feedback. We have worked with clients who felt that the feedback providers were simply "out of touch" and needed to be grounded in reality, which, of course, was precisely what our defensive clients needed to do. Know that, if some of your clients claim that they are simply "misunderstood," it is okay to agree with them . . . to a point.

Help your reluctant clients find convergence with your more willing and open clients. That is, discuss the whole notion of perceptions with them, and help them understand that, in the end, their reputation for excellence in the organization will be a matter of perception more than the actual work they do. Help them use the gap analysis from their 360-degree assessments to draw up a blueprint for how they can alter the perceptions. These blueprints, coincidentally, will be a prescription for more effective behavior. Never take the position that, since everybody seems to think your clients have problems, they are a problem. Gaps can be corrected with perception-altering behaviors.

Connecting Dynamics of a Team to the Coaching Process

The process we just described is not easy. However, as a coach or a manager who coaches, it is your responsibility to get into your clients' heads and hearts and to help them to see the forest for the trees. Help them elevate their perspective and to understand and appreciate how much people's opinions of them matter in the systems scheme of organizations. What people think matters more than many of your clients care to know.

As a coach, this is one of the most career-altering epiphanies you can induce in your clients. The really good news is that the 360-degree assessment is a gold mine of opinions and information. You and your clients can examine their feedback and see just what their greatest challenges are and how they can map out a plan to adopt behaviors that will resonate with people's highest expectations for team members and leaders.

Team Dynamics Summary

Whether a team, which is a dynamic system unto itself, is formed naturally or artificially, it quickly adopts the shared values and beliefs of its members. It also forms a composite personality that is distinct from the aggregate personalities of its members. As a coach or a manager who coaches, your clients need your help and guidance to seriously up their skill sets around team performance. As team members or leaders, your clients have a golden opportunity to add value to the organization and contribute in a collaborative setting. Among the many things that mark people for leadership potential is how well they perform in team settings and, as team leaders, inspire and facilitate others in accomplishing great things.

Leadership at the team level is a highly visible proving ground for leadership at the departmental level, then the divisional levels, and so forth. Too many people consider working on teams to be drudgery and not meaningful. As a coach, you hope your clients will think that way less and less. You will help them recognize opportunities and to exploit them for career success. The contributions your clients make to teams on which they participate or that they lead will be appropriately visible (without being unreasonable) to ensure that your clients derive maximum benefit and recognition from their accomplishments. No good thing your clients do should be done in a vacuum in which they fail to build equity on their performance.

In Chapter 11, you will learn far more concentrated information about how to coach your clients' career aspirations. The opportunity recognition we just mentioned is a part of that. Your clients' careers, which is to say their professional futures, are the culmination of the balance and enhanced knowledge and abilities you help your clients acquire through the Contextual Coaching model and process.

CHAPTER 11

Area of Behavioral Focus: Career

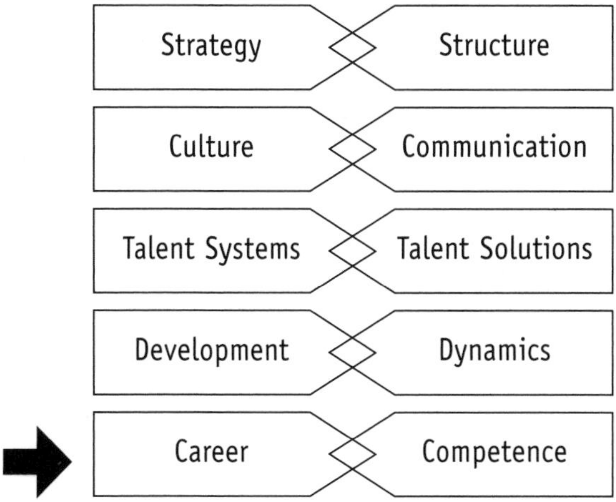

"Coaching is the key to unlocking the inspirational leader inside all of our top executives."

—Gloria Feliciano
Chief Human Resources Officer
GfK Custom Research North America

Career is the ninth component of the Contextual Coaching model and is defined as an occupation or profession, especially one that requires training and education. Moreover, a career can be considered lifework. When considering careers, we think of progress throughout adulthood toward success in a profession or occupation. Very little about the way people manage careers today is the same as it was twenty years ago. In the past, we rarely spoke of career development as an important element in the relationship between an employer and an employee. The employer's role was to train and develop an employee to perform tasks well in order to meet performance expectations. Sometimes this included performance expectations related to a new or accelerated role for the employee. In this world, the employee's role was to take ownership of his or her own career plan. The participation in training that could enhance employees' career potential was managed by your clients. At best, the company might provide career guidance as an optional experience.

In the past, if individuals demonstrated too much commitment to their own career growth, that behavior elicited some degree of suspicion. They were suspected of not paying enough attention to their present job. In the past, career planning was seen as the sole responsibility of the employee, not to be openly discussed. It was a secretive process and, potentially, a sign of disloyalty. An organization could hardly be expected to commit its own resources to this self-serving enterprise. Career development was not considered systematic, it was not strategic, and it was not a partnership between employers and employees.

Times have changed. Enter succession planning. Today, career planning has become a joint responsibility of the company in managing its human capital assets and employees seeking to maximize their options. The company wants to be an employer of choice to attract the best people. Your clients want to be employees of choice who attract the best opportunities. The companies with retention strategies merge these motivations and deepen their reputation as employers of choice by serving up opportunities for employees of choice.

The talent shortage, particularly in key jobs, and its increasing complexities have led many companies to take a new, proactive, and strategic approach to working with employees on their career development. They have merged career planning with talent management and employee development. Clearly, this is a retention strategy. They want to continue to engage their employees in every way so that the organizational population will stay energized about working in the organization and promoting a positive culture.

This partnership means that companies are not simply providing career services at the point of exit for an employee (traditionally known as outplacement). Instead, they are providing processes for internal mobility and career planning through which individuals can identify open roles inside the company, create career plans that follow organizational templates, and identify company mentors to assist them in charting a course for the future. Similarly, as with talent solutions, you as the coach need to help map out your clients' career development opportunities as presented by the company through the coaching process.

The Contextual Coaching process benefits from aligning the career goals of individuals with the organizational definitions of leadership and the organization's overall talent plan and strategy. It is important to work with your coaching clients on how to envision possible career opportunities and how the coaching process can help them move forward with their plans. You might focus on how to build a deeper network of relationships or on how to close some experience gaps in your clients' resumes. Whether it focuses on one or both of these, the work is done in the context of the organization. As a coach or a manager who coaches, your job is to help your clients see and execute on their potential for progress in their current environment.

Why Career Is Important to the Individual

As we stated previously, we too often hear that "everyone hates change." We cannot count how many coaches and consultants have uttered these words, which seem obvious at first blush. But, as we have previously argued, they could not be more wrong. While these words might make us feel better as we are struggling through a reorganization in our company, we need to remember that people like to experience forward progress—especially if they believe they are going to be better off for it.

Everyone wants to know that he or she is getting somewhere. Running on treadmills is good for raising our heart rates, but when we want to move forward, we look for traction to cover ground and change the scenery and circumstances. Hope for a better future is an important motivator for individuals at work. Even if we love what we do right now, we tend to wonder what better scenarios might be waiting around the next corner, scenarios that will stretch us and challenge us to grow personally and professionally, providing new, deeper, exciting, and more fulfilling challenges.

Every individual is different and unique. Some may prefer stability and static experiences and therefore do not seek out new roles or new opportunities. Just as many people, if not more, thrive on the idea of going someplace new and experiencing greater and more stimulating rewards and recognition. Never forget the rewards and recognition at the core of why so many people are excited by change.

As a coach, you are always aware of the career development dimension of your clients' experiences. As usual, your work with your clients begins on the awareness level. Your HR department probably has highly skilled and specialized career development counselors. It is probably best that your client work directly with one of these on succession planning issues. But, you are still responsible for guiding your clients' overall development. Career development begins with learning some of the basics in a comprehensive career plan. You need to track the work being done by your clients' and their career counselors. A career plan typically includes:

Creating as Much Success as Possible in Your Clients' Current Roles. All career paths begin with a foundation on which to build. Your clients need to experience high levels of success in their current positions before they attempt to move to other positions with more responsibility. People are rarely promoted on the basis of potential alone. Oversubscription to their own talent and genius can leave your clients frustrated, disappointed, and, possibly, resentful.

This excessive expectation of rapid promotion is a fundamental but all-too-frequent mistake, especially with younger and newer employees in an organization. Belief that someone's future potential is always balanced with the current performance can be a damaging miscalculation for both your clients and the organization. The absolute best guarantee that your client is ready to move on is a proven record of accomplishment over time. Among other things, greater responsibility in the organization usually means managing others, being responsible for appropriating greater quantities of allocated resources, and increased decision-making authority—none of which are insignificant activities.

Strategizing About the Future. A career plan is like a business plan; it needs to flow from a strategy. We need to be willing to imagine the future we would like to have. There is a technique we use in Action Learning that can help. When working on a problem, we instruct the team in the Action Learning program to write down goal statements that, if fully realized, will solve the Action Learning program problem. This leads them to articulate a business plan that will lead them to achieve the objectives. When it comes to career, your clients need to think about goal statements that will lead them to a satisfying and fulfilling career. From there, we can build out a plan that can lead to advancement.

Focusing in on Personal and Professional Interests. The process of self-exploration is important for working on a career plan or any other talent development initiative. True self-exploration—and learning from it— involves having insight into the areas where your clients are strong as well as areas where they struggle. In career planning, we often use personality-based instruments that are created for career-planning purposes to help focus individuals on the specific job families that are most aligned to their personality and interests. This information can help bring about an "aha" moment and a vision that can inspire your clients to eagerly begin mapping their futures.

Drawing out an Executable Plan for Moving Careers Forward. Having a strategic plan is different from having a goal or a vision. A goal or vision can focus your clients' energies on achieving success. A strategic plan breaks down the steps required to make the goal or vision a reality. With an individual career plan, your clients will outline specific tasks that need to be accomplished and milestones that need to be reached in order to prepare themselves for future opportunities and to respond to future challenges.

Learning How to Market a Personal Brand. We usually associate the term "brand" with commercial products and services. Embedded within the brand is a value proposition, which consumers either buy into or not. The notion of value proposition is often discussed with marketing professionals who hope to build an enduring brand and to create a staff of sales professionals who have the ability to quickly sum up the services they provide. This is the proverbial elevator speech.

When we speak of branding an individual, we are not attempting to look at individuals as consumer products. But we are concerned about building a value proposition that best exemplifies what that person brings to the table. The ability to sum up who an individual is, in a way that resonates with the listener, is a valuable skill for marketing and promoting oneself.

As a coach or a manager who coaches, you will find that convincing your clients to market themselves is often difficult. People often feel that their work should speak for itself and that there is no need to promote the worker. In truth, good work does not speak on behalf of the worker nearly as much as we would hope it would in the best of all possible worlds. Good work cries out to be noticed so that appropriate recognition can be made.

As a coach, you need to help your clients accept and act on the need to get the word out about what they are doing to help their organizations succeed. Your clients do not want to blow their own horns and draw attention to themselves; that would annoy or make their bosses unhappy. But sharing what is happening at a team, departmental, or divisional level is good business. The people above your clients on the organizational food chains need and want to know what is happening. Help your clients avoid becoming braggers about their accomplishments. Help them learn to effectively communicate their accomplishments and the accomplishments of those around them to people who need and want to know.

Building Networks of Relationships. Most people know that job openings are not typically filled by choosing among people who answer newspaper or online advertisements. The vast majority of people chosen to fill existing or newly created roles, especially higher-level roles, achieve that distinction because they have somehow networked themselves into the opportunity. They have joined trade groups, had informational interviews, attended seminars where they have the opportunity to meet others, made use of social networking Web sites, forged relationships with recruiters, or gotten to know their customers extremely well.

We hate to sound utilitarian in our philosophy, but every relationship can lead to something that advances a career. Career planning involves looking at networks and remaining focused on building and strengthening existing relationships and creating new ones. People tend to promote and hire others who make the recruiter or hiring party comfortable. That is a natural byproduct of becoming increasingly familiar with people. Over time, with familiarity comes comfort and trust. With comfort and trust come promotions and other opportunities.

Closing any Gaps in Current Skill Sets, Experience, or Technical Knowledge. Part of your clients' career planning process is being honest with themselves about ways they are simply not prepared for the expanded roles they desire. Closing these gaps can be an effective way to position themselves for advancement. As we have discussed all along, your clients might need to address poor habits and possibly relearn certain habits, engage in training to learn new skills, and expand their proficiency with existing skills. In Chapter 12, we focus more closely on this topic.

You can provide great benefit to your coaching clients by guiding them through the career planning process. As we mentioned earlier, some coaches have specific expertise in the area of career planning and in outplacement counseling. Coaches must be able to competently engage in career conversations with their clients and help map their clients' interests in the context of the organizations' career development opportunities.

Why Career Is Important to the Organization

On the surface, the idea of developing the careers of employees can seem risky. If we invest in our employees for future roles by providing training, education grants, coaching, and job mobility, don't we risk seeing them leave and take those enhanced skills and abilities to our competitors? Absolutely. There is always a risk to investing in your clients who work in what the author and lecturer Daniel Pink calls the Free Agent Nation, where recruiters check in regularly to discuss opportunities in what they portray as greener pastures. Nonetheless, there are several immediate benefits to focusing on career development as a talent strategy within the organization.

First, as we already said in Chapters 7 and 8, investing in the growth and development of your clients will boost retention. One of the reasons new talent chooses to join one organization rather than another is the investment made in growth, development, and internal career opportunities. A talent strategy that focuses solely on acquiring new talent is doomed to fail. New employees will soon find out that there is limited opportunity and that therefore the upside of employment in such an environment is too limited for their tastes.

Retaining current employees presents a similar issue. Organizations have learned over time that there are many reasons why people might want to leave the company, and a huge reason can be that they feel there is no future for them anymore. They were optimistic in the early days, but no more. They feel they have hit the ceiling within the organization and have no sense of where they can go from where they are.

Retention strategies include the process of creating career paths for individuals so that they look inside your organization for opportunities. This is not the case for high potentials or individuals who have a clear future in leadership and are being aggressively groomed for such. Organizations seem to know that they will need future leadership and do not hesitate to invest in future leaders. Retention strategies, on the other hand, involve the larger pool of employees within the organization—the rich talent pool that absorbs and acquires more and more institutional memory and job knowledge each passing day. The organization needs them badly and can ill afford to keep replacing them.

In response to this challenge, organizations need to create an internal labor market that provides opportunity for individuals to experience career mobility. This market should be accessible to all and explicit in determining expectations when it comes to experience, competency, and technical knowledge. Managers should be able to involve themselves in the process in a supportive and instructive manner. To get them to do so requires training and winning over managers, convincing them that it is in their interest to have career conversations with their people. The fear of losing someone to another department is shortsighted and small-minded and misses the point of talent development responsibilities.

If they experience opportunities for growth and career planning, individuals feel more self-realized and in control of their future. In addition to employee retention, the first main benefit that career expertise provides for the company, the second main benefit to the company is employee engagement. People within the organization will develop greater organizational *loyalty* if they see the commitment to their career progression.

This loyalty is realized in employee enthusiasm that translates into effective performance in current jobs. The key to a career progression is having success in the jobs your clients are in now. Individuals who commit to the career development process will learn that they need to focus on getting the current job right so that the right job can be found in the future. We should not underestimate the importance of employee engagement to an organization's success and cultural framework.

The third benefit to the organization from career development systems, right after recruitment/retention and loyalty, is the *employment brand*. This may be the most elusive of benefits of career development systems, but it may prove to be the most valuable. The talent management challenge is about acquiring, managing, and developing talent in a competitive environment. Organizations that prove to be good employers, that focus on people development, and that commit to employee satisfaction can develop an employment brand that becomes known in the marketplace as a great place to work—an employer of choice. This makes it a magnet that will attract new talent into the organization. And the pride that employees feel in belonging to a great employment brand further engages them in their work and the future. Individual concerns and pushbacks never go away, but, in the face of a superior brand, they diminish in importance and urgency.

Companies are not spending money on career development to simply create a feel-good environment. This is a business decision. When people are the most important resource within an organization, developing them for future roles is a wise investment. Failing to do so can cost an organization dearly in many ways and on many levels.

The Objectives and Goals for Career

You can piece together what we have been emphasizing throughout this chapter and get a strong sense for why career development is important to individuals and to organizations. Track along with those reasons and you can extract the objectives. As a coach or a manager who coaches, you have a great opportunity to bring the Contextual Coaching model to life.

You are positioned to help your clients adopt a healthy attitude toward career development. Help them accept that thoughtful, systematic career planning not only is good for them and their future but helps guarantee the organization a progression of strong, talented, highly skilled, and competent employees, as well as a renewable cadre of visionary and strategically savvy leaders. Career development is an area where the benefits to your clients and to the organization could not be more evident. These can translate directly into goals:

- Maximize opportunity for individuals to excel in their careers.
- Maximize opportunity for individuals to prove themselves employees of choice.
- Maximize opportunity for branding the organization as an employer of choice.
- Maximize attraction for new talent.
- Maximize retention of existing talent.

If all of these objectives are met and met well, your organization will have a powerful platform from which to establish continuous improvement in all aspects of human-capital development. Each accomplishment in the area of career development can serve as a benchmark for future career enhancements. Each accomplishment in the area of career development should be exploited for its maximum value for your clients and your organization. As with anything else, the value of even the greatest accomplishments is diminished if the lessons learned are allowed to evaporate or are stuck on a shelf somewhere and forgotten.

Behavior Related to Career

Without actively engaging your clients in career development or at least heightening their awareness of and appreciation for it, the bottom line is likely to be bad news. We are not predicting uprising, revolt, or anarchy. Nevertheless, you are likely to hear comments like, "I don't want to do this forever." Or, "Only the lead sled dog gets a change of scenery." Organizations with a bottom-heavy imbalance in career development wind up with bottom-heavy organizations.

Optimal Behavior for Career

The thing that so many of your clients will find difficult is to take time from the immediate and urgent demands of their jobs to ponder and plan a career path. Yet, that is important for them to do. That is optimal. If your clients have direct reports, your clients need to encourage those people to look at their career paths and to plot a strategy.

In the best of all possible scenarios, your clients will take on a new attitude about career planning, becoming proficient at it and preaching it to others. The propaganda machine should be out in full force when it comes to career development—bulletin boards, newsletters, the Intranet, you name it. Everybody should be thinking about career planning and its flip side, succession planning: "It's good for you and good for the organization."

Underuse of Career

To put it mildly, underuse of career development leaves people without much hope for the future. If they think they will fare well, it is because they are optimistic and appropriately confident or overconfident and headed for a rude awakening. In most cases, when career development is not emphasized, people are left wondering what will happen to them.

As we have mentioned before, people abhor a gap in the story. So when they are left with a gaping hole in their career development story, they naturally fill it in with their interpretation of what is likely to happen to them—almost always bad. They feel that, without feedback, they are being given the silent treatment, which is a sure sign they are about to be fired. If they do not feel an immediate threat of imminent termination, they may simply feel ignored and left to languish, dying a slow death without management nurturing.

Overuse of Career

Too much focus on career development will pull focus away from the job at hand. You might get a lot of people really pumped up about career opportunities, thus improving recruitment. But retention will suffer. Newcomers who have inflated expectations about their soon-to-be meteoric rise to fame and fortune (whatever that looks like in your organization) sooner or later notice that there are older members of the organizational population standing around with blank expressions on their faces.

A little inquiry will reveal that there is no such thing as meteoric ascension in your organization and that the whole thing was oversold. Worse yet is the scenario where people are promoted an average of every quarter and there is nobody left to do the transactional work. Organizations that have a top-heavy imbalance in career development wind up with top-heavy organizations. Top-heavy organizations topple.

How Your Coaching Client Fits into Career

Career development discussions are a great opportunity for you, as a contextual coach, to help your clients understand where they stand in terms of the organization's overall talent strategy. When someone talks to your clients about career issues in the context of your organization, those huge gaps do not appear and people do not need to fill them with worst-case scenarios. As a coach, you can be a great source of relief to your clients.

Your clients also need to know that they must take a proactive approach with their career development and take advantage of developmental activities. Your clients need to seek out the types of career preparation that will best suit them and prepare them to move up to the next level. Training, education, internships, and special-team involvement are only some of the resources your organization offers. Help your clients find out and actively take advantage of all of the developmental opportunities available, whether inside or outside the organization. Encourage them to hurry back and use their newly developed skills, knowledge, and capabilities. (For examples of the underuse, overuse, and optimal use of career behaviors, as well as for suggested reading on career, visit www.WeMakeTalentWork.com and click on "The Coaching Connection.")

How to Introduce Career to Your Coaching Client

The one thing you have going for you as a coach is that career development is all about your clients. People tend to like things that are all about them. As we have been emphasizing, technically speaking, career development is about your clients and the organization. But for all intents and purposes, it will feel pretty much like it is all about them.

This is good because you can get clients' attention quickly. Good workers are not going to drop everything and become career development junkies, but they can appreciate your eloquent way of pointing out to them personally the importance of career development. For example, they can refer back to how it felt for them to be passed over. Nobody likes that feeling. But few people step up and say, "I know it was my fault for not getting more aggressively involved in career development."

To those die-hard organizational loyalists, emphasize the organization's needs and how they might need to take a bullet for the organization and accept a promotion. When that time comes, they need to be ready, lest they let the organization down. As a coach, you must develop the ability to study your clients and identify what and where their triggers are—then pull them. For the self-oriented, the whole concept of career development is about them. To the company man or company woman, it's about going out and winning one for the organization. Most likely, you'll engage your clients somewhere closer to the middle of that spectrum.

Career Behaviors

As you have been tracking the Contextual Coaching process, you have been identifying behaviors associated with your clients and organizational results you want to produce. Career development, the ninth of ten areas of behavioral focus, is about the ways your organization establishes and executes career development as a strategic practice to fortify the enterprise, while at the same time providing practical and effective career opportunity development to your clients receiving your coaching.

In examining, tracking, and modifying your clients' habits, skills, and activities, you are looking to identify ways in which they can benefit from the forward-looking piece of career development as a powerful personal-awareness and goal-setting exercise. You might also inquire as to how your clients are using career as a team-building tool among their direct reports and peers. The following behaviors are part of the Contextual Coaching 360-degree assessment that measures your clients' proficiency in using career as a tool for developing their own careers and/or the careers of their direct reports:

- Demonstrates life balance.
- Offers career advice to others.
- Takes on stretch assignments.
- Proactively communicates career goals.
- Volunteers in situations that promote individual growth.

If you were to place these behaviors before a group of feedback providers and ask them to rank your clients, what would they say? Would they say that the behaviors were overused, underused, or used optimally used by your clients? If you use the Contextual Coaching 360-degree assessment, you will get those answers. Even though using the Contextual Coaching 360-degree assessment is a formal way to assess the overuse, underuse, or optimal use of each behavior in a survey format, you can also use these questions to conduct your own structured interviews with feedback providers, sitting down with them face to face and discussing each behavior.

360-Degree Feedback Questions for Career

A careful assessment of your coaching clients' understanding of the importance of seeking career development opportunities in an appropriate way can be essential to achieving their goals, as well as those of the organization.

Questions for the Coaching Client

As a means of further assessment, here are questions specific to career to ask your coaching clients:

- What are your ultimate career goals?
- What is your plan to attain your career goals?
- What is your commitment to the career aspirations of others.

If your client is an individual contributor or a team, department, or divisional leader, the first question relates to his or her own understanding of career issues. All employees, regardless of rank, have a major stake in understanding their own role in the career dynamics of the organization and must work to ensure that their individual efforts are aligned with the organization's strategic plan around career development. If your coaching client has direct reports, you want to know how his or her management style supports the strategic imperatives of the organization around career development.

The second question also works for both individual contributors and those with teams to manage. Individual contributors and team leaders alike will choose examples to illustrate the depth of their own understanding of strategic issues in addition to examples of how they align personal and team efforts with the organization's strategic objectives. For individual contributors, the third question relates perhaps to peers and might expose where a person is lacking influence. You might want to set up ways this client can demonstrate his or her understanding and savvy around career issues in mentoring or coaching others. This is also a training opportunity for future management responsibilities. For those clients with direct reports, this is a good opportunity to discuss what an important opportunity this can be to achieve strategic alignment between those reporting to your client and the organization's career development needs.

Even if your clients do not manage teams, this is a good exercise to illustrate that being a strategic leader, especially around development of human-capital resources, will have a positive influence on peers. It can be good practice in exercising influence without authority. The earlier anyone in the organization starts talking career development, the better. Knowing who is tuned into organizational career development issues and who is not will ensure that your clients' coaching engagements are aligned with your organization's career initiatives.

Questions for the Feedback Provider

If you are using the Contextual Coaching 360-degree assessment, these will be the questions that your feedback providers will need to answer as they regard your coaching client. You can also use them as the substance and structure of a face-to-face or telephone interview:

- What are the client's ultimate career goals?
- What is the client's plan to attain them?
- How would you describe the client's commitment to the career aspirations of others?

You are looking for rich answers that will give you and your coaching clients material to work with in designing their coaching action plans. The answers you receive to these questions will spell out whether your clients have gaps in the area of career and, if so, the type of remedy that is called for. It should be obvious that just exploring these topics with your clients and gathering data about them will heighten your clients' awareness of the many hats a manager must wear—whether your client is a manager at present or aspires to become one. If your coaching clients are on track to become managers, this is a good opportunity for your client to learn about career development in the context of the organization.

How to Use the Responses to the 360-Degree Assessment Questions for Career

In the 1990s, then–First Lady Hillary Clinton invoked the ancient African colloquialism, "It takes a village to raise a child." In the same manner, it takes an organization to prepare its future leaders. As people at various levels and from different constituencies within the organization provide feedback on your clients' career potential and planning, they are participating in the process.

Their participation should not stop there. Your client should continue to reach out wherever possible to solicit ongoing feedback and career guidance from those who have gone before and those who are well informed about the organization's current and future developmental needs. The feedback from your clients' 360-degree assessments is helpful in plotting their current career coordinates.

More than that, it is an invitation to make your clients' career plans known to a broader population that can help with advice and networking opportunities. You never know where or when the next opportunity will emerge. Without feedback on career paths, people who create and/or facilitate new opportunities might not be aware of your clients' medium- or long-term career development plans and therefore will not be able to assist your clients or take advantage of the value they can add to the organization.

Identify the Gaps

The realistic picture that 360-degree feedback provides should be used to calibrate your clients' current situations. As a coach or a manager who coaches, you must help your clients appreciate this feedback for what it is: a barometer of other people's perceptions. As such, when a gap appears between where your clients think they are positioned in terms of their careers and where others see them, the ruling goes in favor of the feedback providers.

Your clients can argue all day long that they are much better positioned, held in much higher regard, and more broadly recognized than their 360-degree feedback would indicate—but they would be wrong. As a contextual coach, help your clients see the gaps as opportunities to better position themselves as people of potential in the context of the organization. If the organization is calling for people who are skilled at innovation, help your clients bone up on innovation techniques. If the organization needs to improve employee retention, encourage your clients to learn the finer points of what makes employees want to stay and contribute. In other words, go to the gap, whatever it is, and fill it.

Habits

It is doubtful that any of your clients are in the habit of attending to their career status on a regular basis. Career development is not something that everybody jumps out of bed every morning and cannot wait to get started on. Yet, if career development is to best serve the individual and the organization, career development issues need constant attention.

Examining career position, development needs, and progress might never become the mindless behavior we understand to be habitual. Nor should it really be, although undertaking such examinations would be a positive and productive habit to develop. Career development is a strategic endeavor and needs intentional and deliberate focus. As a coach, you can help your clients add regularity to the formula.

Skills

Career development is something that your clients can study and get better at. Career development savvy can be considered a personal and organizational skill. As a contextual coach, you want to help your clients understand that their career development issues are important not only to them and their families but also to the organization.

The company, agency, or enterprise that you and your clients work for needs to have an ever-evolving population of skilled human beings that will help it serve its constituencies and/or create and sustain a competitive advantage. Not only do you want to help your clients become more proficient and efficient at executing their own development; you also want to encourage them to become expert in helping others increase their value to the organization.

Activities

The coursework and practice normally associated with training and development are important when building career development capacity. In many organizations, career development extends beyond formal classroom and online learning. There are management clubs in which peers help one another prepare for expanded leadership responsibilities.

Participation in trade associations or other professional groups can provide valuable and much-needed exposure for people on the move, and also the opportunity to practice leadership and organizational skills. Just as the man with the violin case under his arm told the wayward tourists in New York's Times Square, the way to Carnegie Hall is to "Practice, practice, practice." The more career development activities your clients become involved in, the faster and the better prepared they will be when opportunity presents itself.

How to Discuss the Career Gaps with Your Coaching Client

The internationally acclaimed professional photographer Dewitt Jones said that we must all place ourselves in the "place of greatest opportunity" if we are to reap the rewards that opportunity offers. Jones, famous primarily for his work for *National Geographic,* knows what it means to be patient when waiting for opportunities to arrive, in his case the right lens, the right light, the right sky, the right moment, the right expression. He is also a tireless advocate of preparation.

That is his message to your clients: Prepare constantly so that you will be recognizably ready when the opportunity to move up presents itself. As we previously mentioned, neither you nor your clients will know exactly when or where that will happen, but the worst scenario imaginable is for your lottery numbers to get picked and only then to discover that you neglected to purchase a ticket.

Connecting Career to the Coaching Process

Continuous growth and development and career awareness are subjects you need to keep alive with your clients. The people who look to you for guidance, in your capacity of a coach or a manager who coaches, do not necessarily have the 35,000-foot view that you do. They need your help to be aware of career development issues and how important they are. They need your help to navigate the (for them) uncharted waters of career mobility. And they need your help negotiating their way toward maximum career success for themselves and for the organization.

As a contextual coach, you are serving the needs of the individual and the needs of the organization. Career moves your clients make need to serve both them and the organization if everyone is to win. The best opportunities for the most people—as often as humanly possible—should be your mantra.

Career Summary

In few other arenas are the needs of the individual and the needs of the organization more closely aligned than they are in the area of career. Your clients want to be in the best jobs possible, and the organization wants them in positions where they can bring their best to the effort and be rewarded in kind. Career development is not a one-time or once-in-a-while proposition. As an ongoing occupational and professional concern, especially one that requires training and education, a career can be considered lifework. Training, education, networking, practice, and activities of all kinds are all part of the continuous preparation that will keep you and your clients in the place of greatest opportunity throughout your career journeys.

As a coach or a manager who coaches, help your clients to keep a positive attitude, even if their careers are not moving at the speed or in the direction they desire. Neither you nor they know the precise time and place when advancement opportunities will present themselves. The most and best you and your clients can do is be ready. Do not forget that the activities, practice, and learning that prepare your clients well for expanded responsibilities will make them more effective right where they are.

Looking ahead to Chapter 12 and the tenth and final category in the Contextual Coaching model, we see that competence is at the very core of your clients' abilities to do their jobs and to add value to the organizational equation. In the next chapter, we talk about what competence is and why it is important for you to discuss it with and develop it in your clients. Moving into a role without having the competence to execute it is the antithesis of everything we have discussed in this chapter. Moving into a role without having the competence to execute it will prove costly to the individual and, especially, to the organization.

CHAPTER 12

Area of Behavioral Focus: Competence

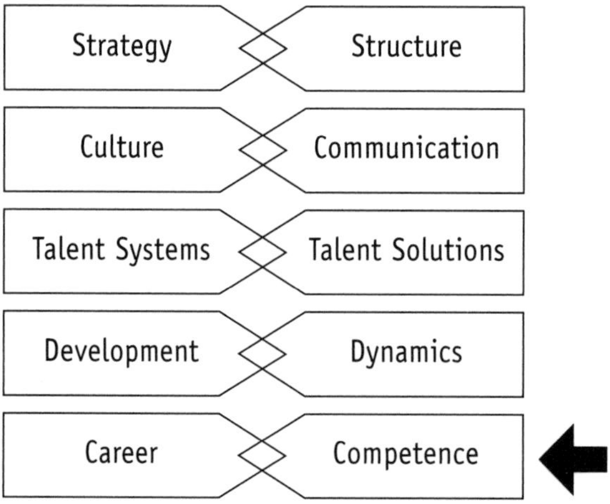

"An Executive Coach establishes a trusting relationship and, through skillful, structured dialogue, deepens the thinking of an executive relative to achieving personal and organizational success. Executive Coaching lights a fire and fans the flame of executive excellence."

—W. Lee WanVeer
Vice President, Learning
Prudential

Competence is the tenth component of the Contextual Coaching model and can be defined as possessing the required skill, knowledge, qualification, or capacity to do the job. Think of someone who works for you who is able to get the job done—the person you can delegate tasks to knowing that he or she will come through on assignments more often than anyone else. This person has earned your trust because he or she has the requisite skill and capabilities to do the work assigned. Generally speaking, most leaders find that being surrounded by competent people is a joy.

Competence is the standard by which we measure capability in a role. Any job description implies specific skills and capabilities that an individual taking on that job ought to possess. When we hire, we use these requirements to screen people. When we manage performance, we measure results and provide feedback on the performance according to these standards. When we promote, we predict that an individual has potential to rise to new levels of competence. When we plan a career, we seek to develop new levels of competence to enhance the possibilities for future success.

Competency models, which are developed by organization development leaders to help managers supervise performance, hire new workers, and promote talent, are meant to be common-sense solutions for establishing criteria and standards and for clearly identifying definitions of success. However, they too often become too complicated, out of touch with the day-to-day work, or so generic that they do not relate to a specific organizational culture. Yet, the idea of having standards for measurement is helpful in the long run.

At the same time, when we speak of competence we actually broaden our Contextual Coaching model to go beyond the context of the organization at large. We consider competence to look beyond the organization and relate to the ways in which our field, marketplace, and competitors identify sets of standards for career potential. Competence in our model includes an investigation of the larger market to determine how the market defines the skills, abilities, experiences, behaviors, and knowledge required for success in key roles. In other words, we ask, what are the criteria for competence?

For instance, leadership is a commonly discussed topic when it comes to competence. We have listed numerous books on competence (at "The Coaching Connection" icon at www.WeMakeTalentWork.com) that help to define leadership. These books look at the topic of leadership across multiple industries and provide insight into the ways that leaders take on specific key tasks associated with their leadership roles.

As a coach or a manager who coaches, you can help your people understand competence on the local or company level, and you are also able to measure progress against goals, hire the right folks, and promote people with potential. By understanding competence beyond your organization, you strive to achieve even higher standards that make you more competitive in the search for and retention of talent.

Why Competence Is Important to the Individual

We partner competence with career in our coaching model to provide the opportunity for you to work with your coaching clients to create a plan for growth that incorporates career management. Here, rather than individual development within a particular job, we focus on the larger path of career management, where competence is measured against talent inside and outside the organization. Individual clients benefit tremendously from creating a plan for improving their talent capabilities as measured against a benchmark that includes competition.

An easy way to understand this is to look at education. If a person plans to become a teacher, he or she will have to acquire the proper education and credentials. People cannot become teachers by having more years' experience than the competition as assistant teachers or substitutes, by having more global experience than the competition, or by joining a teachers' association. They need to go back to school and receive their certification; then, and only then, can they look forward to breaking into the teaching profession in the public schools. In planning their careers, your clients need to understand what skills, education, behaviors, and knowledge they will need to move forward in their field. They need to know what constitutes competence in their chosen field.

We can help them do this by weighing competency models within our organizations and determining the real gaps that might exist. We can also do this through the 360-degree assessment process that has been described throughout this book. The 360-degree assessment typically includes a look at behaviors that become the measurement of competence. The results can reveal areas where your clients excel, areas where they overuse some of their skills, and areas where they have true gaps that need work.

You should also go beyond your own organization and find out what standards are set industry-wide for specific areas of interest. You can often do this through informational interviews with individuals in specific roles. People are usually happy to share why they have been successful and what it takes to get to their level. By comparing your clients' current level of competence to your organization's benchmarks and the benchmarks of the industry, you will be able to create a roadmap toward developing new levels of competence that can open up your clients' career potential.

We have talked about how your clients' promotion offers (or lack of offers) can be decided in conversations (many of them incidental and casual) outside your clients' presence. When your clients' names come up in those conversations about "Who can we get to fill this position?" the ideal scenario is to hear spontaneous remarks like "(Your client) is a competent manager," or "(Your client) is a competent accountant," or "(Your client) certainly has the competence to do the job."

As a coach or a manager who coaches, you want to do everything in your power to help your clients increase their competence. You also want your clients to make their competencies widely known so that the organization can take a quick look to see if your clients are well suited for anything currently open. Competency requires a credential. But, once awarded, that credential needs to become an organizational as well as an individual asset, as you are about to see.

Why Competence Is Important to the Organization

Organizations need to emphasize competence for multiple reasons. The competency models addressed in the organization's talent system provide a measured way to look across an organization and engage in true workforce planning and career management. When it comes to coaching, organizations should include the models and the standards set within their industries in the coaching process.

As a coach, you will focus on the right things when it comes to your clients' careers. By right things, we mean the standards that have been set by the broader organization. Your organization is building a lexicon around competence that influences every talent development process, including individual coaching. The organization will find that individual coaching clients are better able to step up when it comes to performance standards in their current roles and that they are more able to identify a clear path for future success. This can keep individuals engaged, empowered, and committed to the organization.

The organization can also benefit from analysis of how others perceive competence within its field, industry, or practice. These standards can enable the organization to see how competitive it is when it comes to its own talent and to ensure that it is focusing on the right talent initiatives when it comes to current performance and future potential. When the coach is able to utilize this kind of information with the coaching client, the coach is focused on appropriate criteria for growth. Individual growth benefits the person, for sure. But this kind of individual growth also benefits the organization, which is building its bench strength and raising the performance bar.

Individual competence is beneficial not only to the team member who possesses it but also to the organization, which can look at the vast array of competencies within its organizational population and very nearly list those aggregate competencies on their organization chart and monthly financials as assets.

The Objectives and Goals for Competence

The clarity around competency and its associated behaviors is often found within organizational development systems that articulate enduring competencies by level, experience, and/or role. Meanwhile, an organization may also use a specific and unique success model for the top executives of the organization and drive that model within the talent planning process with high potentials. These are often understood as emerging competencies because they can be aligned with the future direction of the organization as it meets its business challenges.

Competence is a helpful way to define the career potential of a person. Aspirations need to be realistic. By noting gaps in competencies, your clients can build attainable career plans. Without this sense, they may have objectives and expectations that are impossible to meet and horribly frustrating. Of course, this kind of frustration affects job performance and employee engagement in the here and now. By noting the gaps that can be managed, especially if your organization provides tools to help your clients, employees have the opportunity to maximize their potential and to limit their liabilities.

Behaviors Related to Competence

In Contextual Coaching, you, as the coach, not only address your clients' career goals, but also help to design future markers of their personal success. As the coach, you attempt to align these markers with the needs of the organization. This helps your clients chart an organizational road map for career progress. Identifying how your clients' competencies align with identified leadership competencies in your organization can benefit current performance as well as the perception that others will have of your clients' capabilities as they build out a plan for the future.

The Optimal Behavior for Competence

As a coach or a manager who coaches, it is up to you to help your clients increase and expand their competence and adequacy. Help them acquire the required skills, knowledge, qualifications, and capacity to excel in what they do. If your clients are responsible for the growth and development of their direct reports, your clients need to help them build skill sets just as you are helping your clients to build their own (although the actual skills may vary).

All of this is about your clients' futures, the future of your organization, and where the two converge. When optimally used, competence is an elusive target. Not that your clients are not becoming increasingly competent by the day, but they can never rest and be satisfied. In a highly competitive marketplace, competence building must be a continuous activity. There is competent and there is highly competent. Help your clients become the latter.

Underuse of Competence

If you and your organization do not consider competence enhancement a serious priority, there will be little of it, and your clients and your organization will pay the consequences. Your clients will experience greatly diminished career opportunities because of their questionable competence. They certainly will not be the assets to the organization that they could be if they and the organization invested in the skill- and knowledge-building activities required to build competence.

Competence and confidence seem to go together. If there is a lack of competence in your organization, there will likely be an equal shortage of confidence. People who lack confidence are not going to compete very effectively against competitors who are confident *and* competent. It will be no contest—with your people getting beaten every time.

Without a healthy culture of competence and confidence, your people will not have the natural internal desire to meet their competitors head on and defeat them. Without a healthy culture of competence and confidence, your people will not transform frustrated energy arising from their defeat at the hands of more competent people into a drive for innovation and performance improvement. Without a healthy culture of competence and confidence, you can expect an organization that is afraid of its own shadow.

Overuse of Competence

In a healthy culture of competence and confidence, it is still possible to overdo it. False confidence and an amplified and distorted sense of competence can lead to disaster. Dangerously undertrained people who are nonetheless confident they can do far more than they have the competence to do invariably wind up embarrassing themselves and their organizations.

Another overuse of competence can come from *over*training. If the organizational population or selected leaders within it are constantly trained at the expense of getting any real work done or accumulating appreciable practical experience, your clients are not going to be any more competitive than they would have been if they had not been trained.

Competence is ideally matched with an appropriate level of responsibility. It is possible, although rare, that someone with tremendous competence is placed in a position far below his or her level of competence and capacity. That is a true waste of human resources. But it happens on rare occasions, as we said. It is much more common to see people with less competence than one would hope being awarded leadership responsibilities beyond (sometimes far beyond) their capacities and capabilities. That mistake brings you and your organization back to the underuse category. (For examples of the underuse, overuse, and optimal use of competence behaviors, as well as for suggested reading on competence, visit www.WeMakeTalentWork.com and click on "The Coaching Connection.")

How Your Coaching Client Fits into Competence

As a contextual coach, you need to get your clients up to speed on the issue of competence. Help them become aware of, accept, and take positive action toward building competence for their own good and the good of the organization. The skills and knowledge you help your clients accumulate in all of the other nine Contextual Coaching categories all add up to remarkable competence. It all works together.

The more you can help your clients master every category of the Contextual Coaching model, the higher the organization's corporate competency rises. It is not merely a matter of people in the organizational population getting smarter. By following the Contextual Coaching model, you can help your organization's collective leadership brain trust become brilliant and well balanced.

As a coach or a manager who coaches, you have an enormous contribution to make to the success of your organization and everyone involved. Competency at the levels we are describing cannot be attained by training and development in the general sense of those activities. Regardless of how well designed and executed the organizational learning plan is, coaching—particularly using the Contextual Coaching process—is the only way to transform the complete person and to achieve total and unquestionable success for the individual and the organization.

How to Introduce Competence to Your Coaching Client

As always, a conversation about what is in it for your client comes in handy. Despite all the well-documented good reasons to increase one's competence, the concept might still seem too foreign for your clients to be comfortable with. The big picture of what constitutes a healthy, vibrant organization is an excellent place to start.

The more your clients can connect the dots between a healthy, thriving organization and their own quality of life, including the security of their futures, the more motivated they will be to expand their own competencies and encourage everyone in their spheres of influence to do the same. Your conversations with your clients must emphasize the interdependence of individual competence and organizational competence.

Competence Behaviors

As you have been tracking the Contextual Coaching process, you have been identifying behaviors associated with the individual and organizational results you want to produce. As a contextual coach, you pay attention to the ways your organization sets expectations for competence and uses its learning organization to increase both competence and confidence. As always, the coaching you do is a laser beam rather than a floodlight (conventional training) when it comes to the intensity and surgical accuracy of the guidance and behavior modification you are offer to your clients.

In examining, tracking, and modifying your clients' habits, skills, and activities, you are looking to identify ways in which they can benefit from competence building as a powerful personal-awareness and goal-setting exercise. You might also inquire as to how your clients are using competence in team building, depending on the number of their direct reports. The following behaviors are part of the Contextual Coaching 360-degree assessment that measures your clients' proficiency in using competence as a tool for developing their own careers and/or the careers of their direct reports:

- Manages time effectively.
- Adapts in light of future trends.
- Demonstrates effective problem solving.
- Shows confidence in taking on responsibilities.
- Exemplifies leadership behaviors valued by the company.

> If you were to place these behaviors before a group of feedback providers and ask them to rank your client, what would they say? Would they say that the behaviors listed are overused, underused, or used optimally by your client? If you use the Contextual Coaching 360-degree assessment, you will get those answers. Even though using the Contextual Coaching 360-degree assessment is a formal way to assess the overuse, underuse, or optimal use of each behavior in a survey format, you can also use these questions to conduct your own structured interviews with feedback providers about your clients' competencies, sitting down with them face to face and discussing each behavior.

360-Degree Feedback Questions for Competence

Like the other components of the Contextual Coaching process, competence is a quality that you can assess by asking questions of both your clients and others in the organization.

Questions for the Coaching Client

As a means of further assessment, here are questions specific to competence to ask your coaching clients:

- What is the most constructive feedback you have received regarding competence in your job?
- What gaps do you believe exist between how you view your competence and how the organization views leadership competence?
- What are some examples of how you plan to close the gaps between your view of competence and how your organization views leadership competence?

The second question relates to your clients' own understanding of their capabilities in the context of organizational leadership expectations. All employees have a major stake in understanding their own roles in or relationships to the leadership competence of the organization and must work to ensure that their individual efforts are aligned with the organization's leadership expectations. If your coaching client has direct reports, you want to know how his or her management style supports the strategic imperatives of the organization, especially as they relate to competence.

Even if your clients do not manage teams, this is a good exercise to illustrate that being a strategic and competent leader has a positive influence on peers. This is a good time for your client to seek a leadership role in an association or professional organization that is starved for leadership. In these types of highly visible situations, your client has a good opportunity to demonstrate leadership competence.

Internally, this can be good practice in exercising influence without authority. The earlier anyone in the organization starts talking about competence, the better. Knowing who is tuned into organizational competency issues and who is not will ensure that your client's coaching engagement is aligned with the need for leadership competence in the organization.

Questions for the Feedback Provider

If you are using the Contextual Coaching 360-degree assessment, these will be the questions that your feedback providers will need to answer as they regard your coaching client:

- What is the most constructive feedback the client has received regarding his or her leadership competence?
- What gaps does the client believe exist between how he or she views leadership competence and how the organization views leadership competence?
- What are some examples of what the client plans to do to close the gaps between how he or she views leadership competence and how your organization views leadership competence?

You are looking for rich answers that will give you and your coaching clients material to work with in designing their coaching action plans. The answers you receive to these questions will spell out whether your clients have gaps in the area of competence and, if so, the type of remedy that is called for. It should be obvious that just exploring these topics with your clients and gathering data about them will heighten your clients' awareness of the many hats a manager must wear—whether your client is a manager at present or aspires to become one. If your coaching client is on track to become a manager, this is a good opportunity for your client to learn about competent leadership in the context of the organization.

How to Use the Responses to the 360-Degree Assessment Questions for Competence

As with any 360-degree assessment, whether you gather the data through a quantitative survey or through structured interviews you conduct or both, the whole point of the exercise is to gather data about your clients that is objective. Otherwise, why not stick with the much easier and quicker self-assessment? When trying to identify potential gaps, it is necessary to use both.

The self-assessment provided by your clients gives you their perspectives. The assessment provided by the feedback providers gives you the objective outside opinion with which you will contrast your clients' self-assessment. It is then up to you to act as a contextual coach, representing the organization, to interpret the expectations of the organization around, in this case, competence.

You will learn what the organization's expectations for competence are from the formal and informal training and learning you experience and from other intentional study. As a coach or a manager who coaches, you will meet and discuss these engagements with your clients' managers—of whom you might be one. You also have consulted with whomever else is available to you to be absolutely clear (or as clear as possible) about the organization's cultural expectations around competence.

Identify the Gaps

If it does not include the organization's expectations for competence in your clients' functions, your clients' plan for achieving success will be incomplete. With the correct organizational expectations in hand, you can more readily see the gaps between those expectations, what your clients identify as their competencies, and what others identify as your clients' competencies. Sometimes you'll have gaps in all three.

That's when you need to appeal to the highest authority available to you to receive a ruling on which interpretation to go with.

In all cases, your clients' managers' interpretations must align with the organizational interpretation before you can go to work with your client on bridging or filling the gaps. If there is a gap between the managers' interpretations and the organization's cultural interpretation, you will be doing your clients, their bosses, and the parent organization a great disservice if you help your clients adopt behaviors that put them at odds with what their bosses and/or their organizational culture demand.

Habits

Once you are assured of this alignment in expectations around competency, you can fine-tune your diagnosis and determine if the gaps between your clients' perspectives and the standard are a result of habits. Are there things that your clients do habitually that knock them off track? Are they off course in their understanding of competence requirements because they unconsciously do things that lead them away from, and not closer to, behaviors that demonstrate the kinds of competence their bosses and the organizational culture expect?

If your clients' behavior in this area is unconscious, there may not be a major disconnect between what they think they are doing and what is expected of them by others. If this is the case, you need to help your clients reframe their understanding of competence from the organization's perspective. Once this is done, your clients' behavior must become consistent with that new interpretation and perspective. You must help your clients replace old habits with new habits that reflect the organization's perspective on competence.

Skills

Nothing displaces misunderstood, inferior, or inappropriate perspective-driven habits better than new skills. Training, coaching, mentoring, thought partnering, and other forms of organizational learning help refine an existing skill set, create a new one, or both. If the new skill set is deliberately adopted as a new behavior, the new behavior will displace the harmful, habitual behavior or other behaviors that were not helping your clients or the organization.

Skills are learned or at least refined if much of your clients' skill sets are the extensions of natural or environmentally reinforced talents or abilities. Adopting new skills that are consistent with organizational expectations around competence must start with identification of what the proper competence looks like, as we mentioned in the section Identify the Gaps. Then the skill building or refinement that you and your clients engineer together can be a finely tuned and surgically precise procedure that will produce in your client exactly what the organization needs and expects in terms of competence from your client.

Activities

Once the new skills your clients acquire or refine are consistent with the competence expectations of the organizational culture, it is time to practice them. The moment a new behavior is introduced into the organization, even if only for research and evaluation purposes, things start to change. Because your clients' new skills-based behaviors are aligned with organizational expectations, these new activities change things for the better.

The activities that your clients engage in day in and day out should reflect this new agenda and the new behaviors. The new or refined skills that your clients possess will not do them any good if they are kept under wraps. It is through the activities your clients engage in that this new understanding of and alignment with organizational expectations is demonstrated.

Demonstration of the new skills is important so that your clients' directs, peers, and other colleagues will see and benefit from your clients' modeling. More than that, executives up the organizational food chains need to see your clients' demonstrated new behaviors to appropriately recognize your clients' accomplishments and to fully appreciate what you have accomplished as a coach. As we have said many times, rewarded behavior is repeated behavior. Without recognition, the new activities and behaviors your clients worked so hard to adopt will begin to slowly diminish and, eventually, disappear altogether.

How to Discuss the Competence Gaps with Your Coaching Client

As with any coaching issue, and especially the ten components of the Contextual Coaching model, competence is important to your clients because of how it affects their career development potential. Their levels of competence affect how well they do their jobs. Understood. But competence needs to be discussed with your clients from a broader and more future-focused perspective. It should also involve the primary definitions of success that exist within your industry.

As a coach or a manager who coaches, you must always remind your clients what is in it for them. You need to address the rewards and recognition they can expect for expanding and deepening their core competencies and refined competencies. Depending on the urgency of any given coaching scenario, you might also need to discuss the consequences of not making the necessary improvements and refinements in competence. In either case, it is critical that your clients be absolutely, positively clear about how important competence is to them and to the organization.

Connecting Competence to the Coaching Process

As a coach, in particular a contextual coach, you deal with things that conventional training and development do not deal with. You engage more individual and personal aspects of your clients than a classroom or online instructor can. When people less intimately affiliated with your clients broach a subject that is as potentially sensitive as competence, your clients might shut them out. Improperly or insensitively approached, your clients might disconnect from or push back against you.

We mentioned that rewarded behavior is repeated behavior. You therefore want to reward the right behavior. That is logical. What makes just as much sense is that inappropriate or nonproductive habits and behaviors are also rewarded. Why else would your clients engage in them? People do things for only two reasons: (1) to get something as a result of the behavior or (2) to avoid something as a result of the behavior.

If your clients become extremely competent at what they do, they might get recognition, or a raise, or a promotion. If your clients are hanging onto their jobs by a thread, becoming extremely competent might mean little more to them than not getting yelled at, reprimanded, or fired. The first is intentional behavior, which means behaving in a way that moves us toward something good. The second example is avoidant behavior, which means doing something to avoid a negative consequence.

If your clients' behaviors have been suspect for a long time, you might need to help them engage in avoidant remediation in the near term. Once you have been able to stabilize their position in the organization, the two of you can refocus on moving toward intentional growth and development in the far term. To build the tallest skyscraper in the world, you must begin by excavating a deep hole in the ground. The building needs to be anchored deep in bedrock to have the strength to stand tall. As a coach or a manager who coaches, you must secure a foundation, in this case a foundation of competence, before your clients can grow their careers.

Competence Summary

Competence means possessing the required skill, knowledge, qualification, or capacity to get the job done. What exactly that means varies from situation to situation and from individual to individual. The essential competencies of a certified public accountant are distinctly different from the essential competencies of a biochemical engineer. The core competencies of a neurosurgeon are distinctly different from the core competencies of the writing team for Lorne Michaels's *Saturday Night Live*.

As a coach or a manager who coaches, you will test and confirm what competencies the organizational culture requires of your clients. You will inquire to confirm that your clients' managers are aligned with the organizational culture's competency requirements.

You will see if the coaching client is living up to standards within your industry. Before you assess your clients' perceptions of their own competencies, you will reconcile any divergence in the managers' understanding of the organization's competency requirements and your own.

Once you and your clients' managers have reached consensus on your clients' requisite competencies and you and your clients' managers are properly aligned with organizational expectations, you proceed to assess your clients' perceptions, understandings, and definitions of competency against 360-degree feedback providers representing a variety of your clients' constituencies. Next come the training, education, and practice that will materially expand and deepen your clients' competencies in the areas where the organization needs them expanded and deepened most.

Then, under your guidance, your clients will address the habits, skills, and activities that will put the newly developed or refined competencies to work. You will regularly remind your clients why the appropriate competencies are important to them as individuals and to the organization. You will also ensure that your clients are demonstrating their enhanced competencies in ways that are visible to organizational policymakers.

Epilogue

"Coaching has a domino effect ...you invest in one and see the ripple impact of the benefits through many."

—Joan P. Lawrence-Ross
Vice President, Learning and Development,
AXA Equitable

Aligning what people do best with what organizations need most: That is the ultimate win for a coach. It is also the ultimate win for your coaching clients, who probably would not have been able to achieve such alignment without your skilled assistance. The organization that pays both you and your coaching clients wins when members of the organizational population start firing on all cylinders.

Whenever possible, you want coaching work to be visible. You do not want your clients' progress and accomplishments to go unnoticed, unrecognized, or unrewarded. You do not want your accomplishments as a coach to go unnoticed, unrecognized, or unrewarded, either. As a contextual coach, you want a win for everyone. In addition, making it known how much coaching improves performance and accelerates growth and development of real potential will spread the good news and help build a coaching culture.

Using Contextual Coaching as your process model for achieving the ultimate Coaching Connection is indeed a Tale of Two Clients. Through Contextual Coaching the Coaching Conundrum is solved once and for all. If your coaching work and the solutions you engineer in tandem with your coaching clients do not serve the best interests of both the individual and the organization, you have more work to do on your own habits, skills, and activities. The coaching connection flashpoint comes when the individual and the organization are both better for the engagement.

The Coaching Connection connects the dots between the need for highly skilled, knowledgeable, and wise coaches and the exponentially increased benefits of preemptive managerial and executive skill and competency building—as opposed to reactive, after-the-fact interventions. The question is no longer "Have we learned anything about coaching through the years?" We most certainly have learned, and proved time and again, that effective leadership does not come naturally to the vast majority of people who are promoted into leadership positions and are paid to lead.

We also know, as we said in the beginning, that leading is not easy for anyone facing high-pressure demands from employee, customer, and the board, internal and external economic challenges, and complex marketplace competition. As a coach or a manager who coaches, you position your best and brightest people, as well as your organization, to meet these challenges. As you coach, you are riding the cutting edge in individual and organization development because the most remarkable and sustainable organizational improvements take place one person at a time.

The Coaching Culture

The organizational improvement that is taking place one individual at a time can become a tidal wave, or an avalanche if you prefer, with the addition of new coaches to swell your coaching ranks. With Contextual Coaching, you now have the blueprint and the architecture to develop well-balanced managers and executives to face the ever more complex challenges of business in the twenty-first century. More than that, you have the lexicon to discuss coaching with organizational policymakers who are not yet believers, as well as with new and prospective coaching clients who can benefit immeasurably from the coaching experience.

One of your ongoing responsibilities is to become an architect and champion of the emerging coaching culture in your organization. You must work to create and maintain a strong bond among your coaches and managers who coach to ensure consistency and a continuity of excellence in the guidance they provide to their coaching clients. Even if you are not in charge of coaching in your organization, you can support and encourage the person who is. Play as much of a role as you can in making sure coaches and managers who coach receive ongoing training and development in the art of coaching. Play whatever role you can in making sure that everyone who provides coaching services in your organization receives ongoing coaching supervision themselves. Just like anyone else, coaches improve when they receive coaching.

Feed the Excitement

At the opening of this book, we urged you to join the excitement. Now we urge you to become part of the engine that drives coaching in your organization and to do everything in your power to make coaching as exciting and attractive to those who want to join your ranks or receive the enormous benefits of coaching. Remember that rewarded behavior is repeated behavior; therefore, you want to reward the right behavior through your coaching. Reward the coaches themselves—starting with yourself—for being willing to coach others and to take coaching seriously enough to constantly improve at it.

Never forget that you are "never not communicating." Make sure everything about how you do your work and everything you preach to others reflects the impact that coaching has made in your job and your career. Be the well-balanced manager or executive that you help others to become through the Contextual Coaching process.

When all is said and done, you have played and will continue to play a critical role in helping your coaching clients and the organization develop. We hope that you will get involved or increase your involvement sooner rather than later because the good you do for your clients and for the organization will have a multiplier effect on more people than you realize. The power of the Coaching Connection begins with you and resides at that critical juncture where you embrace what is best for you and what is best for the organization in the same moment and in the same context. Although you might eventually retire from it, the work of a contextual coach is never done.

Index